RANCHO SANTIAGO COLLEGE
OR MAIN GV1834.55.W47 F74 1985
American rodeo, from Buffalo Bil
Fredriksson, Kristine, 1940-

3 3065 00031 6863

D0687368

American
Rodeo

American Rodeo

FROM BUFFALO BILL ∪ TO BIG BUSINESS

by Kristine Fredriksson

TEXAS A&M
UNIVERSITY PRESS
COLLEGE STATION

Rancho Santiago College
Orange Campus Library

211919

GV
1834.55
.W 47
F74
1985

Copyright © 1985 by Kristine Fredriksson
All rights reserved

Chapter 5 has previously been published in *Sport in
the West*, Sunflower University Press, Manhattan,
Kansas, pp. 62–69, © 1983. Reprinted by permission.

Library of Congress Cataloging in Publication Data

Fredriksson, Kristine, 1940–
    American rodeo, from Buffalo Bill to big business.

    Bibliography: p.
    Includes index.
    1. Rodeos—West (U.S.)—History.   2. Rodeos—Economic
aspects—West (U.S.) I. Title.
GV1834.55.W47F74 1985   791'.8   83-40501
ISBN 0-89096-181-6

CS
85·B1828

Manufactured in the United States of America
First Edition

"In reckless spirit the cowboy is born;
only in long, hard training is he made."

—J. Evetts Haley,
Charles Goodnight—Cowman and Plainsman

Contents

List of Illustrations

Acknowledgments

A number of people have contributed to this publication in a variety of ways, and it is to them that this section is devoted. First and foremost, I owe deep gratitude to Dean Richard E. Oglesby, my faculty advisor at the University of California, Santa Barbara. When I submitted the proposal for a study of rodeo as my dissertation topic, it was with the expectation that the subject matter would be turned down. Much to my delight, Dr. Oglesby not only approved it but encouraged it. His guidance, support, and valuable though often severe criticism were essential to my completing the manuscript. For the section dealing with media images of the cowboy, I am indebted for the direction and advice of Professor Roderick Nash, also of UCSB.

A scholarly investigation of the sport of rodeo had not been undertaken for over thirty years when I began my work in 1978. The pioneer in this field is Clifford P. Westermeier, whose acquaintance I was privileged to make shortly after I began my own study. The continued interest he has shown in my project has been a great inspiration to me. It was my good fortune that Dr. Westermeier's entire collection of rodeo material had been placed in the Western Historical Collections of the University of Colorado, Boulder. After over two years of research at the University of California, I devoted yet another year to the Westermeier Papers, which were an invaluable resource. The Director of the Western Historical Collections, Dr. John A. Brennan, and his staff made every effort to assist me by their generous accommodations, encouraging attitudes, and friendliness.

My sincere thanks go to Bob Eidson, executive vice president of the Professional Rodeo Cowboys Association, who seemed never to tire of my questions, and to his staff, who assisted with much important information and statistics. J. Kelly Riley of the R. J. Reynolds Tobacco Company and Mel Parkhurst of the Wrangler Brand have also been most helpful.

As the photo credits will bear out, a number of institutions and companies have provided the illustrations. I am especially thankful to those which supplied material free of charge: the Justin Boot Company (through Dally Advertising, Inc.), the R. J. Reynolds Tobacco Company, and the American Humane Association. It should be noted that the AHA's contribution of the illustration on page 142 is not to be considered an endorsement of this book or its views.

My fascination with rodeo goes back nearly twenty years. A great deal of this enthusiasm was generated by my instructor, team-roping partner, and friend William Richardson, at whose rodeo school at the T-Bone Ranch in Calabasas, California—which I attended for six years—I learned and came to appreciate the fine points of horsemanship, professional rodeo competition, and just plain cowboyin'. I was a very determined, although at first reluctant, pupil. Bill not only patiently drilled me until every trace of fear had vanished but also, in the process, managed to instill in me many of those indefinable attitudes that make the rodeo cowboy such a distinct individual. I have been able to apply these notions to advantage in nearly every facet of life.

On a personal level, I am particularly fortunate to have had the friendship of Beth and Robert Hillshafer. Their interest and concerned understanding have been of great comfort to me during the long and often frustrating years of seeing this book to completion.

The dedication necessary for the research and writing of a dissertation or a book requires long periods of seclusion. My beautiful and clever calico cat Maybelle has been my constant and loyal companion. Her cheerful and inquisitive presence has strengthened my admittedly curious belief that small animals have been created expressly to keep ladies company.

There is an enormous sense of accomplishment and pride in having a book published, and I hope that many long-time friends will share once again in my *mundus sapientiae dulcis* through this book and beyond. I, for one, am decidedly proud of the end result. In doing this work, I have tried always to live up to my own expectations and to abide by my personal motto of nearly thirty years: *Memoria minuitur nisi eam exerceas.*

KRISTINE FREDRIKSSON
Lubbock, Texas
May 14, 1984

American
Rodeo

Introduction

E ven the most ambitious professional cowboy today actually works only about sixty minutes out of the year. That might appear to be an easy life for someone who can conceivably win over one hundred thousand dollars in that one year. It is hoped, however, that what follows this introduction will explain that one hundred thousand dollars is fair wages for such a small amount of time spent at one's profession.

That kind of work schedule would seem to make for a great deal of spare time, resulting in boredom. This is, to be sure, an occupational hazard of the contemporary sport of rodeo and one with which the contestant has to deal, along with a host of other risks inherent in the profession. But boredom has not always been part and parcel of the contest. In fact, rodeo itself was more or less invented to counteract that very condition—the monotony and loneliness of the life of the working cowboy in the days of the cattle drives and the open range.

At the large roundups during the last few decades of the nineteenth century, representatives of the participating outfits in the district were sent out to pick up stray cattle. These "reps" were good riders, and they used to bring a string of unbroken horses, often called outlaws or broncs, to break to ride for use in their work. Often the reps would challenge the cowboys, and bets were made on the rider or the bronc. Roping contests were also held in a similar way to test the cowboys' skills in that area.[1] At other times, the cowboys from the various camps would challenge each other—with instant rodeo the result, usually including only one or two events, most often saddle-bronc riding and steer roping. (Although an individual cowboy has, in later years, placed bets on whether he or another can ride a certain animal, betting is not something that is condoned at the officially sanctioned rodeos today. However, at the so-called matched roping and riding contests, usually between two top contenders in the event in question, fellow cowboys and spectators will wager on their favorites. These contests are held strictly outside the jurisdiction of the Professional Rodeo Cowboys Association [PRCA], merely as a way of measuring the skill of the participants on a given number of animals.)

What was to become rodeo, as we know it today, was the play of the working cowboy, in which he would indulge during rare breaks from his regular work or when that work was finished. There were no forms of amusement on the trail; the cowboy had to entertain himself. It was quite natural, therefore, that his pastime would be one in which his occupational skills were involved and could be measured against those of others.[2] However, although the cowboy was not the only one who made a game and a contest out of his craft, his were the only skills to have been developed into a professional sport of the magnitude that rodeo has achieved.

The early cowboy contests often took place in the town square of the railhead at the end of the cattle drive.[3] They were something the cowboy looked forward to and were, along with upcoming dances, a topic of conversation in his peer group.[4]

The community that claims to have been the first to hold an organized rodeo, even before the days of the cattle drives, is Prescott, Arizona.[5] Prescott was only a few months old when its first contest was staged on the Fourth of July, 1864.[6] It was only fitting, then, that the town should in addition be responsible for two other firsts twenty-four years later: on the Fourth of July, 1888, admission was charged for the first time, making rodeo a spectator sport,[7] and the first medal was given as a Citizens' Prize to a Juan Leivas, who roped and tied a steer in one minute and seventeen seconds.[8] The Fourth of July became the special day for rodeo and is nowadays popularly referred to as the cowboys' Christmas. It is without a doubt the busiest of all times of the year for the modern contestant. Thirty-eight PRCA-sanctioned rodeos in twenty-two states and three Canadian provinces were scheduled for the Independence Day weekend of 1982.[9]

For quite a few years, however, rodeo remained strictly the amusement of the working cowboy, and many contests later prided themselves on the fact that the participants were real, working cowhands.

The Prescott, Arizona, Frontier Days and the Pendleton, Oregon, Round-Up were among these competitions.

In the fall of 1887, a cowboy tournament was held in Denver in connection with the Denver Exposition. In commenting on the success of the event, the *Denver Republican* pointed out: "Every cowboy who entered the arena did his best, and the untamed broncos and longhorn steers did their best to get away."[10] In another front-page article, E. K. Whitehead, secretary of the Colorado Humane Society, pointed out that a public exhibition of how cattle are handled on the plains should not be conducted by "inexperienced men on green horses."[11]

Rodeo gradually became a profession in itself, at first engaged in primarily by those who did not want or did not care to work at a regular occupation. Later, much later, athletes who were highly suited to the contests became the primary actors in this spectacle, which has been likened to Roman gladiatorial games and the medieval tournaments of knights.

It is the American cowboy, however he may be interpreted, and his contest—rodeo—that have inspired the research reported on the following pages.

1

"Cow-boys' Fun," the Press, and the Public

Even though rodeo has existed as a professional sport for well over one hundred years, the professional rodeo cowboy is only now slowly beginning to be taken seriously as an athlete, as a respectable human being, as a businessman—and as a subject for academic scrutiny.*

The change in attitude that is taking place can be demonstrated by examining the titles and contents of articles about cowboys and rodeo in newspapers and popular magazines over the years (excluding the ones aimed specifically at those following the sport). Earlier in this century, for example, there was a profusion of articles entitled "Ride 'im, Cowboy!" or "Ride 'em, Cowboy!"[1] There were many with references in their titles to the "Wild West" or the "Old West"[2] and with other platitudes that had become synonymous with rodeo in the minds of much of the American public ("Cowboys Are Crazy," "Rip-Roarin', R'arin' Rodeo" [including the dropped g's]) and many that contained such expressions as "cowpoke" and "ornery critters."[3] The *Readers' Guide to Periodical Literature* did not even list articles about rodeo under the subject title "Rodeo" until the volume that covered the period July, 1937–June, 1939.[4] Before that, when looking under that subject title, the reader would be advised, "See 'Wild West Shows.'" From then on, the direction was reversed: when one looked up "Wild West Shows," he would be told, "See 'Rodeo'". However, it was not until twenty years after rodeo was given its own heading that "Wild West Shows" was removed.[5]

*The term *professional* here denotes a contestant winning prize money and/or some other form of consideration for his skill in contests sanctioned by the Professional Rodeo Cowboys Association.

Today, even though many of those who write about rodeo and its cast of characters are metropolitan reporters who know little, if anything, about the sport, it is nevertheless indisputable that rodeo is, indeed, reaching the big cities and parts of the country where once it was a novelty and in some cases even something to make fun of.[6] It is curious and regrettable that many of these journalists still seem to view rodeo from such a distance as to make it nearly unreal, causing the cowboy and his profession to appear too much out of the ordinary to be believable, in contrast to other athletes and their sports. No doubt, sheer unfamiliarity accounts for a good part of this attitude.[7]

Long before rodeo, as such, was something to write about, however, the cowboy—or rather his presumed demise—was the subject of many an article. To be sure, the working cowboy, from whom the rodeo contestant was to evolve, was still a very visible figure in the cattle-business economy. But the changes that had taken place in that industry by the mid-1880s had also served to modify its most conspicuous figure. In the altered circumstances, the cowboy, too, had to change in order to survive.

Nevertheless, the public that had come to know him during the so-called pristine phase of America's cattle industry would have nothing of this change in image. It sought to preserve the cowboy as perceived, bad qualities included, even though that view was more often than not an unrealistic one. As John Baumann wrote in an 1887 essay:

> His admirers are investing him with all manner of romantic qualities; they descant upon him his manifold virtues and his pardonable weaknesses as if he were a demi-god, and I have no doubt that before long there will be ample material for any philosophic inquirers who may wish to enlighten the world as to the cause and meaning of the cowboy myth. Meanwhile the true character of the cowboy has become obscured, his genuine qualities are lost in fantastic tales of impossible daring and skill, of dare-devil equitation and unexampled endurance. Every member of his class is pictured as a kind of Buffalo Bill. . . .[8]

And so, there was created "the cowboy myth," which allowed writers' imaginations to run rampant and to classify almost anyone as a cowboy, depending on the point of view of the beholder. At the same time, the myth was implanted in the minds of those who looked to the cowboy—as the hero of, ostensibly, the last American frontier—for inspiration as well as escape. The cowboy himself became the unwit-

FRANK LESLIE'S ILLUSTRATED NEWSPAPER

No. 1,703.—Vol. LXVI.]   NEW YORK—FOR THE WEEK ENDING MAY 5, 1888.   [PRICE, 10 CENTS.

COWBOY LIFE.—RIDING A YEARLING.
FROM A PHOTO. BY C. D. KIRKLAND, CHEYENNE.—SEE PAGE 162.

"Cowboy Life—Riding a Yearling." The cover of *Frank Leslie's Illustrated Newspaper* for the week ending May 5, 1888, featured this woodcut after a photograph by Charles D. Kirkland, which suggests easterners' interest in cowboy life. Courtesy American Folklife Center, Library of Congress

ting pawn in these efforts to change him into something that he had never been. What is almost incredible is that the mythical view of the cowboy managed to last so long and, furthermore, survived any and all attempts at tearing it down.

Over half a century later, Edward Everett Dale, one of the foremost scholars of the cattle industry and its personages, would find that

> [the cowboys] still retain in the midst of an unfamiliar social and eco-
> nomic order their old-time ideals and state of mind. The conditions
> which produced them have long ago gone forever, but they still persist
> and will remain cow hands as long as they shall live, as a deathless heri-
> tage from the past.[9]

Despite journalistic efforts to lay him to rest, the cowboy perse-vered. Although by 1892 one writer believed that "when barber Des-tiny again has a vacant chair and calls out 'next,' the cowboy himself will disappear,"[10] others saw in the changing cattle industry a means through which the cowboy could survive. In 1886, it had been af-firmed that "the morale of the entire range and range cattle business in the United States now compares favorably with that of other large en-terprises."[11] The increased demand for the cowboy's precision and skill in the new economic order would allow him to remain a fixture in that establishment.

Less than a decade later, writers were beginning to find out that being a working cowboy was, indeed, an occupation that required cer-tain very special qualifications and one that did not attract just any wild and reckless man. It took "a strong constitution," "an active mind," "a steady nerve," and "a fearless spirit"[12] to be a cowboy, one journalist wrote, in what may have been the first enumeration of the qualities that also apply to the rodeo cowboy. The same writer warned, however, that "unless a man has been calculated to be a cowboy and nothing else, he will seek some other occupation at the first conve-nient opportunity."[13]

There are certain definite traits and prerequisites that the working cowboy and the professional rodeo contestant share and that actually select them for their respective occupations and give them a common bond. At first these characteristics were recognized for the cowhand. In fact, already in 1886, the cowboy was said to be possessed of "sports-manlike instincts,"[14] which were manifested in the execution of his daily tasks with his fellow cowboys, even though not yet in any kind of competitive situation. By the turn of the century, the working cowboy had achieved a measure of stature and recognition for his skill,[15] although some still predicted his doom ("it is left for the camera to make him a historic figure").[16]

The cowboy at work held appeal and fascination for spectators; the cowboy at play, even more, in the contests of professional skills he staged in connection with the completion of a trail drive. However, in the earliest days of the sport, only occasional mentions appeared in print, for two main reasons. First, the scenes where these contests took place were usually too far removed to attract more than an occasional curious reporter in search of something new to write about. Thus, the writers of the time were rarely present at the contests that were staged on the trail or in camp, and there was no audience other than the cowboys of the competing outfit or outfits. Second, even if a chronicler did witness the event, he may not have thought it merited a mention. It was not until the mid-1880s—when the days of the open range were numbered and the "cow-boys' fun" was beginning to be considered a curiosity, something that would disappear along with the cowboy himself and his work—that what was to become rodeo attracted any journalistic attention, and then only to set down for posterity something that was believed to be in the last phase of its existence.[17]

At times, cowboy sports were actually presented before gathered crowds, usually as part of Fourth-of-July celebrations. For example, early contests were held in Deer Trail, Colorado; Pecos, Texas; and Prescott, Arizona. For practical reasons, however, these exhibitions remained within the confines of cattle country; consequently, knowledge of the new sport did not reach audiences previously unfamiliar with it.

Then someone came up with the idea of bringing cowboy games closer to the public, to the stage, as entertainment. That someone was none other than William F. Cody—Buffalo Bill. His first public spectacle was presented on the Fourth of July, 1882, in his hometown of North Platte, Nebraska.[18]

It has been argued that the situation in which the cattle industry found itself at the time stimulated the creation of this kind of show. Rangeland had come into private ownership, enclosed by barbed wire. Cowboys from the various ranches would pit their skills against one another, encouraged by the boss-rancher, who would award a prize (a saddle or a suit of clothes) to the hired hand who made the best showing.[19]

Furthermore, being a working cowboy was, by the 1880s, quite often a seasonal occupation, because of the more efficient methods employed by the cattle industry. For up to six months of the year a cowboy might find himself without a job, unless he was lucky enough to be one of the few men who were retained on the payroll of a ranch after the fall roundup was completed. He had to seek a means of making a living in the off-season.

Why, then, did a cowboy, seasonally laid off from ranch work, not take a "regular" job? Rodeo contestants are asked the same question to this day, especially those who barely eke out a living by competing. The answer was the same then as it is now: those who choose that kind of unstructured life-style, born of the trail-driving era and nurtured by the wild-west shows, do not easily fit in a conventional occupation. Early-day cowboys were so proud of their particular work with livestock that it was beneath them to labor at anything else connected with the operation of a cattle outfit, let alone at something outside of it. The man on a horse was in a class above all others. To be caught at the blister end of a shovel would have been to renounce that feeling of superiority.

Moreover, in the early days few opportunities were open in other areas of endeavor. Only three avenues lay immediately before the cowboys, all of which would in short order be phased out by technology— or the law: the butcher shop, the livery stable, and the saloon.[20]

The desire to be employed by no one but himself has also always been a characteristic setting the American working man apart from his European counterpart, and nowhere has that trait been more pronounced than on the western frontier. It is not surprising, therefore, that the cowboy, holding the distinction of being the last frontier hero, has always clung so staunchly to this principle.

The out-of-work cowboy might choose to hire out to one of the many wild-west shows that flourished after Colonel Cody's initial success. By 1885 there were more than fifty of them on the road.[21] As these shows were aimed primarily at audiences in the big cities, not familiar with the West, the cowboy—or the "carnival boy" or "bronc stomper,"[22] as he was sometimes called—stood out as a very unusual individual, coming from a background in which freedom and hardship walked hand in hand.[23] By the late 1890s rodeo, too, had been estab-

10 Cents Per Copy

$1.00 Per Year

The WILD BUNCH

Vol. 1   CHICAGO, ILL., FEBRUARY, 1916   No. 11

COL. LAVELLE

The *Wild Bunch*, the first publication for the wild-west-show trade, began monthly issues in April, 1915. This issue, of February, 1916, featured a Colonel Lavelle on the cover. Courtesy Dorothy Morrell and Skeeter Bill Robbins Collection

lished as public entertainment,[24] although primarily in the western states. Thus, long before rodeo became an organized sport and the participants had virtually unionized, there was such a character as the rodeo cowboy.

The rodeo cowboy and wild-west-show performers of that era have been described as "mostly open-air delinquents, Civil War draft dodgers and out-and-out renegades," who would intersperse their riding and roping with drinking, fighting, and the wrecking of saloons and then repeat the performance in the next town on which they descended.[25] Even the *Cheyenne Daily Leader* tended to look down its nose at the cowboy, but that was before he became a familiar sight at the annual Frontier Days, during which Cheyenne, since 1897, has played host to the largest rodeo in North America. In 1882, that paper carried the following comments, reprinted from an eastern publication:

> As you mingle with these boys, you find them a strange mixture of good nature and recklessness. You are as safe with them on the plains as with any class of men, so long as you do not impose on them. . . . Morally, as a class, they are foulmouthed, blasphemous, drunken, lecherous, utterly corrupt. Usually harmless on the plains when sober, they are dreaded in towns, for then liquor has the ascendency over them. They are also so improvident as the veriest "Jack" of the sea. Employed as cow-boys only six months in the year—from May till November—their earnings are soon squandered in dissoluteness, and then they hunt to get odd jobs to support themselves until another cattle season begins.[26]

The article went on to illustrate the point further, while admitting that there were exceptions—"a white sheep among the black."

The Cheyenne newspaper's decision to reprint what had been written by an eastern observer and the absence of a disclaimer indicate, it would seem, that the publisher agreed with the writer's comments. It is unlikely that, by reprinting the piece, the paper wished to indulge the eastern and British cattle interests so important in Wyoming Territory at the time; these interests depended greatly on the cowboys for their success and would undoubtedly not totally have welcomed the observations in the article. Furthermore, since the author admittedly had not had an opportunity to view the cowboys during the off-season months, the image the cowboys presented, as a group, during their brief visits to town was what he recorded. It was that image which remained in people's minds.

A scene from a wild-west show. Courtesy Tad Lucas Collection

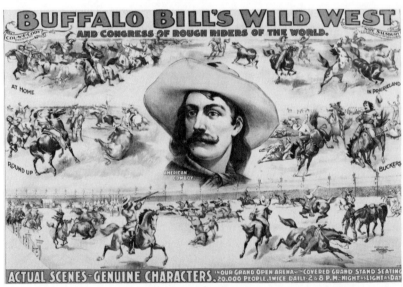

"American Cowboy," poster for Buffalo Bill's Wild West. Courtesy Buffalo Bill Historical Center, Cody, Wyoming

The sympathetic press, on the other hand, from early on tried to emphasize the positive side of the cowboy. In 1912, the *Calgary Daily Herald* wrote in his defense:

> There rises up the distorted image of him in his most reckless moment. . . . The personal qualities of the cowboys are visible enough, but their services to civilization are scarcely thought of. . . . The strange, burned and gloomy country over which many of the cowboys roamed yet awaits its sacred bard, and no master's hand has yet set down the manly and generous cowboy life under the sun and the stars.[27]

The unfair judgment this writer mentioned was only one of the factors that worked against the early rodeo cowboy. Along with other elements, many beyond his control, it eventually led to his contributing to the caricature.

The early cowboy was habitually trusting, simply because those he was used to dealing with were usually honest. Many westerners prided themselves on never needing any written contracts or agreements in a business transaction because honesty and integrity were traits characteristic of everyone. But by the end of World War I, motion pictures had put the wild-west shows virtually out of business, and a figure known as the rodeo promoter began to make himself known. To these more worldly men, the trust the cowboy displayed was easily interpreted as naïveté and a weakness to be exploited. When a cowboy, tempted to enter contests advertising attractive prizes, traveled many miles—at his own expense—only to find those prizes merely a ruse to get him there, it was small wonder that he took matters into his own hands, often surprising the promoter with his astuteness. Accustomed to settling differences as they arose, like his earlier western counterpart, he resorted to violence to get what he believed was his. The exploitative promoter or the unfair judge could expect to meet instant justice. Stock contractor Leo Cremer remembers rodeos circa 1917 as "five to six hours of casually run events, often enlivened, however, by a good variety of fistic encounters when some contestants well braced with red-eye would undertake to whip a judge or fellow cowboy." To the cowboy, all promoters were a bad breed of people, not to be trusted. It did not matter to him whether the rodeo was a long-established one or not; promoters were all looked upon with the same suspicion.[28]

The havoc the cowboy wreaked was, needless to say, detrimental to both his reputation and that of the fledgling sport.[29] The well-behaved cowboys, serious about competing and about making a success of rodeo, were believed to be cut from the same cloth as those who caused disturbances. By early in the century, the community that wished to hold a rodeo was becoming hesitant to have the cowboys come, only to cause destruction and violence. (Then, as it often is now, the rodeo was a community effort, something that unified people in working toward a common purpose.)[30] After a few years of bad experiences, committees in certain localities refused to organize any more contests. The public would simply not come to watch a collection of reputed hoodlums.

These unfortunate circumstances had turned the contesting cowboy into something he had not wished to become. Wherever he went, he was made aware that he was not a desirable character. This manifested itself in his appearance as well as in his behavior. Belligerence was a natural defense mechanism he called upon in standing up for his rights. Having to fight for what he felt was justly his made him into a sullen, suspicious individual, which, in turn, did not help his already poor image. He neglected his appearance, just as he himself felt slighted.[31] He simply did not care. The first two or three decades of the twentieth century were truly an unpropitious and trying period for the sport. It survived only because its participants were determined not to let it die.

Most competing cowboys in the early days were from the area in which the contest they entered was held. Ranch cowboys who did not follow the circuit but competed only in local contests did not show the lack of care of the more professional rodeo competitors. At the Pendleton Round-Up, which prided itself on being strictly a contest of working cowboys, the contestants showed up in "gaudy shirts" that contrasted with the dress of the rest of the townspeople. Angora chaps, dyed in brilliant colors, were in vogue, and those who wore leather chaps adorned them with silver conchas.[32] This clothing demonstrated the pride the cowboy felt in being able to show off his skills on familiar ground in his home territory.

As the rodeo cowboy was increasingly denounced by society and as he continued to face often unscrupulous promoters and judges and illusive prize money, he retaliated by failing to appear for events he had entered, for reasons such as drunkenness and gambling or on any other pretext.[33] He became a shiftless person, ready to take whatever he

Three "champs" at Pendleton Round-Up, Pendleton, Oregon, 1915. *Left to right:* Lee Caldwell, Yakima Canutt, and Jackson Sundown.

Riders at the Trinidad, Colorado, Fair, 1910.

could but prepared to give only what he wanted to give. If all he could get out of rodeo was what he considered a good time, that was what he was going to have. In spite of all the factors working against him—self-generated and others—he was determined to make himself a permanent fixture, thereby defying those who predicted the waning of his existence.

As a consequence, the economic situation of the rodeo contestant was an extremely precarious one. If he was lucky enough to join a wild-west show, his position might be more secure. Even so, there seemed to exist in him a penchant for reckless divertissements, something for which rodeo cowboys are noted, as they are for their ingenuity in devising such amusements. (The cowboy still has an eye for the sensational, even if he no longer needs to use that talent as a means of attracting attention).

This tendency is well illustrated by the behavior of the participants in the 101 Ranch Show, which appeared at Madison Square Garden in New York City for the first time in 1905. All working cowboys from the Millers' 101 Ranch at Ponca City, Oklahoma, they had no need to use their off-duty pastime as a form of rebellion; rather they saw in the occasion the opportunity to expend an overabundance of energy.

> They'd all booze it up and [after hiring a car] they'd ride up and down the streets, whooping and yelling like prairie wolves at a kill. If it was a wet night and the pavement slick, they'd come helling it down the street till they found a broad place and then, without checking speed, they'd whip the cat around just to see how long it would spin on the pavement before lining out again. They took in all the leg shows, drank everything in sight, and prized up hell in general whenever the notion struck them.[34]

That New Yorkers would find the cowboys wild is no wonder. Even after more than a dozen years of World's Championship rodeos at Madison Square Garden, the inhabitants of that city found cowboys a rather questionable breed. They failed to comprehend that the once-a-year apparition was a human being and not a personage lifted from the movie-theater screen or a radio program. The cowboy suffered from these misconceptions, which naturally slowed down the general acceptance of him as an athlete and of his occupation as a sport.

James Cox pointed out with foresight in 1894 that "it is doubtful

The 101 Ranch wild-west show's horsedrawn calliope, parading through the streets of an unidentified town. Photograph by Vance Dillon, courtesy Bruner Collection, Western History Collections, University of Oklahoma Libraries

whether any human being in any age or generation has ever been so absurdly caricatured and misrepresented as the cowboy." Indeed, as late as 1940, "the New Yorker [felt] indignant at seeing a cowboy in person in high heels as if he saw Peter Pan or the Mad Hatter." The city people felt that "Americana ought to keep its own place and not bob up Eighth Avenue."[35] To the New Yorker, and probably to many others, for the first few decades or so of the twentieth century the cowboy remained just that—Americana. This image was frustrating and inhibiting to those who saw in the sport a way of carrying on a tradition while still making a living. Their belief in themselves and their contest was strong enough to make them seek for their group a fairer deal.

2

A Greater Future for the Game

During the first few decades of the twentieth century, rodeo began to emerge as a competitive spectator sport in its own right. It more and more divorced itself from the circus and carnival elements of the touring wild-west shows, where the cowboys' roping and riding exhibitions had been only one small part on the program of many and varied acts by military drill teams, Bedouins and Cossacks, snake charmers, sword swallowers, and the like.[1]

However, in view of the bad name the cowboy had acquired and the irregular manner in which contests were held, it became clear that, if the sport was to continue, something would have to be done to improve existing conditions. Rodeo's image was one of "wild, loose-figured men who . . . followed the unorganized shows at the turn of the century,"[2] and that image persisted at least in the minds of the public through much of the next few decades. As a result, rodeo's popularity declined.

A major complaint voiced by the cowboys was directed toward the management of the contests. While the responsibility of the cowboys themselves to provide attractive entertainment for the public was not overlooked, it was generally believed that most problems could be solved if the rodeo committees arrived at some kind of organization and coordination.[3] The producers of rodeos quite frequently staged poorly organized shows. Often the rodeo performance would be an endless series of slow-moving contests of several hours' duration. This did not serve to stimulate either the spectators' interest in a sport with which they were rather unfamiliar anyway or the cooperation of the cowboys.

The first important step taken to correct the situation was the formation of the Rodeo Association of America (RAA). With a point-awards structure ready to be implemented by January, 1929, it was organized

> in order to insure harmony among them [the rodeos] and to perpetuate traditions connected with the livestock industry and the cowboy sports incident thereto; to standardize the same and adopt rules looking forward towards the holding of contests upon uniform basis; to minimize so far as practicable conflict in dates of contests; and to place such sports so nearly as may be possible on a par with amateur athletic events. . . .[4]

This was not an organization of cowboys. Rather, it was an association of rodeo committees, designed to correct shortcomings in what had caused the contestants' complaints and unhappiness: the rodeo itself.

With headquarters in Salinas, California, the RAA set out to put rodeo on a sounder footing than it had enjoyed to date. North America was divided into fifteen territorial districts, each presided over by a vice-president, a member of the association's board of directors.[5] At the recommendation of the vice-president of the district in which a given rodeo operated, the organization or committee in charge of that contest could apply for membership in the RAA. After an initial application fee of $35 was paid, annual dues were assessed at two percent of the purse* offered at that particular member show, with dues set at a minimum of $35 and a maximum of $150 per year.[6]

One of the many grievances of the cowboy had been the dishonest and misleading advertising that had beckoned him to compete. This problem was solved in part by an RAA rule that required member rodeos to publish the amount to be paid in each event in the *RAA News* at least thirty days before the rodeo was to take place. In addition, sixty days prior to the contest, the rodeo had to file with the RAA a statement of the purse to be paid in each recognized event, including the entry fees, by event, and whether or not these were to be added to the purse. The recognized events were bronc riding (i.e., saddle-bronc riding), bull or steer riding, calf roping, steer roping, steer decorating, steer wrestling, team roping, and wild-cow milking.

---

*The purse is the money put up by the individual rodeo committee. With the cowboys' entry fees added, it constitutes the prize money.

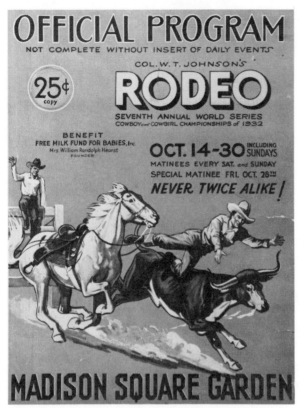

Elaborate programs were issued to acquaint eastern audiences with the western sport of rodeo. On the left is a program for the 1932 rodeo held in Madison Square Garden (courtesy Everett Bowman Collection). On the right is a 1929 prize list for the cowboys entering the Chicago World's Championship Rodeo, organized by Tex Austin, an early promoter noted for his showmanship and generous purses.

The grand entry at the fourth annual World's Championship (or World Series) Rodeo at Madison Square Garden, 1929. Photograph by Century, New York City

To qualify as a member show, the rodeo had to include at least four of these.[7]

Part of the effort "to place such sports so nearly as may be possible on a par with amateur athletic events" involved the revision of the score-keeping system. Up until this time, several rodeos had claimed that their winners were world champions simply because they had won their event or events at that particular rodeo. Being proclaimed a world-championship rodeo increased the drawing power of a contest and attracted more and better cowboys by offering the winners greater prestige. As a result, however, there could be several world-champion cowboys in each event every year. Indignant, Tex Sherman (former Buffalo Bill's Wild West bronc rider and later a rodeo announcer) wrote in his column "Rodeo News" for the magazine *Hoofs and Horns*, "every wild west show on the road today is advertising the shows as a championship rodeo, and every one of their riders is hailed as an 'honest to goodness' champion and I can safely say that many of those world champions have never seen a genuine rodeo."[8]

Nevertheless, the long-running rodeo in Madison Square Garden, New York City, was advertised as the World's Championship Rodeo well into the 1940s. To this day there are oldtimers who insist that they were world champions by virtue of having won their event at one of the contests that persisted in doing this kind of advertising.

The RAA established a point system in order to determine more equitably the true world champions. By this system, which awarded one point per dollar won in any recognized event, the title winners and the all-around champion were named at the end of each year. Points were not given for increased prizes (for instance, when a local business offered money), however, or for that part of the final prize money that was made up of entry fees.[9] This was very significant, and it indicated that further action would have to be taken to satisfy the demands of the contestants.

Judges had long been another object of the cowboys' complaints. Success in rodeo in the early days was not necessarily based on performance. In order to have skill recognized, it was almost essential to have a friend among the judges. If a cowboy went into a strange territory to compete, he stood but little chance to win. Even bribery was not unheard of: for giving a winning or placing score, the judges would take part of the contestant's winnings.[10] This, of course, further contributed to the distrust the cowboy already felt. If there was cheating

Bob Crosby (*left*) accepting the Roosevelt Trophy as the all-around cowboy winner at the Pendleton Round-Up in 1927. Photograph by R. R. Doubleday

The Sam Jackson Trophy, first given in 1929, succeeded the Roosevelt Trophy as the prize for all-around cowboy winners at the Pendleton Round-Up. This picture shows Ike Rude, the 1931 winner.

in the sport, the blame had to lie with the rodeo officials because, as one multi-event contestant, the late Bill Linderman of Red Lodge, Montana, once said: "Rodeoing is about the only sport you can't fix. You'd have to talk to the bulls and the horses, and they wouldn't understand you." Thus, the RAA stressed to its member rodeos the importance of the careful selection of all officials connected with the competition.[11] However, the problems of this aspect of rodeo were not solved merely by such an admonition.

Once the cowboys, too, finally organized, they felt their strength was such that they could make heavy demands concerning judges and other arena personnel. A petition that the cowboys themselves be allowed to select officials was presented at the RAA convention in Ogden, Utah, in January, 1938. This prompted RAA President Maxwell McNutt to observe, "In what sport in the United States is the contestant granted the right to say 'I am both contestant and judge'?"[12] However, cowboy organization did not immediately take care of the problem of judges. Quite some time was to pass before the members, as well as their leaders, would feel comfortable within the framework of their new structure. Even after cowboy and rodeo organizations became quite autonomous and sophisticated, this controversy sometimes took a violent turn. Again following in the footsteps of his earlier counterpart, when no regular recourse existed the twentieth-century cowboy took it upon himself to correct an injustice and to get what was rightly his. This was a vestige of the time when law had not yet reached the western regions of sparse settlement that were the cowboy's place of work. If something had to be done, there was no one to do it but the cowboy himself.

The seriousness of the situation became apparent in August, 1949, when Herbert Frizzell, a member of the Rodeo Cowboys Association (RCA), shot a judge at the Big Springs, Texas, rodeo. A stray bullet also killed a bystander. Finally, in 1954, after a world-champion cowboy had struck down a judge at a Detroit rodeo for giving him a no-score for the second time,* the RCA ordered the suspension of any cowboy "attempting to fix, threaten, bribe, influence, harass or coerce the judges at any time between the opening and closing dates of the rodeo in or out of the arena."[13]

Vast improvements have been made since then in the area of rodeo

---

*He was disqualified for the remainder of the competition.

Smokey Branch on the saddle bronc Glass Eyes, Garden City, Kansas, 1923. Photograph by R. R. Doubleday, courtesy Wyoming State Archives, Museums and Historical Department

judging. In 1978, the Professional Rodeo Cowboys Association introduced a concept known as the Pro Judging System. Administered by a Judges' Commissioner, the program called for twenty full-time, salaried judges and an equal number of part-time associate judges, all experienced in competition, to judge most PRCA-approved rodeos for the year. The funding was to be derived from a combination of sources: producers, committees, contestants, and a percentage of the purse. The judges had to attend Pro Judging seminars, held periodically throughout the country.[14]

The concept was expanded in 1982, when it was renamed the Pro Officials System and underwritten by Wrangler. The name was changed to distinguish the judges (officials) employed directly by the PRCA from regular contestant judges (cowboys from the PRCA membership selected to serve as judges at a particular rodeo). For its initial year, a budget of $550,000 was created, toward which Blue Bell, Inc.— manufacturer of the Wrangler Brand—contributed $200,000. Eight officials were selected from a field of numerous applicants and retained at an annual salary of $18,000. These men judged from 20 to 28 PRCA rodeos each, for a total of 190 for the year. In 1983 the program expanded to include two additional full-time officials and six to eight part-time employees. The administration, scheduling, and payment of salaries are handled through the office of the Director of Pro Officials at PRCA headquarters. As they had under the Pro Judging System, the officials have to attend seminars and orientation sessions in order to keep up with changing rules of competition, besides satisfying such other requirements as are essential to the proper execution of their tasks.[15] The initial dream of having salaried judges officiate at all PRCA rodeos may never be realized. That would require some eighty employees, which, in light of the budget already necessary to manage even the current program, seems prohibitive, at least for the time being.

The importance of today's rodeo official or judge is emphasized in the PRCA rule book:

> The decision of the judges will be final and may not subsequently be overturned by action of the PRCA, its officers or directors, or any other party. Any judge, however, who does not perform his duties in compliance with these rules, or who otherwise abuses his position, will be subject to disciplinary action by the PRCA board.[16]

Considering the problems confronting rodeo in the 1930s, the formation of the Rodeo Association of America was an auspicious first step in the effort to come to terms with them.

The cowboy himself still had no organization to speak for him at that time, however. In fact, he could conceivably be even more exploited by the united front of rodeo management. Yet cowboys were still somewhat reluctant to form their own association. One explanation for this is that individualism has always been a very strong trait in the cowboy. This inbred independence worked against any kind of grouping together. The idea of organizing did not itself repel him; westerners had resorted to that solution before and had formed livestock and cattlemen's associations to promote the common welfare and interests of the range. There had even been isolated attempts by working cowboys to unionize, with a view to obtaining better wages and with the ultimate cooperative goal of making everyone a cattleman. For instance, during the years 1884–87 many cowboys belonged to the Knights of Labor, which had assemblies throughout the West.[17] However, the organization was largely unsuccessful in its efforts to realize the cowboys' aspirations, and only one cowboys' cooperative ranching enterprise resulted—the 3CCC (3 Cowboys Cattle Company). Although, by and large, organization had worked for the western man, the pride and independence of the cowboy—and particularly the rodeo cowboy—caused him to look upon almost every effort made toward organizing with a certain degree of suspicion.[18]

His characteristic individualism was reinforced by the structure under which early contests were conducted. Then, as now, the rodeo cowboy was responsible for all expenses relating to his travels from one rodeo to the next. In this aspect, rodeo is different from many other sports, and it is quite possibly this element that has made the rodeo cowboy's situation so difficult for the uninitiated to understand. The wild-west-show performer, on the other hand, received a salary set by the contract under which he was hired. As an outgrowth of this practice, there existed for several decades something called a contract rodeo, in which the cowboy was given a flat weekly or monthly salary for his performance. In the more familiar contest rodeo, he was on his own: he paid his way to the rodeo, paid the entry fees and other expenses, and received the payment only if he won or placed in the events in which he competed. This only served to reinforce his sense of independence.

There were other practical obstacles to organizing, as well. Such an effort required that a large number of cowboys be present in one location at a given time, so as to formulate the ground rules to which the members would be held. The rodeo cowboys were scattered geographically to a far greater extent than today, when annual rodeos in many locations bring a great majority of contestants together several times a year. Moreover, transportation in the early years of rodeo was not as readily available as today, especially for those who also had their roping or steer-wrestling horses to take along. When several ropers and steer wrestlers could get together and travel at one time, they would occasionally get the use of a baggage car or horse car for their horses and equipment as well as themselves.[19] But often they had to find their own means of transportation. Even when horse trailers began to be used in the mid-1920s, most of them were homemade contraptions unsuitable for the extensive and rapid travel needed to follow the circuit, as later cowboys could do.[20] Finally, especially before the formation of the RAA, rodeos were scheduled on a haphazard and rather undependable basis, although some contests had already become regular annual features in their respective communities.

Despite these obstacles to forming a united front, there was a very early attempt to organize by cowboys and cowgirls contesting at the Jefferson County (Colorado) Fair held at the Stockyards Stadium in Denver, in 1910. The participants formed the Broncho Busters' Union and demanded five dollars a day for contesting wild-horse riders.[21] However, money was apparently not the only consideration in their decision to unionize.

A developing professional pride seems to have motivated them. It could well be that these competitors resented the favoritism shown the ropers and hence decided to form their own professional union. Moreover, of all professionals, the cowboy may be the one to discourage imitators and impostors most vehemently, and the *Denver Republican* reported that "the 'horning in' of irresponsible individuals who are but poorly vested in the art of sticking to a saddle without 'pulling leather'"* threatened the respectability of the "ancient and honorable profession" of the real cowboy.[22] However, nothing further was heard of the organization, and it cannot be established whether the members' demands were met at the contest in 1910.

* *Pulling leather* is touching any part of the saddle or animal during the ride and results in disqualification.

Nonetheless, from all indications, the idea of some form of union remained alive among the cowboys. In 1916 wild-west-show performer Fay Ward presented a proposition for such a measure in the monthly magazine of that trade, *The Wild Bunch*. It contains startling parallels to what was eventually achieved several decades later. Mr. Ward proposed an organization that would arrange its own contests through so-called camps in various states. The members, after having duly proven themselves competent, would support both the contests and the management for the organization, as well as fellow-cowboys under a doctor's care and those who had "crossed the Great Divide" without leaving funds for funeral expenses. Ward demonstrated not only an unusual insight into the cowboys' peculiar needs but also an extraordinary anticipation of future developments destined to constitute what he termed "a greater future for the game."[23] However, his ideas apparently remained just a dream, with no steps taken to realize them.

Gradually, however, rodeo cowboys recognized that the odds were against them as they faced a powerful and well-organized rodeo management with an impressive number of member rodeos adhering to its dicta. By the 1930s, more cowboys than ever were making their living by competing in rodeos, not just entering for a lark. Many participants had long felt cheated by the low prizes offered at most contests.

An opportunity to change the situation presented itself in 1932, at the National Western Rodeo in Denver, which the year before had become a part of the Stock Show and Horse Show. It had already been established as a midwinter gathering place for most of the country's top contestants because of the generous purse it offered as well as the congenial atmosphere the stock-show management provided the cowboys. What came about was the idea of timekeeper M. D. Fanning. His discussions with the cowboys had revealed a desire for some form of organization that would not only raise the standards of the sport but also provide funds to take care of those who were injured while competing. There was even talk of a permanent fund for "those scarred and broken veterans whose usefulness in the show world had passed."[24]

At a meeting of "all riders of prominence" on the afternoon of January 19, there was formed "a protective association of cowboys designed to raise the standards of rodeo personnel all over the country and place rodeo performances on an equal plane with other competitive sports."[25] The organization, tentatively named the Cowboys Association of America or the Cowboys Rodeo Association, boasted of ninety-five

Cup winners, including Everett Bowman (*second from left*) at the Oregon City Frontier Days, Oregon City, Idaho, mid-1920s. Courtesy Everett Bowman Collection

Rodeo competition, added to the show in 1931, has consistently drawn major contestants to the National Western Rodeo Stock Show and Horse Show in Denver. This picture, taken in January, 1932, shows (*left to right*) Billy Wilkenson, Hugh Bennett, Oral Zumwalt, Jake McClure, Dick Truitt, and Everett Bowman. Courtesy Everett Bowman Collection

members from the start. A fund of three hundred dollars was collected at once by passing the hat and was expected to grow to five hundred dollars before the run of the show ended. Eight committees were organized, one for each branch of rodeo,* and these were charged with working out individual plans for the entire association's approval. Announcer Abe Lefton of Los Angeles was appointed chairman.

The primary function of the new organization was "to compell [sic] certain annual rodeos to pay more money to performers."[26] The participants made it clear that their action was not to be interpreted as a criticism of the National Western contest, which from the very first year had been a favorite of the cowboys. Another purpose was to develop a point system for the selection of a champion at the end of the year. Nothing was said of how this plan would be coordinated with the point-awards arrangement already in use by the Rodeo Association of America, however. The champion, to be selected by the cowboys themselves, would have to be "skilled in every department of the sport from steer wrestling to bronc riding."[27] Thus, even though cowboys in the earlier days of rodeo more often than not competed in several events, the championship scheme worked out by the organization appears to have been overambitious. The cowboy of the time was certainly more versatile than today's rodeo contestant, simply because competition was not as stiff, but it would have been very unusual for anyone to excel in more than two events. Furthermore, as a rule, each man concentrated on either the timed or the rough-stock events and did not mix the two areas necessary for winning the championship under this plan.

In the next few years, nothing further was heard or written of the cowboy union that had had such a promising beginning. Rodeo contestants continued to earn little money and to be plagued with unfairness and deception. What brought matters to a head was the first serious *rodeo* cowboy strike. Previously there had been only some half-hearted attempts at using the strike for leverage to solve occasional problems at rodeos, such as at Alliance, Nebraska, and Colorado Springs, Colorado, in the early 1920s.[28] However, working cowboys had struck before. Some of these early rebellions have gone on record.

---

*Heading the various committees were Buck Lucas, Fort Worth, Texas; Fred Beeson, Arkansas City, Kansas; Johnny Schneider, Livermore, California; Elmer Hepler, Carlsbad, New Mexico; Earl Thode, Casa Grande, Arizona; Hugh Bennett, Fort Thomas, Arizona; Eddie Woods, Emmett, Idaho; and Smokey Snyder, Kimberly, British Columbia.

Charles "Sharkey" Irwin on the saddle bronc Magruder, Ski Hi Stampede, Buena
Vista, Colorado, 1927.

In the spring of 1883, cowboys in the Texas Panhandle struck for a wage increase of from thirty to fifty dollars. The *Fort Collins Courier* reported:

> The movement of Texas cattle will be impeded this year unless the owners and cow-boys agree upon terms in the Pan-handle country. . . . The novelty of the strike is that the men have struck before work has begun, and the serious feature is that it is in anticipation of the spring work, or the regular annual round-up which can not go on without them.[29]

Reportedly, the strikers, about two hundred strong, were armed and determined to resort to any means in order to secure a raise to fifty dollars a month from the thirty to forty dollars they were earning. Already at this time, the cowboy had clearly demonstrated what drastic measures he was prepared to resort to in order to obtain what he believed was due him. He was, then as now, sure of who he was and what he deserved. While striking, the Panhandle cowboys took jobs as streetcar drivers in the cities, where the regular drivers had, at that time, also walked out.[30] This could be an indication of a beginning sense of belonging in a structured society: the cowboy was awakened to the fact that he was not the only professional whose lot had been overlooked and needed improvement. In 1886, cowboys in Wyoming Territory struck for a five-dollar-a-month pay increase. That conflict called attention to the importance of the cowboy and his skills. "The occupation of the cowboy is one gained only by long experience upon the range. It is not the acquisition of a day. The stock owners will probably accede to the demands as now is the time competent hands are most needed."[31]

From 1886 to the 1930s was a long interval, but the first three and a half decades of the twentieth century had provided enough of a learning period for the cowboy to win confidence in himself as a participant in a sport that was—despite everything—gaining a membership. It had also become a profession; as cars and horse trailers came into widespread use, cowboys began to follow rodeos for a livelihood, such as it was.[32]

By the second half of the 1930s, many other occupational groups had already organized. Time and conditions were ripe for the cowboy, too, to make another attempt at it. Even though he had failed several times before, he had eventually come to realize that such a step was possibly the only solution for the survival of his sport—and of himself.

3

An Order to Represent Our Ideals

Ironically, what brought matters to a head and irrevocably changed the direction that the sport was going to take was a man who, at least in his own publicity, was called "truly the 'angel of the rodeo.'"[1]

It is generally held that Col. William T. Johnson of San Antonio, Texas, had founded the Madison Square Garden and Boston Garden World's Championship shows (in 1926 and 1932, respectively) and produced them annually for several years. However, recently uncovered documents seem to reveal that rodeos were held in Madison Square Garden on an annual basis prior to 1926. Substantiating this conclusion is the fact that two large New York City hotels began sponsoring rodeo trophies prior to 1926. In 1920 the McAlpin Hotel began awarding the McAlpin Trophy to the "champion woman rider of the world" each year at the Cheyenne Frontier Days, and three years later the Roosevelt Hotel began to present the prestigious Roosevelt Trophy to the all-around cowboy who won the Cheyenne Frontier Days and the Pendleton Round-Up in one year.[2] By 1936, however, Colonel Johnson was well ensconced as producer of both East Coast events. In the official program for the Boston show in 1936 (November 2–11), he declared, "It's goin' to be tougher than hell; if a cowboy claims to be a champion, let him come to Boston and prove it."[3] Indeed, the cowboy did.

As has already been mentioned, one of the several reasons why previous efforts to unionize had been unsuccessful was the difficulty of assembling a large enough group for such important action to be effective.[4] At the Boston Garden show, however, which traditionally followed the Madison Square Garden World's Championship Rodeo, most of the top contestants of the time were gathered. Furthermore, the month-long stay in New York, just prior to the Boston rodeo, must have served to bring about an even greater sense of cohesion and cooperation among the cowboys.

The RAA rules stipulated that the purses offered had to be published well ahead of the rodeo dates in the official *Bulletin*. (The Bulletin appeared in the monthly magazine *Hoofs and Horns*, designated in March, 1936, as the official publication for the RAA's announcements.)[5] This enabled the cowboy to decide whether or not it was worth his while to enter any given rodeo. However, there was nothing that stated that those moneys had to be a given minimum amount. Bearing in mind that the cowboy—then as now—was responsible for all expenses connected with the pursuit of his occupation, it is clear that it was very difficult for anyone to make a living as a rodeo contestant. The purse at the 1936 Madison Square Garden contest (October 7–25) had been $45,000 which averaged out to $1,760 for each of the twenty-six performances.[6] By comparison, that year's Cheyenne Frontier Days (July 22–25) had offered $7,500 plus added entry fees, to be spread out over the four performances.[7] In 1936, the purse for the entire eleven-day contest at Boston Garden was $6,400[8]—so small that even the winner of an event would hardly cover expenses. In order to compete in New York City and Boston, many cowboys traveled three thousand miles. Furthermore, the stay at each contest ran into weeks, which of course added to the cowboys' expenses. Contestants, used to traveling the distance to the East Coast rodeos every fall, had come to expect that the money offered would make their trip worthwhile. It was their last opportunity for the year to compete for substantial sums of prize money and to earn points toward the RAA world championships. In previous years they had not had much reason for disappointment. In time, however, as their profession had developed, they had also come to expect more.

No records were kept before 1945 of exactly how much a full-time competitor made, but two articles in *Time* made reference to the amount some of the contestants would earn in a year during the period under discussion. In 1935, according to a computation made by the publication, the average income was $2,000; two years later, it was $3,000.[9] By the standards of the day, an annual income of $2,000 was certainly not at the low end of the scale: by comparison, a dentist made $2,391 and a public-school teacher $1,227.[10] There was even in the rodeo profession one exceptional case of the famous lady trick and

With Best Wishes "Tad"

One of the top female stars of early rodeo was Tad Barnes Lucas. Courtesy Tad Lucas Collection

bronc rider Tad Lucas, who by 1935 was earning $12,000 a year.[11] One cannot, however, get a complete picture of the financial situation in rodeo at the time simply by considering Lucas's earnings. Although trick riding was at times a competitive event, it was also considered a contract act, along with trick roping, clowning, handling of trained animals, and so forth. The performers worked on a contract basis for a given amount of money per show. Thus, unlike the contestants, they did not run the risk of coming away from a rodeo with nothing. Although contract entertainers also had to pay their own way, they were at least assured of a salary after fulfillment of their obligation to the committee.

Money was truly the most important issue at Boston. However, if that had been the sole problem, what was to evolve would never have taken place. This time, there were other grievances as well, which prompted the action that followed. The need for set rules for the various events and for competent judges also loomed large.[12]

On October 30, three days before the first performance was scheduled, the following petition, signed by sixty-one cowboys, was delivered to Colonel Johnson.

> For the Boston Show, we the undersigned *demand* that the Purses be doubled and the Entrance Fees added in each and every event. Any Contestant failing to sign this Petition will not be permitted to contest, by order of the undersigned.[13]

To prove their intentions were serious, the cowboys had, ahead of time, secured their train tickets for the return home, as well as shipping authorizations for their horses.[14]

When the contest opened its eleven-day run, the cowboys refused to compete by unanimously voting to strike. Determined to go on with the rodeo, Colonel Johnson hurriedly attempted to find other riders to fill the gaps: 130 cowboys were reportedly en route to New York from a Chicago show, and others were contacted as well.[15] When these contestants learned of the situation, however, almost to a man they backed the strikers and refused to come to Boston. Sixty-one of the top names in rodeo watched and booed from the stands the first night as stable grooms, chute men, ex-jockeys, and wild-west-show performers tried to ride saddle broncs, while the band played "Empty Saddles in the Old Corral."[16]

The following day, the cowboys announced to the newspapers that they were leaving the city. However, they chose to remain at least long enough to see what effect such a public statement would have.[17] By that evening, Colonel Johnson had agreed to increase the purse to $14,000 for the fourteen performances. A portion of this sum came from the added entry fees, while George V. Brown, manager of the Boston Garden arena, himself contributed $1,250. In addition, Colonel Johnson gave $20 to each of the first-nighters who had watched the opening while still on strike.[18] In return for the concession he had made, however, Johnson expected the cowboys' cooperation. Thus, to the customary release clause in the contestant's entry blank was added the following rider:

> IT IS DISTINCTLY understood and agreed between Col. W. T. Johnson and myself, in consideration of the strike that has been made, I will abide by any and all rules and regulations of the show and all rules that have been published in the New York Prize list and I will not agitate nor form a strike nor will I use my influence to keep any contestant that did not cooperate with the strikers here from entering any show at any time or at any place. I further agree and promise that I will cooperate in every way possible to make this show a success and will work under the instructions and abide by rules of Col. W. T. Johnson.
>
> I AGREE that this instrument be binding on my heirs, next of kin and assigns.[19]

The main issue had been a fair share of the prize money, and the cowboys had won. Realizing that their course of action had produced the desired results, they deemed the time right finally to make their united front a permanent one. Who would know when they again would come up against a storm such as that which they had just weathered? Thus was formed, on November 6, 1936, the United Cowboys Turtle Association.[20] Shortly, the word "United" was dropped from the name, and it became the Cowboys Turtle Association (CTA).

There are several divergent stories about how the organization acquired its name. One has it that, during the meetings, one cowboy said, "Now let's don't give this outfit no highfalutin' name, let's take it slow like a turtle."[21] Another source attributes the name to a joke made by one of the organizers to the effect that "we've been slow as turtles doin' somethin' like this"[22] and that therefore the cowboys

Cowboys' walk-out at the 1936 World's Championship Rodeo in Boston. *Mounted, left to right*: Everett Bowman, E. Pardee, Red Thompson, Jake McClure, and Everett Shaw. *Standing*: Dick Truitt, Rusty McGinty, Eddie Curtis, Hub Whiteman, and Hugh Bennett. Photograph by *Boston Daily Record*

The cowboys present a desk set to George V. Brown, manager of the Boston Garden, 1936[?]. *Left to right*: Everett Bowman, Hugh Bennett, Herman Linder, Everett Shaw, and Rusty McGinty.

should be called turtles. Still another story explains the name by the fact that the cowboys of the time often wore turtleneck sweaters instead of shirts.[23]

Regardless of how the name was derived, however, the name Turtle stuck, and the reptile became the symbol of the new organization, represented on its letterhead and on hat and belt pins. Its motto was "slow but sure."[24]

The main purpose of the CTA was

> to raise the standard of rodeos as a whole and to give them undisputed place in the foremost rank of American sports. This is to be done by classing as "unfair" those shows which use rules unfair to the contestants and those which offer purses so small as to make it impossible for contestants to make expenses. The Association asks a fair deal for contestants as well as rodeo organizations and hopes to work harmoniously with them.[25]

If this could be accomplished, it would at the same time give rodeo a greater audience appeal. How this was going to be effected was laid down in four rules, three of which dealt with strikes, an action that had been all-important for the success of the step that had just been taken.[26]

The rules were brief and fit on one single typewritten page. To show how important it was for the cowboy to improve his economic situation, the first rule imposed a heavy fine (five hundred dollars) on any member who competed at a rodeo where the cowboys had agreed to strike.[27] The organization had given the member a powerful weapon in the strike, but he was at the same time very much aware that misuse of that tool could work against him. The third rule provided a safety valve in that it stipulated that *all* members had to approve a strike before a list of signatures could be sent to the committee of a rodeo whose purse was not satisfactory. It forbade the individual walkout by any one member for reason of dissatisfaction.

The fine imposed on strikebreakers or violators was to go into a trust fund and be used for expenses in lawfully negotiating with the committee of a rodeo being struck. This was detailed in the second rule, which also stipulated a one hundred-dollar fine for "disgraceful conduct." This rule set the annual dues at five dollars and delineated some of the duties of the nonsalaried officials.

In the fourth rule, another problem of long standing was dealt with—judges. The CTA (referring to itself as "the Union") declared that it had the *right* to demand capable judges at the rodeo. However, it would not interfere in any one member's personal disagreements with a judge or with another member.[28]

The original board of directors of the Cowboys Turtle Association,[29] selected from among the top contestants of the time, consisted of the following officers:

Rusty McGinty .... President
Eddie Woods .... Vice-President
Hugh Bennett .... Secretary-Treasurer
Everett Bowman .... Speaker (i.e., spokesman for
                                     the members)

In addition, each rodeo event had its representative:

Dick Griffith .... Bareback riders
Bob Crosby .... Calf ropers
Eddie Curtis... Bronk riders
Hub Whiteman.. Bulldoggers
Paul Carney... Steer riders

The slate of officers changed somewhat after the first formal elections were held during the Southwestern Exposition and Fat Stock Show Rodeo in Fort Worth, Texas, in mid-March of 1937.

The rodeo committees now had their organization in the RAA and the cowboys theirs in the CTA, both for the purpose of furthering their common interests. This did not mean, initially, that CTA cowboys could compete only at RAA rodeos, nor that these member shows required that contestants be Turtles.

However, despite organization, all did not run smoothly. The cowboys' surprise at finally having the strength to be heard collectively and in many cases having their demands met had some unfortunate consequences. To a degree, the first victory at Boston inspired an overnight confidence, which, on occasion, caused their newly discovered strength to be misused over the next few years. More important, the cowboys' power had not been tested. They had a united voice, but they had different ideas as to how to go about getting what they wanted. Sometimes the very knowledge of their newfound strength prompted some to make claims seeking contests to abide by the CTA rules, an action that was resented by the more conservative faction of the membership. On several occasions, the Turtles on short notice called a strike before a rodeo at which their demands, as set forth in the rules, were not met. The fact that this could be done in such an unpredictable fashion made the association appear intimidating to rodeo committees. This tenuous situation was, for a while, a threat to the very existence of the sport, for the lack of trust and dependability that the cowboys displayed could easily have led either group to decide to give up on the other. The arbitrary manner in which last-minute exactions often were made was quite naturally resented by the rodeo committees, and those of upcoming contests quickly became hesitant to deal with the CTA: if they failed to meet the demands the CTA might make, the rodeo would be endangered.[30]

The association enlisted the help of the RAA to have member shows guarantee the average at one hundred dollars per day in each event, in addition to having entry fees or their equivalent added into the total prize-money amount. In this matter the CTA displayed the typical impetuousness of a new organization.

As the CTA rapidly grew in confidence, it proceeded to make further demands of the shows under the purview of the RAA, which was the central scheduling agency for contests. These were presented in the form of an ultimatum to that organization on April 20, 1937. This action was taken in spite of an agreement not to make any further claims, entered into with the RAA at its convention in Reno, Nevada, January 29–30, 1937. There, delegates from the CTA had participated in an effort to iron out the obvious difficulties that existed and to lay the groundwork for increased cooperation in the year ahead. The RAA had agreed to divide the prize money (percentage of total to first-, second-, and third-place winners) and to issue points according to the Turtles' specifications.[31] In return for this concession, a promise had been made by the cowboys to finish out the year 1937 without causing further problems, provided the RAA rodeos kept their part of the agreement by securing the guarantee to that effect at least thirty days before any given show. The promise had been repeated later the same year by Everett Bowman.[32]

Regardless, the CTA persisted. The organization was merely a few months old, yet its advance had been such that it stood to jeopardize seriously the sport it had been formed to protect and improve. It used its powerful weapon—the strike—by threatening to walk out on some of the largest rodeos in 1937.

A strike, the second in four months, was imminent the night before the first performance of La Fiesta de los Vaqueros, held February 19–22 in Tucson, Arizona. The reason was that one of the CTA members had entered that contest after violating a rule. The CTA had demanded that the Pima County Fair Commission, sponsor of the show, accept the blacklist it had developed upon organization in order to police its members; by allowing the blacklisted cowboy to enter, the committee had betrayed that trust. Therefore, for the strike to be averted, it was necessary to deny that cowboy the right to compete. Yet, even though the committee returned his entry fees and reimbursed his expenses, thereby ostensibly coming to terms with the CTA exactions, immediately following this settlement further demands were made—now with regard to the selection of judges, an area of complaint of long standing. Finally, after a compromise had been reached, the show was allowed to proceed.[33] (The California Rodeo at Salinas did use cowboy judges for the first time that year. This was a decided victory for the cowboys, although not without controversy.)[34]

Several other big RAA contests in 1937 were threatened by strikes by the dictatorial Turtles. Many member-shows were by now unwilling to deal with the RAA for fear that problems with the contestants would ensue, and chose to go nonprofessional (i.e., to allow no Turtles to enter). According to the noted rodeo historian Clifford P. Westermeier, the CTA "had been reduced to an organization of monopolists, strikers and unreliable racketeers."[35]

In the fall of 1937, after almost a year of intense contention, war was finally declared on the CTA. The Pendleton Round-Up presented its stand to the CTA members in the form of a sign on the rodeo-office door, which read "No Turtles Need Apply." Because of the officials' refusal to allow the Turtles the right to select judges, the show that year was an amateur event,[36] with local and nonmember cowboys taking part. Those who entered the contest had to sign an affidavit vouching for their amateur status. Nevertheless, the show was a success and broke attendance records of long standing, the front page of the *East Oregonian* proclaiming that "'hayseed' cowhands showed thousands of visitors they need make no apologies for their lack of professionalism."[37]

Troubles similar to those at Pendleton, where committees sought to exclude the Turtles from their contests, were reported at Ellensburg, Washington, that year, as well as at other contests. The situation went so far as to provoke several important rodeos into announcing their intention to follow in Pendleton's footsteps in 1938 by reverting to amateur contests.[38]

In spite of it all, CTA cowboys persevered. The purse at the 1937 Madison Square Garden rodeo was thirty-eight thousand dollars; *Time* reported that the average annual income for a contestant was three thousand dollars, and it was estimated that about thirty cowboys made from eight thousand to fifteen thousand dollars per year.[39] Evidently, despite troubles, the economic situation was improving.

By 1938, many large, established rodeos intended to relinquish their membership in the RAA because of the repeated troubles these contests had had with CTA members, who were seeking, as best they knew how, to enforce the rules governing their organization. (Ironically, had these rodeos, in fact, given up their RAA membership, the cowboy would have been no further along than he was at the turn of the century. His organization would have had little significance.) The controversy kept boiling. It became quite apparent that the CTA, in making its demands over the past two years, had not acted with the consensus of the majority of its members. The conservative faction of the association suffered from the actions of the more vociferous and radical members—as did the entire sport, for that matter.[40] Its leadership was insistent and overwhelming and often had not consulted the entire membership. Even though all wished to see a realization of their platform, most preferred to go about it in a more businesslike manner than had been used to date.

The conflict between the two organizations drew the attention of the press, which by this time had demonstrated an increased awareness of the sport. However, the RAA requested that the controversy be kept out of the papers until it had been resolved.[41] This indicates clearly that the organization was anxious to continue its efforts to reach some sort of agreement favorable to both itself and the CTA. Possibly it blamed itself in part for what had taken place and saw weaknesses in its own structure and operation.

To restore harmony, eight rules were drawn up at the RAA convention at Ogden, Utah, in January, 1938. These were designed to avoid controversy in the coming year. (That money was still the foremost consideration is evidenced by the contents of Rule I, which covered that important aspect: "At all shows or rodeos for the year 1938, all entrance fees must be added in each event to the prize money." Earlier, the entry fees paid by the cowboys had frequently ended up in the coffers of the committees, which often had sought to pad the pockets of their members at the expense of the cowboys.) If a member rodeo wished to deviate from the rules, as approved by the RAA, such a change had to be printed in the prize list sixty days before the rodeo and in the *RAA Bulletin* thirty days before the contest.[42] This important stipulation was intended to eliminate the earlier complaint of misleading and fraudulent advertising, which had often cheated the cowboy. It gave him the choice of whether or not he wished to compete at any given rodeo.

The lockout at Pendleton in 1937 was reported in an article in the *Saturday Evening Post*, but not until the summer of the following year. Although the subject of the piece was the Round-Up in general, ostensibly to publicize the 1938 show, the headline, "No Turtles Need Apply," drew unwitting attention to the controversy: it was written by Wanden M. LaFarge, who was later made honorary CTA member No. 1 for her assistance in writing the organization's *Articles of Association, By-Laws and Rules.*[43] In the article, the circumstances surrounding the 1937 Round-Up were merely mentioned in passing and not meant to condemn either the cowboys or the Round-Up committee for their actions. However, it was the national exposure of the continuing battles that served as an eye-opener to the Turtles. For the second half of 1938 and into 1939, their demands were considerably toned down.[44]

Ogden, Utah, had been the scene of the latest—and to date most successful—peacemaking effort. Ironically, that city was to provide the ammunition for the next (and last) Turtle strike, the entente notwithstanding. It was by this time a year and a half since the agreement had been entered into, but it was obvious the cowboys could no longer uphold it. They made this clear in connection with the Pioneer Days Rodeo, July 21–24, 1939.

A purse of $3,100 had been advertised. However, CTA President Everett Bowman declared from Salt Lake City, where he was competing in the Covered Wagon Days Rodeo (July 22–24), that no CTA members were to take part in the Ogden show. This walkout by the Turtles was caused by the refusal of Mayor Harman W. Peery of Ogden (also president of the rodeo committee) to increase the prize money to

$4,100. Bowman stated, "For 150 cowboys 4,100 dollars isn't much prize money to divide. We spent that much in gasoline coming here." The decision to strike Ogden was made by some of the directors of the CTA, including Hoyt Heffner, Everett Shaw, and Hub Whiteman.[45]

At this point, around fifty cowboys, among them Burel Mulkey, Kid Fletcher, Smokey Snyder, Dick Griffith, and Fritz Truan, all leaders in their events, staged a rebellion. They decided to participate in the Ogden rodeo regardless of the walkout dictum. Their action was prompted by a compromise by Mayor Peery, who did, in fact, increase the prize money to $4,100, while adding an extra performance, to take place in the afternoon of Monday, the twenty-fourth. In short order, however, CTA officials imposed a $500 fine on each of the dissidents; furthermore, some of the individuals would not be permitted to enter the upcoming Cheyenne Frontier Days, July 25–29.

Bowman defended the actions of the association by asserting that, although the Ogden purse had been advertised at $3,100, there had been no indication as to how the money was to be divided. Moreover, he claimed, the Cheyenne Frontier Days officials, too, had apparently neglected to publish such a breakdown, while also refusing to increase the total purse by the amount requested by the CTA. The members of the rebellion issued a statement, requesting the CTA to retract its ban on the Pioneer Days show. They were also determined to ignore the fines.[46]

The Sunday (July 23) edition of the *Salt Lake Tribune* carried the following headline on the front page: "Rodeo Riders' Association Head Resigns, Turtle Association Rift Assumes National Aspects." As it turned out, Everett Bowman's resignation in July of 1939 was only temporary. Not only had his orders been disobeyed by some fifty "rebellious 'buckaroos,'" as the paper put it, but the RAA seemed to side with those rebels. RAA Secretary Fred S. McCargar felt Bowman had failed to live up to the agreement not to call a strike over prize money just before a show. Apparently he did not hold as valid Bowman's criticism of the lack of a published breakdown of the purse. In a telegram sent to Burel Mulkey (CTA saddle-bronc director and leader of the dissenters) jointly by Frontier Days Committee Chairman R. J. Hofmann and stock contractor Verne Elliott, the dissenters were assured that they were welcome in Cheyenne and that "no penalties will be tolerated."[47]

An atmosphere that was in general more conducive to sportsmanship and fair play began to prevail in rodeo. At the same time, committees as well as the public began to look upon the professional rodeo cowboy in a new light. Complaints became rarer, as each side came to understand what it was the other wanted. Once this important realization had taken place, both could finally begin working toward their common goals.

The following, in summary, were the demands; in retrospect they seem very simple and basic:

Contestants' demands:

1. Fair and reasonable purses offered and distributed so that it will offer best chance to make money.
2. Fair entry fee and *added* to purse.
3. Competent arena help, judges, etc.
4. "Official" RAA events open only to proven contestants.
5. Separate classes for "amateurs" and "beginners" and the fact advertised.

The RAA book made no mention of professional or nonprofessional contestants. It was generally believed that the qualifications of the cowboy should be evaluated to determine his eligibility to compete in an RAA event for official points and the chance to win official championship titles.[48] However, it would seem that holding membership in the CTA automatically provided such eligibility. Nevertheless, as already discussed, a nonmember was also allowed to compete at RAA shows.

Management's demands:

1. Contestants to enter far enough in advance of opening date to allow scheduling.
2. Proper dress, proper equipment on first day through final performance.
3. Contestants must have entry fee.[49]

The members of the fledgling association had in its first few years tested their power—often with unfortunate results. As western men, they were doers, not parliamentarians, and the long, drawn-out discussions back and forth, which always become necessary in organizations of this scope, frustrated them. It took some time to realize this, perhaps longer than necessary, because of the impertinence of those members who expected changes to happen overnight.

Although the fellow cowboy's interest was uppermost in his thoughts, President Everett Bowman did not always take into consideration the fact that the rules that applied in situations where big business and the fate of several hundred members were decided were different than those in dealings on a one-to-one basis. He has been accused of stubbornness and lack of foresight, but he is nevertheless unanimously credited with the leadership that laid the foundation for organized professional rodeo.

In the original rules, as stated, a fine was imposed for "disgraceful conduct." Now, with an organization that cared for his well-being, the cowboy's attitude and appearance changed drastically, and the association did much to encourage such a change.[50]

For the first time, the rodeo cowboy had definite guidelines for his appearance and conduct, which helped make him a respectable figure and which placed his sport "on a par with [other] amateur athletic events." For quite a while he had existed without these directions, and that period had not been a happy one for him and his contests. He may have believed he could live and prosper without express standards, but doing so had proved disastrous and had almost spelled his doom. The cowboy would demonstrate that he was capable of living within a framework of rules, as his counterpart—the working cowhand—had been able to do in the past.

Cow country had had its own, unwritten etiquette, but several of the large ranches had, in addition, made several very specific rules for the working cowboy to follow, or his employment would be terminated. Charles Goodnight had three rules for his employees: no gambling, no drinking, and no fighting. Goodnight, an extremely capable cowman but a stern disciplinarian, would at the beginning of a cattle drive draw up an agreement, not only concerning each man's duty but, even more important, also regarding his conduct. As manager of the J A Ranch in the Texas Panhandle during the years 1877–87, he had made an agreement with the managers of the neighboring Espuela and Matador ranches not to hire anyone who had been "discharged elsewhere for theft or drunkenness."[51]

The management of the XIT Ranch of Texas, under Abner Taylor, in 1888 posted no less than twenty-three rules in each of its camps, three of them relating to conduct. Apparently, a great many employees appreciated the rules, which doubtless must have given the ranch and, in turn, its many cowboys a good reputation in a formerly lawless territory. One hand, in thinking back, commented that it would have been "best for all concerned if all companies had been as strict."[52]

It is an interesting parallel that both the working cowhand and the rodeo cowboy had to undergo the transformation, in the eyes of society, from a bad, undesirable character to a trustworthy and respectable one—another tie between the sport and the industry from which it sprang. By 1939, the rodeo cowboy had completed that change and had prescribed and enforced rules that he himself had been instrumental in formulating. His future looked promising.

4

A Germ of Professionalism

While the controversies of the 1930s were going on, rodeo continued to gain a following as a spectator sport. The contestants, too, began to acquire respect and recognition as a group of professionals, which they were despite initial lack of organization. Indeed, if the term *professional* can be defined as anyone who makes his living from a given endeavor, then many rodeo cowboys were professionals already at the beginning of the 1930s. In fact, they had been so for quite some time before that, in the much broader sense of the criterion: "As soon as it becomes enjoyable enough to the spectator for the charging of admission, a sport contains a germ of professionalism."[1]

One of the decade's first tests of the cowboys' professionalism came with the creation of the National Western Rodeo in Denver in 1931. This was an addition to the National Western's Stock Show and part of the Horse Show, which in that year celebrated its silver jubilee.

The National Western Rodeo became from the start a favorite of the cowboys. Although not an RAA member until 1944,[2] it nevertheless paid out a substantial amount in prize money, drawing the top names to the city to compete. It replaced the Tucson, Arizona, rodeo—La Fiesta de los Vaqueros—as the first rodeo of the year and was one of the very first indoor rodeos ever held.

There had been quite some discussion by the Stock Show board before deciding to add the rodeo feature as a last-ditch effort to rescue the show from its financial difficulties. The main argument had been the reputed unsavory character of the cowboy. This concern had apparently been unfounded, however, as the manager of the National Western Stock Show, Horse Show and Rodeo, Courtland R. Jones, admitted at the end of the first year's rodeo:

These men are good fellows. They're busy all the time, and they've got to keep in condition to do what they do. They are men; all the way thru [sic]—as fine a bunch as I've known, and I hope they'll come back to our show in the future.[3]

Mr. Jones showed his appreciation of the caliber of men he had brought to Denver by sending a personal letter to each of the contestants, who in 1931 numbered over 150.[4]

Denver was impressed with the cowboy contestants and treated them well and fairly in the contest. There were no complaints. The competition ran smoothly, and everyone was content. Although the city had long been an important center for the cattle industry in the Rocky Mountain area, it had also taken on a very cosmopolitan character through that segment of its population connected with other business interests. The addition of the rodeo to the long-established horse show therefore introduced the sport to a new audience. That it was an immediate triumph was shown on the annual Society Night, when Denver's elite flocked to the stadium to cheer the added attraction.

Cowboys were, in fact, beginning to be noticed by the press, and not only in negative circumstances. They were, of course, most conspicuous when appearing in the eastern rodeos, held in the fall, and thus it was at that time that they drew the attention of the major popular news publications. *Popular Mechanics* featured the cowboy and rodeo in 1926; *Newsweek* followed in 1933, *Time* two years later.[5]

Simultaneously, two magazines appeared—aimed at first directly at the horseman, then, gradually, at the cowboy and the emerging rodeo enthusiast. The first of these was *Hoofs and Horns*, which was styled "A Western Range Publication." Established as a monthly magazine on July 24, 1931, it was for many years published in Tucson, Arizona, with Ethel A. ("Ma") Hopkins as managing editor. *Hoofs and Horns* directed itself in the beginning primarily to cattlemen but soon began to devote its pages more and more to rodeo, listing upcoming shows and their dates and officials. By the June, 1934, edition, it included the RAA standings and rodeo results. The RAA declared *Hoofs and Horns* its official publication in 1936 and printed its *RAA Bulletin* for the first time in the March, 1936, issue.[6] CTA news first appeared in December, 1936, and on July 27, 1937, the CTA selected *Hoofs and Horns* as its official organ at a meeting in Cheyenne, Wyoming. The "Cowboys Turtle Association" column began with the April, 1938, edition.[7]

Ethel "Ma" Hopkins, editor of *Hoofs and Horns* from 1931 until 1954. Courtesy Willard H. Porter, Oklahoma City

Attesting to the fact that *Hoofs and Horns* (selling for ten cents an issue or one dollar per year by subscription) was widely read among cowboys was a new service that "Ma" Hopkins made available in April, 1937. The magazine offered to forward mail to traveling cowboys. If a letter could not be delivered, it would be published in the following month's magazine.[8]

In January, 1936, the *Western Horseman* magazine came into being in Lafayette, California, with P. T. Albert as editor and publisher. It termed itself "Official news of the Palomino Horse Association, the Contra Costa Horseman's Association, the Hayward Rodeo, the Livermore Rodeo, Atascadero Golden Spur Club, the Mother Lode Rodeo, the Reno Rodeo." A quarterly in its first year, the *Western Horseman* switched to bimonthly publication in 1937; in 1949 it became a monthly magazine. Although at first local in scope, covering only central California events, the *Western Horseman* nevertheless served an important function from the beginning: the California rodeos, because of the long season, attracted many of the top cowboys from all over the country, and they received favorable press exposure through the magazine.

With the September–October, 1943, issue, the *Western Horseman* began publication in Reno, Nevada, with Graham M. Dean as both publisher and editor; from the next issue on, Dean was strictly publisher, and Merrill S. Gaffney became editor. In 1948 the publication became a member of Speidel Newspapers, Inc., "a national service and research organization devoted to publications in the best interest of our country and our homes."[9] With the July–August, 1948, issue, the magazine moved to Colorado Springs, Colorado, which has been its headquarters since that time. It had by then become a publication for horsemen all over the nation, and now claims to be the world's leading horse magazine.[10] Moreover, from the very earliest issues on, there appeared well-written articles on rodeo and rodeo cowboys, which undoubtedly did much to help the sport and its participants gain acceptance and popularity in wider and wider circles.

As a result of these efforts, rodeo began to expand to areas where contests had rarely been held before. Several of the larger fairs in the East and the South added rodeo to the program: the Eastern States Exposition in Springfield, Massachusetts, included a rodeo in 1933, and the Mid-South Fair in Memphis, Tennessee, and the Southeastern Fair in Atlanta, Georgia, followed suit in 1935.[11] A column,

"Eastern Rodeos," written by Herbert S. Maddy, became a regular feature in *Hoofs and Horns* in the spring of 1935.

As more eyes were opened to the sport, many began to engage in it for recreation and as a hobby. Several wealthy men in the East devoted themselves to rodeo on a large scale. Al Hernig, millionaire milk dealer in Pennsylvania, had a barn outside Philadelphia filled with western dogging, trick-riding, and roping horses; his stable even included a bucking horse. In his private rodeo arena, Hernig staged shows for friends, in which he himself rode. Another easterner, New Jersey silk-mill owner Lew Weber, gave free shows to guests at his rodeo grounds on the Black Horse Pike.[12] Fraternal and civic organizations in the East began to realize rodeo's potential as a fund-raising medium for local charities, something of which their western counterparts had long been aware.[13]

The following notice appeared in the December, 1934, number of *Hoofs and Horns*:

> The Director of the New York Public Library desires to obtain copies of *Hoofs and Horns* from July 24, 1931 [first issue] to April 5, 1933, in order to complete the file. It will be much appreciated by the Director and also by the present management of *Hoofs and Horns* if anyone having copies of these early issues will forward them to *Hoofs and Horns*, P.O. Box 790, Tucson, Arizona.[14]

The New York Public Library never obtained these issues. Its holdings begin with the October, 1933, issue and continue through that of August, 1954,[15] at which time *Hoofs and Horns* was consolidated with another publication, *The Buckboard*. The fact that the library was even aware of the publication, and also wanted copies of it, can only be interpreted as a definite indication that rodeo was a growing phenomenon.

By mid-decade there was no question that rodeo had secured a foothold nationwide. In 1936, the nineteen-day Madison Square Garden rodeo was seen by nearly a quarter of a million spectators; Cheyenne and Pendleton could boast of audiences of 100,000 each, Denver of 105,000. By that year, rodeo had become the featured attraction of the entire National Western Stock Show,[16] and it contributed in good measure to the ever-broken attendance records.

Bruce Clinton, a regular contributor to *Hoofs and Horns* and, later, to the *Western Horseman*, wrote many articles, in his rather forceful style, supporting the cowboy and his endeavors. Mr. Clinton was possibly the first writer to recognize that rodeo was emerging as a bona fide sport and that its participants were athletes, not circus performers. Moreover, rodeo was here to stay:

> The rodeo seems to have passed the stage of a *small-time attraction*, held only in the rural districts and witnessed only by the country folks. It has left the country and found popularity in the *largest cities* of our United States, and has, from all appearances, become a permanent fixture in the world of sports and amusement.[17]

The 1930s were a transition period for the cowboy in more ways than one. As noted previously, it was a time in which he founded an organization that would give his game greater stability. But it was also an interval during which he himself underwent some changes in order to become the athlete required to perform. When competition became keener as the sport grew, he had to begin taking himself and his efforts more seriously.

To early contestants, rodeo was basically having a good time, because, usually, they also had another way of making a living, most likely from ranching, whether they were owners or working cowboys. Besides, a living could scarcely be made from the meager moneys paid at rodeos of the time. Thus, when asked whether he was going to the Cheyenne Frontier Days one of those early years, steer roper Ike Rude of Buffalo, Oklahoma, replied, "Cheyenne? Hell, yes! I'd go there just to hear the band play."[18] Several years later, in 1947, he was number one in the steer-roping standings; in order to attain that status he undoubtedly had revised his attitude in the intervening years. To stay successful in the sport, the contestant had to arrive at a new and more discriminating reason for his participation: he had to make up his mind to pursue rodeo as a career and a profession.

While these changes were taking place, there was quite some discussion as to who was the better cowboy, the one who worked on a ranch or the one who had gained his experience solely in the arena. The argument actually seems to have been brought on by an unwitting lack of definition of the two species that had resulted from the emergence of the professional rodeo contestant. One defendant of the old-time (i.e., ranch) cowboy was an E. W. Thistlethwaite, who in a letter published in *Hoofs and Horns'* April, 1937, issue claimed it was the

Ike Rude after roping a steer at age 16 in 1910.

more highly trained roping and steer-wrestling horses and the lighter and better equipment that made the "contest hands" good:

> A man can learn to be a bronk rider or a calf roper without getting out of the city limits of Chicago or New York while those contest riders are cowboys and good ones, there's just one helluva lot of them that *ain't!* [19]

In conclusion, he wrote, "if these modern boys used the old timers['] horses and equipment, they would slow up considerably and nobody but a fool would argue otherwise." [20] In retrospect, though, it seems only natural that, since seconds and points are at stake, the contesting cowboy should pay a great deal of attention to his equipment.

Bruce Clinton continued over the years to stand up for the cowboy-athlete. He is quite possibly also the first to have used the term *professional* with regard to the cowboy: in the article "Modern Cowboy Contestants" in the July–August, 1940, issue of the *Western Horseman*, he wrote: "When speaking of the 'modern contest cowboys' I am referring to the professional rodeo cowboy whose name appears regularly in the 'win columns.' . . ." [21] It is indisputable that Clinton's efforts and those of others in that regard must have served to instill further confidence in the cowboy himself. Knowing that someone took his side and spoke for him before a large readership must have added to the cowboy's self-assurance during those rather trying times.

Clinton deplored the lack of coverage of rodeo by sportswriters: while the high-salaried athletes in other sports were prominently featured, the cowboy—whose pay depended entirely on his winning ("true sportsmanship")—was virtually ignored. "If all athletes had to pay entrance fees," he said, "there would be fewer sports events." [22] Clinton felt that, despite the skill every successful rodeo contestant had to acquire through diligent practice, cowboys had commonly come to be looked upon, through "vivid fiction," as "an ignorant lot of illiterates, uncouth in every respect." [23] Although conditions and public opinion have changed for the better, there are some who still hold to the old "vivid fiction" in assessing the cowboy.

The RAA itself was trying to have rodeo recognized in reference books. In the May, 1940, *Bulletin* it was reported that the association had contacted the publishers of the *World's Almanac* to ask that the names of the world-champion cowboys be included. [24]

The RAA was also anxious to place rodeo in the proper light before the public. In 1942, it offered a fifty-dollar award to the person who could prepare an article that fairly described the sport and the organization behind it. This was in reaction to a piece that had appeared in a national magazine (unidentified) and that had contained many errors.[25] For the first time, therefore, the organization took pains to go outside of the *Bulletin* to reach a public that had become more and more important to the sport. By the end of the year, several submissions had been received; none, however, met the criteria that had been established. Indeed, the RAA secretary reported that "every one built up bucking horses in their particular area and didn't give an all-around picture of the contests." As a result, the plan for the article was changed to read as follows:

> No living horses could be used and no contest, contestants, clowns and announcers, etc., names be used in the story.
>
> The story primarily is to straighten out the different events that are carried and to kill many of the illusions that have been built up regarding trained bucking stock.[26]

Nothing further was heard of the contest throughout 1943, however, and it can be presumed it was overshadowed by the ever-increasing news of World War II and its effect on the rodeo scene.

There were several other ways in which the growing popularity of rodeo manifested itself. By the late 1930s, for example, the quarter horse, traditionally the working companion of the cowboy, had begun to be included in special classes at horse shows.[27] As the cowboy himself had come to be recognized, so had the most important tool of his trade. By 1941, rodeo's popularity had grown to such proportions that an organization called Rodeo Fans of America was formed. The initiator was Dr. Leo ("Two-Gun") Brady, a dentist from Endicott, New York, who was a member of that city's rodeo committee and had been a fan of the sport for over twenty-five years.[28]

It is rather significant that such a movement should have originated in the East. Spectators in the western states took rodeos for granted: they were held with great frequency throughout most of the year in communities that were usually not far apart, and the westerner could attend a contest almost any time he wished. The easterner, however, might have only one opportunity a year to witness a rodeo, and that occasion became a very special event. When the cowboys departed after the contest, the West left with them. There became a definite need for an organization that would keep the spirit of rodeo alive until the following year. Furthermore, an urban situation was more conducive to the creation of this kind of establishment, as it depended on the close interaction of its members to implement its goals.

The main branch, called the National Arena, was located in Waverly, New York, with Dr. Brady as president. Other branches, called corrals, were established in Washington, D.C.,[29] Chicago, and in several localities in New York, Connecticut, Maryland, and Pennsylvania.

The public played a very important part in steering rodeo onto a firm course. Those growing numbers who had taken a liking to the sport would not tolerate the disputes and controversies that had taken place and that threatened the contest's future. To add to the pressures, there were also humane-society protests, not only over the use of inferior stock but also over the treatment displayed by unskilled (amateur) contestants.[30] (The role of humane associations in rodeo is discussed in detail in chapters 10 through 12.)

The RAA and the CTA were both to blame for the damage that had occurred, and both organizations recognized that collaboration was of the essence to rectify the situation. From the experiences of the late 1930s, the RAA came to an understanding of its responsibility to the contestants to provide good stock, competent help, and optimum conditions in which to compete, in order to decrease the risk of injury and loss of points. The organization also realized the importance of satisfied spectators in order for the sport to flourish. More showmanship was introduced, as well as an increased use of contract acts for entertainment to please the public. A trend toward evening performances could be seen, in which lighting effects and spotlighting were used to enhance the events in the arena. An added advantage was the fact that the stock would perform better in the cooler temperatures of the evening. Furthermore, nighttime shows had greater drawing power,[31] even though, quite often, the ticket prices were higher than for the matinée performances.

With the RAA member rodeos providing better conditions, the cowboy had every reason to cooperate. The amateur shows that had temporarily taken the place of many RAA rodeos became fewer. James Minotto, a former Italian count who had taken a liking to the western way of life and rodeo in particular and had become a member of the CTA's advisory committee, warned in 1939, "Whenever amateur shows take the place of real rodeos, the days of good rodeos are gone."[32] Attendance at amateur contests dropped rapidly when the public realized their inferior quality. As a result, those who stood to gain by a good turnout—the rodeo producers and local business people—became dissatisfied with these shows. Rodeos that had prevented Turtles from participating began to return to professional performances.[33]

At the same time, the RAA began to take a greater interest in the cowboy's welfare. It began to weigh the merits of established practices by discussing whether points should be issued to the cowboy if the member rodeo in which he competed had not paid its dues to the organization. The consideration was the contestant, who was not at fault if a rodeo was in arrears with its RAA dues. The association also felt that rodeos should publish increased purses in the *Bulletin* so as to encourage the entry of contestants who would have stayed away if the purse had not been augmented.[34] However, at its 1940 convention in Houston, Texas, the RAA decided, at the request of the cowboys themselves, that points would be issued only for the money paid out, *excluding* added entrance fees. In this manner, a contestant would at least be assured of fairness in the issuance of points.[35] Whether or not he elected to compete at rodeos where entrance fees were added to the prize money became his own option, allowing him to enter such a rodeo for the opportunity to win the extra money, although not additional points. This solution was a compromise, which, for the time being, was adequate until the next step could be taken. At the same convention, the RAA amended the basis on which the dues of member rodeos were assessed. Henceforth they were to be figured strictly on a percentage of the prize money offered, and not also on a percentage of the entrance fees, as had been the case until this time.[36]

Some rodeos in 1940 found a means of having lower dues assessed by using entrance fees solely as day money (paid out to the winners at each performance) or by giving the entry fees as final money (given to the cowboys with the best scores for the entire contest). This lowered the percentage on which the dues were to be paid. However, it cheated the cowboys out of valuable points. The matter was taken up at the 1941 RAA convention in Salinas, California (January 23–25), where the decision was made to leave it up to each rodeo to distribute points in any way that was fair, as long as these were given both for day money and for final money at those contests where entrance fees constituted a portion of either.[37] As long as only a portion of the entry fees was added, the cowboy still had considerable work ahead of him in order to accomplish his goals.

Nevertheless, the results of the efforts by the RAA to improve conditions for the cowboy were reflected in the increasing number of contestants who became CTA members. Competing in rodeos under the auspices of the two organizations had become attractive and could even be profitable.

The CTA raised its dues on January 1, 1940, from five to ten dollars per year.[38] By August of that year, the association had 1,346 members.[39] Provisions were made to include not only contesting cowboys but also contract performers, such as cowgirl bronc riders, trick riders, trick ropers, clowns, and announcers,[40] who by this time had begun to play increasingly important roles in rodeo performances.

The following letter from a new CTA member, sixteen-year-old J. D. McCormick of Council Grove, Kansas, to Hugh Bennett, secretary-treasurer of the association, serves as an illustration of what kind of people constituted the membership:

Dear Sir,

I enclose check for $5 for my 1940 Turtle dues. As I am just 16 years old, I do not make many shows. I do not believe I can afford $5 for the Benefit Fund at present. I think this fund is certainly a good thing and will pay it as soon as I can.

This summer was the first time I ever depended on what I made at shows for a living. The Turtles were good to me at all the shows. At Cheyenne I was broke and I rode over to the Turtles banquet one evening with Barton Carter. I was waiting for the meeting to start so I could go in and Mr. Bowman told me to come on in and eat. I believe I appreciated that meal as much as any I have ever eaten.

At this meeting I realized what a fine thing the Turtle Association is for the cowboy and what a good job it is doing. I had been told by men who had rodeoed a long time that before the organization started there was a real need for something of this nature.

I rope calves and ride bulls. If you could have my card and button to me by Christmas I would appreciate it, because it is my Christmas present.

Sincerely yours,

J. D. McCormick

December 14, 1939

[*Hoofs and Horns*] Editor's note: Since the Turtle dues are $10.00 this year, Everett Bowman says that he will pay the other $5.00 for this boy and he can pay him back just when he can.[41]

The CTA was naturally anxious to attract such members as would do credit to the organization and to the sport. The second of the original four rules that governed the CTA stipulated a one-hundred-dollar fine for "disgraceful conduct." So as to encourage further the acceptable deportment of the members, the directors, at a meeting held in Dublin, Texas, in 1941, set additional fines to be imposed: twenty-five dollars for a third offense (presumably related to competition) and fifty dollars for a fourth. In the case of a fifth violation, the cowboy would be blacklisted.[42]

The conditions that had been established through the endeavors of both the RAA and the CTA boded well for rodeo in the new decade. Bruce Clinton declared, "At last the American people are Rodeo Conscious."[43] What was soon to follow became a test of how strong the sport had actually become and of the significance it held for America.

5

Riding for Day Money

In 1940, an estimated 105 RAA rodeos were held in the United States; the average CTA member entered 30 of these.[1] This was a promising beginning for the sport in a new decade. Seven years later, with more than 130 rodeos to choose among, the average cowboy still entered only 30.[2] Nevertheless, this does not indicate a lack of growth.

The war in which the world was enveloped definitely had an influence on rodeo, just as on every other facet of life during those years. However, World War II proved actually to be beneficial to the sport. The reasons for this statement will be examined here.

On the surface, something on the order of a global war seemingly could have nothing but a disastrous effect on any activity, but especially on those not essential to existence, such as sports and entertainment. Already by 1941, 28 percent of the regularly scheduled rodeos in the United States and Canada usually held in connection with fairs had been canceled.[3] Not too many years before, rodeo had been added to many fairs to boost attendance.

The nature of the sport requires that the rodeo cowboy be a relatively young man. As a result, he was eligible to be drafted under the Selective Training and Service Act, which went into effect in the fall of 1940. By mid-July, 1942, about one hundred CTA members were reported to be in the armed forces.[4] Among them were Fritz Truan, all-around world champion cowboy in 1940, and Gene Autry, well-known actor and singer in western films and owner of the Flying "A" Ranch Stampede, which had been formed in 1942 to revive elements of the wild-west show.[5] Truan joined the U.S. Marines, while Autry signed up with the Army Air Corps.

Enlisted cowboys retained their competitive spirit even as soldiers.

During World War II, *Hoofs and Horns* often used patriotic cowboy-soldier themes on its covers, as for this July, 1943, issue. Drawing by Olaf Wieghorst, courtesy Longhorn Publishing, Inc., Walsenburg, Colorado

One such soldier-cowboy boasted, "I'll ride those fighter planes for day money every time I climb aboard and show those Japs they are just riding for mount money."[6] The Cowboys Turtle Association sought to keep account of those members who were in the service and published these names in the official publication, *Hoofs and Horns*. The magazine once again offered to assist with the forwarding of letters to cowboys, this time to cowboys overseas.[7]

The many restrictions brought on by the war—tire and gasoline rationing, curtailment of public gatherings along the coasts and military roads, and so forth—raised the question of whether rodeos could still be carried on in the altered circumstances. President Roosevelt had declared that baseball must continue, in spite of the war, as a morale builder. Rodeo had by this time built up strength among its participants as well as its followers, and this enabled it, too, to persevere. In fact, the very elements that had made it possible for the sport to endure its own difficulties during the formative years were enlarged upon now to serve a higher and national purpose. The realization and application of this strength made rodeo not only survive the war but also come out of it possessed of a more purposeful direction: the circumstances brought on by the war helped the sport begin to find its place in the social scheme. Those connected with rodeo were able to take a negative set of conditions and make it work in favor of the sport and of the country as a whole.

In an article in the March, 1942, issue of *Hoofs and Horns*, the arguments for the continuation of contests in wartime were set forth.[8] Rodeo—like baseball, among the oldest of American sports—was considered a morale builder. The spectators identified with the contestants, and because courage was such a vital element in the competition as well as in war, some of that quality was instilled in them at every rodeo they attended. Furthermore, it was stressed that those cowboys who were not in the armed services owed it to their fellow contestants who were serving their country to keep the sport alive in their absence.

The aspect of competition would obviously change because of the war. With many men between twenty-one and thirty-five years of age in the service of their country, the age of those available to participate in contests was higher. This was believed to set an example of courage for young and old, "because a cowboy never quits!"

To fill out the ranks of contestants, the CTA would permit non-

Far Away in the Fox Holes

A recurrent theme in wartime rodeo publications was the importance of continuing the sport as a morale booster for the boys on the front. This *Hoofs and Horns* cover appeared in June, 1943. Drawing by Henry Roth, courtesy Longhorn Publishing, Inc., Walsenburg, Colorado

member working cowboys to enter local rodeos. This would in turn increase the membership, should these decide to give up ranch work for rodeo.

Another advantage of having local contestants entered was of course the increased interest and attendance of the population in surrounding areas. Without audience support, rodeo would find it difficult to survive. Especially in wartime, the rapport between the contestants and the spectators was essential. Audience involvement was never more important, and it was up to the announcer to see to it that this link was firmly established. The cowboys were urged to "make the public feel that you are THEIR boys, just as they feel toward the men in uniform."[9] In a curious sense, the competing cowboys represented, to people at home, the fighting men overseas, and parallels were drawn between fighting the enemy and conquering the animal in the arena.

The first recognized rodeo to take place in wartime was the National Western in Denver, held January 10–17, 1942. Speculation ran high as to what effect the war would have on attendance and participation. As the first large rodeo since the United States entered the war, it would be looked to as an indicator of what could be expected of future events. The Stock Show itself took on a new significance by stressing the importance of the livestock industry in the war effort, as manager Courtland R. Jones proclaimed, "More and better beef is going to win the war."[10]

For the first time in the rodeo's twelve-year history, each of the fifteen performances opened with a grand entry, in which 150 mounted cowboys and cowgirls participated.[11] The color and patriotism displayed in such a parade heightened the desired social consciousness. The restated direction of all aspects of the Stock Show inadvertently also pointed up their common origin: the cattle industry. Despite the decrease in the number of rodeos that had taken place, the National Western of 1942 proved that rodeo was still as popular a sport as ever. At the end of the eight-day run, as many of the 110,000 Stock-Show visitors as could crowd the Coliseum had seen the performances.[12]

Immediately before the opening of that year's show, the RAA convention was held in Colorado Springs, Colorado (January 8–10). The association's president, R. J. Hofmann, who throughout the war campaigned vigorously for the holding of rodeos, emphasized the importance of wartime rodeo in his opening address:

During times of stress, there is always a need of some sort of outlet for play and there is a definite need for building up the morale of the people as well as that of the soldiers. Near many cities where rodeos are held are some large cantonments of soldiers, and there is no form of entertainment in the world that pleases soldiers more than rodeos.[13]

Army camps all over the United States began to take an interest after a successful all-soldier rodeo held at Camp Roberts, California, in the fall of 1942.[14] Rodeo producers were urged to contact the commanding officer of the camp in their area, offering to stage a rodeo. To attract more soldier-contestants, the entry fees were kept low; soldiers who wished only to watch from the stands were charged a small admission fee, while the general public had to pay more.[15]

By spring, 1944, a plan had been worked out through rodeo producer and livestock contractor Joe Bessler, an army staff sergeant stationed in Redwood City, California. Through his Rodeo Department, Special-Service officers could obtain information on how to organize an army-camp rodeo. Likewise, stock contractors could get from Staff Sergeant Bessler the particulars required for this type of show. All profits from these contests were to go to Army Relief.[16] Just as many peacetime rodeos had been held for the purpose of raising funds for worthy causes, those in wartime now took on that same function.

The successful efforts on the part of the armed services to bring rodeo to the camps were a sign not just of the popularity of the sport; the high degree of participation by the soldiers demonstrated the influence it had by now achieved. Holding rodeos at military camps, where men from all over the country were stationed, served to make the interest nationwide in scope.

The enthusiasm that the soldiers showed for the sport was instrumental in spreading it to other countries. By the close of the war, there was hardly an overseas U.S. military installation that had not seen a rodeo. In the south of France, a weekly contest was held for the U.S. Army Special Service Branch "in a fine big coliseum." This was reportedly enjoyed by soldiers and Frenchmen alike.[17] An Inter-Allied Rodeo was held in Australia before seventy thousand spectators in 1943. In 1944, soldiers in Italy staged a three-day Fourth of July Rodeo; 185 contestants, representing every state west of the Mississippi, participated in the six performances. At a contest in Ramgarh, India, that year, servicemen from no less than twenty states took part, and the prize money consisted of 420 rupees, donated by Special Service.[18]

Sgt. Cecil Jones competing in the saddle-bronc riding at an early wartime rodeo in Hayward, California. Photograph by Ernie Mack, courtesy *Western Horseman* magazine, Colorado Springs, Colorado

Army rodeo in Ramgarh, India, 1944. Here, the grand entry features the U.S. flag and the China-Burma-India flag. Photograph by U.S. Army Signal Corps, courtesy *Western Horseman* magazine, Colorado Springs, Colorado

A Sergeant Hexom of Waukon, Iowa, acting as rodeo clown in Ramgarh, India, rodeo. Photograph by U.S. Army Signal Corps, courtesy *Western Horseman* magazine, Colorado Springs, Colorado

To help men in the service keep up with news of the sport, Califor-nia stock contractor Harry Rowell and Sears, Roebuck and Company donated two hundred dollars each, in 1944, to make *Hoofs and Horns* available, particularly in U.S.O. station reading rooms. In addition, the magazine was sent to officials of those towns in England where U.S. troops were stationed. American cowboys in England had been denied permission by British authorities to organize contests, and the spreading of information about rodeo through the magazine was an effort to make local representatives gain an understanding of the sport.[19]

Meanwhile, on the home front, the restrictions imposed by the war continued to force several of the large contests to be canceled. This was particularly strongly felt on the West Coast. For one thing, the East Coast had far fewer rodeos, and those that were held were sched-uled only during the summer and fall of the year. Furthermore, the East Coast was not thought to be nearly in the same degree of danger from possible invaders as was the West Coast.

The California Rodeo was canceled in 1942, along with a host of other contests. Not only was the city of Salinas located on the mili-tarily important Highway 101, but the rodeo grounds were used as a detention camp for the evacuated Japanese population in the state.[20] Other fairgrounds, too, in California were used for this purpose, to the indignation of horsemen.

The entire West Coast from the Canadian to the Mexican border and including Arizona and New Mexico was designated military areas one and two. Within this large territory no public gatherings of five thousand or more could be held without sanction. The only estab-lished rodeo within this zone to be held in 1942 was La Fiesta de los Vaqueros in Tucson, Arizona. The issues of the *RAA Bulletin* were filled with lists of names of well-established contests that would not be held that year. There were some who resented the fact that baseball and football games were allowed to be played, while rodeos and horse shows, usually held in less congested areas than the ball games, did not receive the same support from wartime authorities.[21]

However, others saw in the cancelation of the major western rodeos an opportunity for establishing new contests in communities where none had been held before. This was a trend that had begun during World War I in an effort to use the rodeos to raise funds for the war cause. Some of the contests thus created had continued and were by the time of World War II annual events.[22] Thus, it was not long before rodeo in that war, too, became a tool for raising money. The 1942 Cheyenne Frontier Days (July 21–25) invested 75 percent of the profits in war bonds and donated the balance to the Red Cross.[23] Other rodeos and horse-related events were held with great success for fundraising and war-bond-selling purposes.[24] As during World War I, new rodeos sprang up. One such rodeo organized to aid the World War II effort was the Kamloops Stampede in British Columbia, Canada, initiated in 1941 to help raise money for milk for the children in Britain.[25] It is still an annual event.

The Cowboys Turtle Association immediately particpated in the war-bond drive. By early 1942, the organization had $10,000 worth of U.S. defense bonds held in trust at the Valley National Bank in Phoenix, Arizona.[26] By the end of the war, the CTA, by then the Rodeo Cowboys Association, had $20,910 in war bonds.[27]

The RAA, determined to see the sport continue during the war, urged committee members of canceled rodeos to help organize those that were still being held, not just to preserve the sport but also to make rodeo available for the soldiers to enjoy. One colonel wrote to the secretary of the RAA that the rodeo held in his particular locality "was one of the finest morale builders for the army of any other community event."[28]

Rodeo had always been a civic affair and an object of communal pride. Wartime conditions heightened this feeling. It could be noted that those who served on rodeo committees or in other ways assisted in the production of a local rodeo usually took the lead in a community's defense activities.[29]

For the contests that did continue, a war clause was included in the contract. According to this clause, the show had the right to cancel at any time without notice. There was fear among RAA leaders that the possibility of lower attendance figures and overestimation of profits could place a rodeo in the embarrassing position of not being able to pay off the prize money. This is yet another expression of the increased concern the association showed for the contestants. Because of the restrictions on travel imposed by the war, the RAA advised local rodeos to concentrate on the spectators in their own communities by making the shows more interesting, not only to those who would normally attend but also to those who had not before seen their hometown rodeo.[30] By midyear 1942 rodeo attendance had actually increased over 1941. The RAA attributed this happy fact to two factors: the organiza-

Freckles Brown, who would go on to be 1962 world-champion bull rider, competing in army uniform in 1943 World's Championship Rodeo, Phoenix, Arizona. Photograph by DeVere

tion of rodeos in new areas attracted the curiosity seekers, and those contests that were still being held were more than ever sought out by spectators truly interested in the sport.[31] From all appearances, rodeo had successfully weathered its first wartime year.

Cancelation of rodeos was not the only plight imposed on the contesting cowboy by the war. While reportedly sales of saddles and harnesses were on the increase,[32] the horseman who bought a new saddle in wartime years would find it lined with carpeting instead of sheepskin. Wool was no longer available to saddlemakers as the government needed all sheepskin to be had for clothing for soldiers.[33] On the other hand, horse owners could profit from the army's need for animal products: horsehair, used for airplane-cushion upholstery, rope, and various war products, sold for four hundred dollars a ton.[34]

In 1943, RAA President Hofmann continued his campaign to carry on all rodeos possible, while adhering to the travel restrictions that tire and gasoline rationing had imposed. He impressed on the shows the need to cooperate with his request, as well as with government stipulations relating to troop movement and other travel. Rodeo had, in the first year of wartime, proven itself as a morale builder, not only for those in the military but for civilians as well, and it continued to be looked upon as such an agent. This was the primary reason its existence should be continued, despite adverse conditions.[35] The secondary motive in attempting to maintain the contests as before was to keep the interest of the audiences alive so that rodeo could resume on a full scale when the war was over.[36]

However, the lower purses being offered at those shows that were allowed to take place brought on situations similar to those that had led to the Boston Garden compact. The reduced prize money caused arguments among the contestants, who demanded more money of rodeo managers. Discord also occurred among the managers themselves. The RAA urged cowboys to avoid bickering over prize money— especially as such unfavorable news could reach the press—and instead refrain from entering those contests whose prizes they deemed insufficient.[37]

It was generally believed by the executive committee of the RAA that allowing as many rodeos as possible to continue would result in an immediate expansion of the sport after the war.[38] Time would prove the committee members were right.

The perseverance on the part of the association's management paid

We Have No Field Representatives

Read by More Contestants and Fans Than Any Other
Rodeo Publication

HOOFS AND HORNS

Trade mark registered in U. S. Patent Office

Vol. XIV, No. 6   TUCSON, ARIZONA, DECEMBER, 1944   FIFTEEN CENTS PER COPY

Drawing by Henry Roth.

Home On Furlough

Returning soldiers found the sport of rodeo thriving, as this *Hoofs and Horns* cover, December, 1944, suggests. Drawing by Henry Roth, courtesy Longhorn Publishing, Inc., Walsenburg, Colorado

off. Although 1944 began with few definite rodeo dates scheduled,[39] the number of contests held that year actually increased from the previous one.[40] The growth was attributed in part to the new contests that had been organized as fund-drive efforts. Moreover, by the second half of the year, several war-canceled shows had been reinstated. The patriotic theme continued: at the Southwest Exposition and Fat Stock Show Rodeo in Fort Worth, Texas (March 10–19), fifty-dollar war bonds were substituted for trophies to event winners. The prize money was an impressive $23,275, plus entry fees. Other rodeos, too, were able to offer higher dollar amounts.[41]

The 1944 Madison Square Garden Rodeo (October 4–29)was reported to be forty performances of "a bang-up show." It was recorded by the Office of War Information for broadcast to U.S. armed forces overseas. Earlier efforts by American rodeo interests to instruct the British in the ways of the sport had produced some effect: the British Broadcasting Corporation covered the Madison Square Garden contest and conducted interviews with contestants and the arena manager.[42]

As the world entered the last year of the war, rodeo had demonstrated that it not only had survived its own internecine conflicts and emerged stronger as a result but also had weathered with confidence all the restrictions demanded by the war and grown in spite of them. Rodeo had become synonymous with patriotism in a way it never had been before, an association the sport was to develop further in the years to come. In the process, it had developed a sense of identity about itself and its origins, which helped it retain the place in postwar American life it had so recently earned. Moreover, the dispersion of U.S. soldiers to combat areas all around the world had contributed to making the sport known and popular in many places it would otherwise never have had reason to reach. Rodeo was ready to enter a new and important phase that pointed it more than ever toward the future.

6

The Beginning of the Future

Since 1938 there had existed an organization that to a degree complemented the efforts of the RAA. This was the Southwest Rodeo Association (SRA), formed to enable contestants from that region who chose not to compete outside their area to win the prizes offered by that association. Should these cowboys also enter rodeos in other parts of the country, they earned RAA points as well. Rodeos in the Southwest were induced to retain membership in both the SRA and the RAA, and full cooperation existed with the CTA.

In March, 1942, the name of the SRA, which by now included members from ten states, was changed to the National Rodeo Association (NRA).[1] After a few years of the NRA's existing side by side with the RAA, it became apparent that it would be in the best interest of rodeo if the two organizations merged. Such a merger would result in an increase in the trophy money for each event.

The fundamental difference between the practices of the two associations was that the NRA had been giving a larger percentage of the membership dues back to the competing cowboys in the form of awards. The NRA and its supporters felt this strengthened the organization by having the larger part of the prize money come from the contributions of its members. In contrast, the RAA supplemented awards only when no trophy donor existed in a given event. Those who felt strongly that rodeo was a community concern and that each committee should be responsible for adequate prizes favored the existing RAA policy.[2]

The climate in which the sport existed at this particular time was conducive to change for the sake of better conditions, higher standards, and increased professionalism. Surviving the war and even being strengthened by that experience had given rodeo the incentive to seek out methods whereby further improvements could be made. Also, by this time the membership had come to include new and younger men, who displayed a more progressive attitude than the older cowboys, and even among the older group there were many who had returned from armed service with more open-minded views and a new sense of self-worth.

Two important measures, taken early in 1945, were designed to signify "much progressive action."[3] Everyone agreed that the sport had reached a point at which it was necessary to establish national headquarters. Until 1942, all record keeping and most of the correspondence had been handled by Josie Bennett, Secretary-Treasurer Hugh Bennett's wife. The office had been the trunk of the couple's car.[4] Despite the primitive conditions, her work had nevertheless been impeccable and businesslike. Letters were typewritten on printed letterhead on a portable Royal typewriter, and records of the members were neatly kept in a metal card file. In the spring of 1942, the CTA had set up a permanent office and hired its first salaried employee: Fannye Jones (later Lovelady), who became the secretary-treasurer and worked out of her home in Phoenix, Arizona.[5]

Although the rodeo publication of the day, Hoofs and Horns, reported that the 1945 decisions took place at one historic meeting of the Turtles in Fort Worth, Texas, in mid-March of that year, an eyewitness, Earl Lindsey, remembers the development of events somewhat differently. According to Lindsey, dissatisfaction with the name Turtles had been expressed at a CTA membership meeting held during the 1944 Madison Square Garden rodeo (October 4–29). This issue was again brought up at a directors' meeting during the Houston rodeo (February 2–11) in 1945. At that time, it was decided to change the name to the Rodeo Cowboys Association. The reasoning behind this was explained: "The name 'Turtle' does not have any connection with rodeo business, cowboys, nor anything connected with the West; is confusing to the public, and is entirely out of place for the purpose of our organization." It was also conceded that "the Turtle name" had been abused in many instances.[6]

Toots Mansfield, 1943 calf-roping champion from Bandera, Texas, became the RCA's first president. The directors were also selected at this time. A few weeks later, at another meeting held during the Fort Worth rodeo (March 3–18), it was decided to retain as business manager Earl Lindsey, a Texas businessman and formerly a representative of

Josie Bennett (*left*), wife of timed-event contestant Hugh Bennett, was responsible for all record-keeping of the Cowboys Turtle Association from its founding in late 1936 to 1942. At that time Fannye Jones Lovelady (*right*) took over the duties and became the CTA's first salaried employee.

Toots Mansfield, first president of the Rodeo Cowboys Association, shown in calf-roping event, early 1940s.

Gene Autry's organization.[7] At this time, Mrs. Lovelady resigned her position.[8] Lindsey's duties were intended to go beyond mere routine correspondence and bookkeeping. He was to be the cowboys' spokesman in negotiations with rodeo committees. Also, he was to act as public-relations agent, assuring the committees of the contestants' eagerness to help make the shows successful. National headquarters were established in the Sinclair Building in Fort Worth.

Those present at the meetings where these decisions were made concluded the changes to be "the greatest thing that ever happened for the benefit of the cowboys." They predicted that, as a result of the reorganization, the association would, within twelve to eighteen months, be established as "trustworthy, desirable, and in demand at all rodeos in this country."[9] It may seem that the cowboy organization had already acquired these qualities. However, the sentiments during the war, which had helped propel rodeo to national prominence and importance, diminished as peace was restored. People's energies were channeled into other, more diverse efforts to rebuild after the ordeal. The rodeo cowboy was again on his own, but he had had the foresight to take measures to ensure the continued growth and popularity of his sport.

The reaction to the changes that had taken place was not totally unanimous within the membership. There were within the association contestants who had been members since the first days of the CTA and whose careers in rodeo dated back to the 1920s. To some of these, it was rather alarming to see their organization take such a significant stride forward as had been done by the decisions at the Houston and Fort Worth meetings, into a future that they had no way of projecting. The man who, once again, acted as spokesman—this time only for that conservative faction—was Everett Bowman. He had in February of 1945, just prior to the Houston meeting, resigned his post as president, one he had held since 1937. Bowman openly criticized the developments that had taken place, rebuking the directors for not allowing the membership to vote on the decision to engage a business manager. It was his opinion that all dues-paying cowboys were, as "stockholders," entitled to have a say in the matter. In his disapproval, however, he ignored the fact that the association's directors—selected by vote of the entire membership—had acted in its behalf. Article 11 of the *Articles of Association, By-Laws and Rules* of the Cowboys Turtle Association defined the directors' functions specifically:

The legislative and rule-making power of the CTA shall be held by the Board of Directors. It shall have general supervision over the business and affairs of the Association; with the power to make, adopt, alter or amend the by-laws as hereinafter specified. *It may make all rules which it considers necessary to carry out the purposes of this organization, and any contracts incidental hereto.* [10]

Bowman further called the whole idea extravagant in view of the manager's $7,500-a-year salary plus undefined travel expenses:

I always felt that any time we had to go outside of the Cowboys to get someone to run the business, the thing was sunk, according to my way of thinking. I still think our cowboys are plenty capable of running their own business. [11]

However, the transactions in the new association's meetings were final: the Rodeo Cowboys Association was, indeed, in operation.

One of the first actions taken was the formation of a point-awarding system. As in the RAA system, a point was to be awarded for each dollar won. This was to be retroactive to January 1, 1945. At the end of the year, a champion would be named in each event, but, unlike the RAA, there was—initially—no all-around world champion.* In order to have a rodeo qualify to award RCA points, upon approval of the prize list its committee paid a membership fee to the organization, the amount depending on the size of the prize money at each particular show. In the first year, such membership was voluntary. Beginning January 1, 1946, the show automatically became a member once its prize list had been deemed up to RCA standards[12] and was, in return, required to pay dues.

The RCA goals appeared to be a repetition of those of the original Turtles:

1. To organize the professional rodeo contestants of the U.S.A. for their mutual protection and benefit.
   a. To insure a just amount of prize money.
   b. To require that all entrance fees be added to prize money.
   c. To secure competent, honest judges and officials in all events.

---

*In 1947, at the request of Levi Strauss & Company, a long-time trophy donor, the first RCA all-around world champion was named, after the end of the season. The first man so chosen was Todd Whatley, riding- and timed-event contestant from Hugo, Oklahoma.

Todd Whatley, the RCA's first all-around world champion on bull #12 (K) at La Fiesta de los Vaqueros Rodeo, Tucson, Arizona, 1947. Photograph by DeVere

2. To raise the standards of the cowboy contests so they shall rank among the foremost American sports.
3. To cooperate with the management of all rodeos at which members contest.
4. To protect the members against unfairness on the part of any rodeo management.
5. To bring about honest advertising by the rodeo committees, so that the public may rely upon the truth of advertised events in which it is claimed that members of the association will participate.
6. To work for the betterment of conditions and of the rules governing rodeo events in which the members of the Association participate.
7. To establish a central place of registration for the rodeos, names of contestants, the prize money, and other particulars in which members are interested.[13]

These goals were reestablished as the transition from the CTA to the RCA was made. The association entered into this new phase of its existence with a firmer commitment from its members than ever before, which placed it, for the first time, on a solid business foundation. For that reason, this time the changes were destined to bring about what the cowboys had sought to achieve since their first attempts to form a union to protect their interests and advance their sport.

However, alongside the RCA there still existed the RAA and the NRA, each proclaiming its own champions each year. Consequently, there could be three different world champions in any one event, or one cowboy could win three separate championships in the same event.[14] This, needless to say, detracted from the importance of any one award. With two rodeo associations and one cowboy association, the latter was clearly the underdog, and many committees were annoyed with the influence the cowboys attempted to exert in trying to get their association's awards considered the most important of the three.

An initial meeting to work out a possible consolidation of award systems was held in Tucson, Arizona, in late February, 1945. As the rodeo contestants had very much at stake in this connection, they were not excluded from the discussions. In early April, the Rodeo Cowboys Association and the NRA conferred in El Paso, Texas. At this meeting, which RAA representatives were unable to attend, it was decided to defer final action on any of the various plans until a later date.[15]

Further efforts to arrive at a solution came in the spring of 1946, when the RAA and the NRA consolidated into the International Rodeo Association (IRA).[16] Its goal was to secure more prize money for the cowboy by attracting national advertisers to support the sport. This effort was the precursor of the developments in later years, in which commercial sponsorship was to become the mainstay of the sport. The new organization would have liked to work out an agreement with the RCA to name an all-around cowboy each year.[17]

With some rodeos approved by both the IRA and the RCA and some by one or the other, it was inevitable that the existing system would lead to controversy. In 1947, the IRA declared that some so-called better rodeos would be "open shows"—that is, contests that anybody could enter. This ran counter to RCA's avowed policy of protection of the strictly professional contestant. An "open show" was, in the eyes of the RCA, an amateur show. An agreement was reached on "all phases of rodeo activities" at a joint meeting in Stockton, California, early that year. IRA President R. J. Hofmann pompously announced, "All is quiet on the Potomac tonight."[18]

That year, the RCA named its first all-around cowboy.[19] Now there could be not only two champions in each event but also two all-around champions.

For the next seven years, efforts were made to work out this dilemma. At the IRA convention in Reno, Nevada, in November, 1948, RCA delegate Bill Linderman suggested that measures be adopted to allow only one cowboy in each event to be declared champion for the year. Linderman also recommended that, failing that, at least the all-around championship be jointly awarded by the two organizations. Already suggestions had been made that one of the two associations drop its point-award system, allowing for one set of standards and one set of champions each year.[20] If one of the two was to do away with its point-award system, the IRA felt itself the more qualified to continue as before. That organization, composed of powerful rodeo committees representing well over a hundred rodeos, was in a better position to negotiate for higher prize money and more trophies to benefit the contestant. Unlike the RCA, the IRA—subsidized by those committees—did not need excess profits and could therefore more unselfishly work to secure a better financial deal for the cowboy. The only area where the efforts of the two organizations would be combined would be the actual details of a single point-award system. The IRA further favored a final or championship show. It already held such a contest, having declared the Grand National Rodeo at the San Francisco Cow Palace the final contest of the season. Although the Grand National was also an RCA-approved rodeo, the cowboy association objected to the compulsory attendance required in order for contestants to be named champions, or, as the IRA proclaimed them, the year's "Rodeo Kings."[21]

Another and more serious area of RCA disapproval of the IRA's proposal was the fact that the latter organization awarded its points on the basis of one per dollar of purse only, not counting the entry fees.[22] The cowboys had from the very beginning of organization vehemently insisted on the addition of entry fees to the purse to form the total prize money. As a consequence, they expected such moneys to be included when figuring the points that determined the year's champions.

The two organizations continued to specify ways to make the achievement of the all-around championship more complicated. This was perhaps in an effort to establish criteria for the inevitable day when a single set of standards would exist. In the summer of 1951, the RCA announced that it would recognize as IRA all-around champions only those who had won at least three events, of which one had to be a riding event, one a roping event.[23] The following year, the IRA declared that, to qualify, the all-around champion had to be a competitor in both a riding and a roping event. However, two events still sufficed.[24]

For a few more years, two sets of champions continued to be named— the IRA winners at the Grand National Rodeo in San Francisco and the RCA champions at the National Western in Denver, two months later. Finally, in July of 1955, a rather inconspicuous announcement proclaimed that the IRA had decided to drop the word "champion" from its point awards. The high-point winners received their awards and checks at the end of that year, but they no longer had the title of champions.[25]

To the RCA, the titles conferred by that association were, as they had always been, those of the bona fide champions. RCA's newspaper, *Rodeo Sports News*, merely acknowledged the IRA decision by printing an explanation of the RCA point-award system on the front page of the July 1, 1955, edition.[26] This system was now the only one in force. No mention was made of the fact that the IRA had stepped back and the RCA system now determined *all* world championships. It was apparently clear, without stating it, that the association had emerged as the more important for the professional rodeo contestant as well as for the followers of the sport.

After 1955 the IRA disassociated itself from rodeo competition by no longer distributing awards to top contestants. It involved itself more in the management of rodeos and in related activities, such as the sponsorship of the Miss Rodeo America pageant. In time it changed its name to International Rodeo Management and, under that name, is still in existence today.[27]

The reorganization that had taken place in 1945 was not solely responsible for the rapid growth of the professional rodeo in the years that followed. There were other factors as well that played a part in this development.

Lex Connelly, rodeo announcer and former contestant, tells the story of the first few years of professional rodeo after the war. Probably more involved with the sport in all its aspects than anyone—as a member of the RCA board of directors for six years, as manager of the RCA, as first secretary-treasurer of the National Finals Rodeo Commission, as producer of the National Finals Rodeo for three years, and as manager of the Cow Palace in San Francisco—he remembers: "Rodeo had a jump on a lot of things coming out of the war. It did very well and just kind of exploded."[28] The RCA had a membership of about two thousand by 1947.[29] All of a sudden there were more rodeos, and the attendance was good at all of them. Surprisingly enough, the reason apparently was neither that people needed this kind of diversion after the bleak war years, nor that there was a resurgence of desire to celebrate old-time values by witnessing a recreation of the old West, as a stabilizing factor after the period of danger and uncertainty. The real reason was not nearly as profound as that. The increased popularity of rodeos is attributed by Mr. Connelly to the lack of personal recreation that was available then.[30] Now, many more people than in the mid-1940s and early 1950s engage in one or more forms of sports rather than being just spectators. This has in no way, however, hurt rodeo attendance, which has continued to increase year after year. The explanation for this lies in the inherent lack of identification with rodeo events. While it is relatively easy to take up and become reasonably proficient in the game of tennis, for example, it is extremely difficult for the average spectator to find an opportunity not only to learn rodeo events but also to become a skilled rider or roper. The existence of this factor makes rodeo an attraction unlike any other spectator sport and is one of the reasons for the ever-rising attendance figures.

Furthermore, in the late 1940s and early 1950s, rodeo received a great deal of national publicity. Coverage of rodeo by national magazines more than doubled during the fifties. The sport and its players, some of whom became well-known personalities, were featured regularly in *Time, Newsweek, Life,* the *Saturday Evening Post,* and *Sports Illustrated.* Rodeo even found its way into *Better Homes and Gardens,* the *Ladies' Home Journal,* and *Business Weekly.* Through this national publicity, the sport attracted many very athletic young men, including some who were not ranch raised or ranch oriented. These newcomers, through their intense desire to become rodeo contestants, surmounted the difficulties imposed by their background in achieving their goal.

Bull rider Harry Tompkins, originally from upstate New York, later of Dublin, Texas, was a prime example of these new recruits to the sport. World-champion bull rider in 1948, 1949, 1950, 1952, and 1960 and high in the standings in the intervening years, he is considered one of the best athletes the sport has ever seen.[31] The fact that he lasted so long in the most dangerous event of all is proof of his athletic ability. Harry Tompkins and a few contemporaries were forerunners of a trend that was to accelerate in the coming decades, during which the rodeo contestant became less and less an apostate ranch hand.

The 1950s have been referred to as the golden age of rodeo. While admitting that today's competitors, in general, are better athletes than those of earlier years, Mr. Connelly makes a point of saying they are no better than such champions of yesterday as Jim Shoulders, Casey Tibbs, or Harry Tompkins. In the golden years, a relatively small number of cowboys competed on a full-time basis, and, as a consequence, the great ones dominated the sport completely. They would even be advertised as attractions at many rodeos, though they were just a few of many contestants; their names had become so well known that this kind of advertising was effective. This was the closest rodeo had come, up until that time, to other professional sports in terms of audience attraction.

A great many RCA members in the earlier years would go to only five or six rodeos annually. The "weekend cowboy" is more noticeable

Casey Tibbs on the saddle bronc Pay Day at Omak, Washington, 1954. Photograph by DeVere

Bill Linderman, steer wrestling at Lone Pine, California, in the 1950s.

Dean Oliver, calf roping, Reno, Nevada, 1960.

Jack Bushbom on the bareback bronc Dry Gulch, third go-round, National Finals Rodeo, Los Angeles, 1964. Photograph by DeVere

today with mobility so much easier. There are also about five times as many rodeos today as thirty-five years ago. In 1940, for example, 106 of a total of 200 rodeos were RAA sanctioned; in 1982, the Professional Rodeo Cowboys Association (PRCA) approved 651 contests.[32]

The National Intercollegiate Rodeo Association (NIRA) was formed in 1948 and contributed enormously to the wider acceptance of the sport and its participants. In spite of objections by some college officials, it did not take long for rodeo to become a standard college sport on campuses throughout the western United States. Sportswriters optimistically foresaw the day when institutions would hold out the same advantages to promising rodeo contestants as they did to would-be football players.[33]

Harley May of Oakdale, California, was the first champion to come out of college rodeo. He was instrumental in the founding of the NIRA and became its first all-around cowboy.[34] A student at Sul Ross State College, Alpine, Texas, he became world-champion steer wrestler in his first year as a professional contestant in 1952. Another successful cowboy from the early college ranks was Cotton Rosser of Marysville, California, a student at California Polytechnic College, San Luis Obispo. He is now the owner of the well-known Flying U Rodeo Company, engaged in stock contracting and the production of numerous rodeos along the entire West Coast.

Rodeo on college campuses flourished after the war, as ranch-raised youths who had been in the service returned to continue their education. They were distressed to find that their activities were at first looked upon not as a sport but merely as a side show.[35] However, with the backing of the NIRA, the students were persistent and devoted themselves to their endeavors with the assuredness that their somewhat more mature age and recent war experience had given them. They were attracted to the sport because they stood to make more money than in a conventional occupation and also because, by this time, the rodeo cowboy had become a respected figure, even in his home area. Before the war, and particularly before the cowboys organized, he was regarded by ranchers—by the very element from which he stemmed—as undependable, too lazy to hold down a job. He would have trouble finding work unless he knew the rancher from whom he sought employment. The rodeo cowboy had truly been an outcast among his own people. Time had reversed that condition.

Harley May on the saddle bronc Blue Smoke, Cheyenne Frontier Days, Cheyenne, Wyoming, in the 1960s. Photograph by DeVere

The rodeo cowboy had become accepted and respectable. The reason for this was that, as rodeo improved, it attracted men who were more serious and who therefore were given society's stamp of approval. The sport continued to receive public recognition through syndicated wire-service columnists, popular magazines, and television coverage. Because of its visual qualities, rodeo lent itself to that kind of exposure. It was successful, and, as a consequence, acceptance followed.[36]

This was the beginning of a trend that was to grow in years to come and set a powerful pace for future developments.

7

Looking for a Place in the Limelight

Hoofs and Horns had been the official publication of both the RAA and the CTA. When the latter association was reorganized and renamed the Rodeo Cowboys Association, the magazine became that association's organ as well, but not for long. While *Hoofs and Horns* continued to be published, *The Buckboard* was created in July, 1945, to be the RCA mouthpiece. When the association's office moved from Fort Worth to Denver in December of 1950, the publishing duties were leased to the Argus Printing Company of Sidney, Iowa.

This arrangement was not altogether satisfactory. The RCA office was unquestionably the center of information, incoming as well as outgoing, about professional rodeo. It proved inconvenient and time-consuming to have to send such information out to be disseminated to members through a publisher several hundred miles away. It also became increasingly important to be able to serve the membership in a more immediate manner. Consequently, the semimonthly *Rodeo Sports News*, in tabloid format, began publication out of the association's Denver office with the November, 1952, issue.* Gene Lamb served as its first editor and continued in that position until 1958.

However, the organization was well aware that, if the growth and public recognition that had begun were to continue, it had to take an active part in also placing the sport in the public eye outside of the membership and the arena. To that end, in January of 1955, the Rodeo Information Commission (RIC) was created. This was a joint effort on the part of the contestants themselves and the rodeo committees, both

---

*With the change of the RCA name to the PRCA in 1974, *Rodeo Sports News* followed suit, becoming, as of the issue of April 19, 1978, *Prorodeo Sports News*.

of which groups stood to gain by such cooperation. The support came in part from the members' dues to the RCA, in part from contributions from the committees, based on the purse of each approved rodeo. It was the commission's function, through its news director, to furnish rodeo news and articles to newspapers and magazines across the country.

Those responsible for the formation of the commission recognized that it was not prejudice against the sport that kept rodeo from being written about as often as other athletic events. Rodeo had by this time clearly overcome that disadvantage. It was simply a lack of knowledge and information that made journalists hesitant to cover rodeo events and contestants. Rodeo did not have the trappings of other sports: leagues, teams, high-powered publicity machinery, and well-known personalities. In most locations, it was a once-a-year affair. Consequently, in order to sustain an interest, it was necessary to keep the local followers informed about what was happening in rodeo in the rest of the nation, the rest of the time.

Although the results of the commission's efforts were slow in coming, a slight increase in rodeo attendance could be discerned already in its first year of operation. This was even more remarkable in view of the fact that other sports and outdoor entertainments experienced a decrease during that same period.[1]

The commission realized that, with the work it had before it, it was going to take time before much progress could be noticed. Changes in the attitudes and editorial policies of the press do not happen overnight. However, by the fourth year, some of the desired effects of the commission's labors were beginning to make themselves evident. It was no longer just the stories generated by the news director that found their way onto the pages of the press. Journalists and photographers also began to take the initiative for coverage of rodeo and its contestants, inspired by earlier exposure by the commission. This coverage included a few syndicated regular columns. As a result, the work and responsibilities of the commission's staff increased as it sought to explore the opportunities offered by the growing attention.[2] However, rodeo continued to be what one observer called "America's Greatest But Least Recognized and Understood Sport."[3]

Television, curiously enough, was not regarded as a medium through which wider exposure for rodeo could be gained. The medium was probably accountable for the declining attendance figures not only in motion-picture theaters but also at sporting events in the early and middle 1950s, and it was therefore looked on as more of a threat than a promotional tool. True, a few cowboys were beginning to appear on entertainment programs such as "To Tell the Truth," "This Is Your Life," and "Name That Tune,"[4] but this benefited the contestants as individuals more than the sport as a whole.

RCA President Toots Mansfield stated in 1950 that "when the rodeos are televised, we don't feel very sorry when a promoter comes around with a sob story about all those empty seats."[5] By 1958, the RCA was limiting network telecasts of contests to two a year.[6] This restriction is rather amazing, in retrospect, considering that the two NBC telecasts that year brought rodeo before one hundred million viewers.[7] Indeed, it is plausible (and ironic) that the attitude held by the RCA at the time retarded the achievement of its dream of national recognition of its own sport.

Nevertheless, the leaders of rodeo, in analyzing the situation, came up with a different answer. They reasoned, television and newspaper coverage notwithstanding, that rodeo did not have an annual focal event to which the public's attention could be directed. Baseball had its World Series; other sports culminated in finals of one sort or another. Rodeo did not have anything to offer that tied the year's contests together; champions were named at the end of the season, based on the amount of prize money won, but their achievements were passed over virtually unnoticed, except among their peers and the truly avid followers.

After an RCA board of directors meeting in Cheyenne, Wyoming, in July, 1958, an announcement was made of the formation of the National Finals Rodeo Commission (NFRC). This was a seven-member, nonprofit corporation whose function was "to produce and direct an annual National Finals Rodeo on behalf of the sport as a whole in order to bring national attention to rodeo and to win for it long deserved public recognition as one of America's leading spectator sports."[8] A plan had been under discussion for the past two years, although no steps had been taken until this time. The inevitable results of such an event as a National Finals Rodeo would be not only increased coverage by news media but also more and better-informed spectators. One hundred twenty-five cities across the country were invited to provide the site and sponsorship for the first contest. After an eight-thousand-mile inspection tour of various possible locations by the NFRC's ex-

President Dwight D. Eisenhower receiving the first ticket to the National Finals Rodeo in 1959. Presenting it are (*left to right*) John Van Cronkhite, executive officer of the National Finals Rodeo Commission, Jim Shoulders, and Harley May.

ecutive officer, John Van Cronkhite, the commission chose Dallas, Texas, with the city of Dallas and Texas State Fair as sponsors.[9]

The RCA retained the large theatrical agency of William Morris, Inc., to represent the organization in the sale of television rights. However, after much inaction, the negotiations were taken over by Lex Connelly, the commission's secretary-treasurer. Through his efforts, the Columbia Broadcasting System bought the rights to the telecast of the first National Finals Rodeo (NFR), held in the Livestock Coliseum in Dallas, December 26–30, 1959.[10]

As the novelty it was, the five-day event was a success. It brought together not only top contestants but also, for the first time, the stock contractors, who jointly furnished their most outstanding animals to the contest. It was the plan of the NFRC to hold the Finals in a new location every three years. This was one more way in which the commission could further its aim of making rodeo more noticeable around the nation.

The site for the second three years (1962–64) was the Los Angeles Sports Arena. Here, the commission encountered a set of problems, traceable to the nature of the new host city. The transient quality of Los Angeles was especially pronounced during those early years of the 1960s, when literally thousands of people daily migrated to Southern California. The ensuing lack of social cohesion ran counter to the unified community effort that the production of a rodeo usually enjoys in more stable localities. Moreover, the Los Angeles Finals lacked the civic financial backing that Dallas had provided. As a result, the event became a strictly commercial venture. Nevertheless, it met with success. Television ratings were high, and, for the first time, California sports writers devoted space to rodeo.[11]

The 1963 Finals were scheduled to open just a few days after President Kennedy's assassination, and that tragedy, needless to say, negatively affected the financial success of the event. The next year saw an increase in receipts, although they still did not equal those of 1962; a fifty-thousand-dollar debt resulted.[12] From a publicity standpoint, however, the contest served the purpose for which it had been created.

When the time came to select the location for the 1965 National Finals Rodeo, Oklahoma City, Oklahoma, was chosen.[13] That year's contest coincided—appropriately—with the dedication on December 9 of the National Cowboy Hall of Fame and Western Heritage Center, which had been over eleven years in the making. Sponsorship for the rodeo was provided by the Hall and the Oklahoma City Chamber

Program for the first National Finals Rodeo, held in Dallas, Texas, in late December, 1959.

of Commerce. This was by far the most successful of all National Finals Rodeo contests until that time. The location, the hospitality of the sponsors, and the importance that the event, then in its seventh year, had achieved combined to secure for Oklahoma City its designation as the permanent site for this annual finale of the professional rodeo season.

From the inception of the National Finals Rodeo, the rule for selecting contestants has been to choose only those cowboys who, by December, are the top fifteen in their respective events. To be one of those fifteen has been the all-consuming goal of every professional contestant since the Finals' beginning, the goal he never loses sight of throughout the entire year of competition. For eleven months each year the cowboy prepares himself to qualify. If he does, he stands to share in the nearly three-quarters of a million dollars in prize money offered in the ten performances* and even to achieve the ultimate triumph of the professional rodeo cowboy: to "win the World."

In what has been called "a foolish surrender to television," the rules for determining world champions were changed in 1976. Still, the top fifteen cowboys in each event would qualify. These were named PRCA champions before the Finals. However, the world championships were to be based not on total money won for the year (including the Finals) but on the most money won at the National Finals Rodeo. Similarly, the all-around world champion would be the cowboy who won the most in two or more events at the NFR.[14] The PRCA champions (i.e., the Finals qualifiers) entered that contest with zero points, each with an equal chance to become the world champion in his event. In some cases, the man who would have become champion in his event under the old format also won the championship according to the new structure. In other instances, however, some who were lucky at the NFR won the world title, whereas had the old rules applied they would have finished the season further down the list.

The system, first tried in 1976, took away an important element in the rodeo cowboy's competitive existence. Since the beginning of point systems, it had always been the year's total winnings that had determined the champions. Making just the prize money at the NFR the criterion for a world championship removed from that contest both the significance that was inherent in it and the reason for which

---

*Figure based on the total payoff at the 1982 National Finals Rodeo, which was $700,860 in the five standard events and barrel racing. In addition, $36,300 was paid out at the 1982 National Finals Steer Roping, held September 11–12 in Laramie, Wyoming.

it had been created. Under the new rules, with all fifteen contestants starting out with a clean slate, the Finals became just another opportunity to win a good sum of prize money while possibly also becoming world champion. It was no longer, as it had been, truly the culmination of eleven months of intense competition.

After two years of applying the so-called sudden death system, it appeared that success was assured. As far as television was concerned, professional rodeo now had its very own World Series. However, after the sudden death system was used for the third time in 1978, there appeared in *Prorodeo Sports News* early in 1979 an announcement pertaining to that year's NFR, which advised readers that "the 'sudden death' scoring system which has been used at the NFR during the past three years, has been eliminated. Season earnings of qualifiers will be added to the NFR purses to determine the world champions from 1979 on."[15] The change back to the former system was, at the time, attributed to the fact that the purse at the 1979 NFR ($350,700—an increase of $60,000 from 1978) would still make the world titles "up for grabs."[16]

The early-day rodeo contestant had frowned on organizations and committees, and on the restraints such bureaucracy would entail. However, his counterpart in the 1950s held the exactly opposite view. He felt that the only way rodeo could properly move forward, as it grew, was through the combined efforts of everyone connected with the sport. By the late 1950s, rodeo had admittedly reached big-business status, with the all-around champion for 1959, Jim Shoulders, winning nearly 33,000 dollars, and it was considered that "big business needs wise counseling and sound advice." Thus, early that year, the National Rodeo Foundation was formed. Its primary objectives were:

> To study programs, plans, problems and trends related to the sport of rodeo, to meet in consideration of these things and to make recommendations for the continued advancement and betterment of the sport.
>
> To raise money for a central fund to be used to carry out the purposes of this organization and to finance activities on behalf of rodeo as a whole as determined by the board of trustees.[17]

The foundation consisted of a twelve-man board of trustees: six represented RCA rodeo committees in different geographical regions, three were livestock contractors, and three were contesting members of the RCA. Delegates in each category were selected from within their own group. This was the first effort to provide a meeting ground where representatives from all groups involved in the sport could discuss common problems and make the policy that would guide rodeo in the years to come.[18] Some of the recommendations offered in the first few years of the foundation's existence were to make a training course available for rodeo judges and, again, to limit the number of rodeos to be televised by the networks.[19]

It would appear that, in its zeal to make conditions more favorable for the cowboy while placing the sport in a more conspicuous position in the public eye, rodeo had overorganized. By 1967, it was felt that those interests that needed to be served could be better looked after with some consolidation of the various commissions. Therefore, the Rodeo Information Commission merged with the National Rodeo Foundation and became the Rodeo Information Foundation (RIF) governed by a nine-member board of trustees still representing the three segments of the earlier organization: committees, stock contractors, and contesting cowboys.

The aim of the RIF was still to provide exposure for the sport. However, the consolidation was regarded as a measure that could better accomplish this goal while at the same time strengthening the RCA, which now had tighter control of the RIF's activities.[20]

Still staffed by only two persons, the foundation's duties grew every year. The 1970s saw the so-called new breed of cowboy emerge: well-educated, articulate young men who made good material for media coverage. A new generation of reporters was also becoming prominent. The two groups of professionals worked well together, and the cooperation produced in the early 1970s not just high-caliber news articles but several excellent books on the modern professional rodeo contestant. The cowboy was further brought before a large and increasingly more interested audience through the Academy Award–winning documentary film *The Great American Cowboy* and the feature films *Junior Bonner* and *J. W. Coop*, all released in 1972.

The foundation's staff furnished press kits, photographs, and news releases to an ever-growing mailing list. In 1973, a further consolidation took place. First, the foundation's charter was dissolved. Next, the function of media liaison was given to the Rodeo News Bureau under the direct jursidiction of the RCA. Finally, as the association sought to increase its supervision of all activities relating to the sport, continuing a trend that had begun with the formation of the RIF, the group that had constituted the Rodeo Information Foundation became the RCA's Rodeo Advisory Committee. The committee's function was to serve as the connecting link with the business world,[21] which was beginning to be considered both as a more and more important segment to cultivate and as a source from which to draw support in a number of ways.

As professional rodeo grew at an unprecedented rate in the 1970s, its association began to recognize the opportunities that the establishment of closer ties with the business world would produce. The PRCA, as a nonprofit corporation, was prohibited from embarking on income-generating endeavors. In order to enable the PRCA to secure funds to expand and improve its activities, as well as its service to members, a revenue-producing subsidiary of the association named Professional Rodeo Cowboys Association Properties, Inc., was formed early in 1977. Through the new corporation, the PRCA negotiates with commercial award sponsors and handles product licensing and endorsement, as well as a host of other income-related efforts.[22] The new organization also has taken over the publication of *Prorodeo Sports News.* The publicity and public-relations duties continue to be handled by an office of the PRCA, now renamed the National Media Department.

The Rodeo Advisory Committee is still in existence as a seven-member board but because of the more highly professional caliber of the National Media Department staff the committee's function is now more nominal. The department prepares a variety of literature to aid all media, the rodeo committees, and the public. Its publications are superbly designed and produced and cover all possible facets of the sport, its participants, sponsors, and statistics. Once a week, over one thousand copies of a three-page news release are sent to newspapers, magazines, radio and television stations, rodeo committees, saddle shops, and even garages—any place of business that a contestant or rodeo enthusiast is likely to frequent. The PRCA also makes a variety of films and video cassettes available to interested parties.

In its public relations as well as in every other area, rodeo has caught up with other businesses and sports with incredible rapidity and in some cases has surpassed them. The days are long gone when the contestants had to be admonished to refrain from actions that might end up in the press and cast a negative light on the whole profession. The fact that it was precisely men from within that profession who made it all come about is especially significant.

8

Getting to the Top

To say that rodeo has undergone many changes during its 110-or-so years of existence is an understatement. It would be almost impossible to single out one change that was more momentous than another. To a great degree, one development led to another, and the pattern of change can be seen as a natural chain of events.

One important area in which the sport differs from conditions of even a generation ago is that more and more competitors today are arena trained, having received their preparation in 4-H, high-school and college rodeo, or at a rodeo school. In fact, it is estimated that, whereas about one-third (approximately seventeen hundred) of the more than five thousand full members of the PRCA have attended college, only about half of the membership has ever worked on a ranch.[1] This was not always the case.

Long before young men began to be drawn to rodeo, the working cowboy had for quite some time fascinated the uninitiated. Special excursions were arranged to see him perform his tasks. Equally intriguing was actually participating in his chores or, better yet, becoming one of his group. Indeed, few individuals have been surrounded by as much mystique as the cowboy or been the subject of as great an amount of emulation as that attempted by those who desired to be part of his fraternity. In 1891, for example, the following letter was printed in the *Stock Grower and Farmer*, which was published in Las Vegas, New Mexico Territory, and devoted to "The Pastoral Interests of the Great West":

Bridgewater, Mass., June 23, 1891.

To the Stock Grower.

Dear Sir:—I am a young man 22 years old and having a great desire for a cowboy's life thought I would write you for information concerning a cowboy's life. First, what wages are paid a green hand, and is their [sic] work the year round. Is there likely to be plenty of herding for years to come or not. I am use [sic] to roughing it: I have been brought up on a farm. Are cowboys as a rule a good class of men. When would be the best time to come and what would I need to bring with me. Can you buy as cheap out there as you can here. I like your paper very much. Respectfully, W. A. Cass.[2]

As the sport of rodeo grew in importance and scope, those who had never had the opportunity that ranch life offered as an early training ground began to demand a means whereby they could learn the required skills some other way. The famous 101 Ranch in Ponca City, Oklahoma, for example, served for years as a school for future wild-west-show performers, in addition to those sons of rich easterners who could afford a working vacation, learning regular ranch work just for the fun of it.[3] Another early effort to create a situation where the sport could actually be learned was at the Cheyenne Mountain School at Colorado Springs, Colorado, where in 1933 Superintendent Lloyd Shaw sought to adapt rodeo to the sports program of a modern school.[4] In the 1940s, some of the champions of the day, notably Everett Shaw and Shoat Webster, learned to rope at Fred Lowry's Ranch School near Lenapah, Oklahoma.[5]

Generally, however, there were not enough academic opportunities for the rodeo-cowboy aspirants in the first few decades of professional rodeo. In 1940, most hopefuls still were advised to count on two or three years of "trouping on the circuit" to become oriented and develop into "a finished performer."[6] That was to remain the cowboy's only recourse for nearly two decades.

In 1954, six-time calf-roping world champion Toots Mansfield began operating thirty-day sessions for those who wanted to perfect their skill in that event.[7] The first regular rodeo school opened in 1962, when five-time all-around world champion Jim Shoulders began to offer six-day courses in the three riding events at his ranch in Henryetta, Oklahoma. From the start, students from all over the United States and Canada, ranging in age from fifteen to thirty-four, signed up. In such a

Toots Mansfield's calf-roping school, Big Spring, Texas, in the early 1950s. Photograph by Willard H. Porter, Oklahoma City short time as six days, the most important lesson a newcomer could learn was, as Jim Shoulders put it, "whether he's got any business in rodeo."[8] Shoulders was still conducting sessions in 1982. Among top-ranked rough-stock-event riders to come out of his school is his own son Marvin, a major contender for the world-championship title in bull riding in the mid-1970s.

Since Shoulders opened his school, a number of other professional cowboys have started their own training programs for students and seem to have no trouble filling their sessions with those eager to learn. It is more and more common for young hopefuls, as well as those who are already competing, to attend a rodeo school. For the latter group, the school becomes a training camp, an opportunity to polish the performance and correct a problem that could have stood in the way of winning.

There are many examples of successful contestants who had never been on a horse until they became adults. These men have found, in the rodeo school, a shortcut to the top. Even a late starter can definitely fare well. The key to it all is athletic ability; the second prerequisite is determination, known to the cowboys as "try." If the skill is not there, however, those qualities will matter little.

Saddle-bronc rider John McBeth, world champion in his event in 1974, did not have the advantage of a rodeo school when he started out in the early 1950s. In his role as an instructor, he clearly believes in the benefits such training offers, provided the student is serious of mind and purpose: "They know something about what they're doing, whereas, when I started, there was [sic] very few people that knew, and those that did were reluctant to tell you."[9] Winning—wanting to win, *having* to win—is what motivates the cowboy. However, while it propels him, that drive is also the most difficult aspect of being a rodeo cowboy and something only he himself can deal with. McBeth does not teach how to win—that has to come from the cowboy himself. He teaches how to *ride*: "I don't ever mention the word "win," myself. I try to play up the feeling, the good feeling from within, that one gets when making a good ride on a good horse, and the money kind of takes care of itself."[10] Calf roper Jeff Copenhaver, who has roped since age eleven and was the 1975 world champion in his event, says, "You've got to learn to win by thinking. A top roper keeps getting better; a good roper is no better next month than he was last month."[11]

The arena training gives the contestant a coordination and a precision that would be impossible to achieve in a ranch-work situation. Furthermore, having a bona fide champion as an instructor cannot help but instill determination and the desire also to go after the highest honors in rodeo. The students display an almost awed reverence for their teacher; this is possibly the only time a rodeo cowboy is called "Mister."

Six-time all-around world champion Larry Mahan teaches one further element in his sessions: survival in rodeo—that is, how to get from one contest to the next without a car, how to borrow clothes, how to live on next to nothing, and how to put up with having to share a motel room with ten other cowboys and maybe find the bathtub the only available place to sleep.[12] Without such prior knowledge, many a newcomer to the sport would be in for a rude awakening.

Most likely, those who decide to become professional rodeo contestants are aware of the negative side of the sport. However, the drive that put them and rodeo together in the first place overrides any drawbacks and makes everything else incidental.[13] Rodeo becomes the one thing that matters.

The transition from college rodeo and rodeo school to professional contesting was once quite difficult to make. The newcomer was regarded with some degree of suspicion and scorn by those who had made it the hard way. Now that the majority of new contestants come from the college ranks and arena training, the transition is becoming a smooth and natural one. In his new environment, the new cardholder will find men who only a few years ago were where he is today.

It would be a rather expensive proposition for today's rodeo cowboy to go to Cheyenne (which in 1982 offered $370,194 in total money, the highest payoff that year in North America) if all he expected to get out of the trip was to hear the band play, as Ike Rude had been willing to do about sixty years earlier. He cannot afford to be in the game just for the fun. The rodeo cowboy is, indeed, still a fun-loving person because the nature of his work allows him to get to know himself better than most people ever do, and therefore he is in a position to enjoy whatever life has to offer by doing away with all pretense.

One advantage the cowboy has over the great majority of working people is the way he feels about his work, living it twenty-four hours a day by the choice he has made. Like Ernest Camron in the novel *The Bronc Rider*, the rodeo cowboy might be said to have "an almost naïve . . . romanticism." Cam in the story

avoided social contacts with all but his own breed; he despised any activity suggesting routine. He had, in effect, created a world of his own,
but a real world of action and variety, achievement and sometimes mis-
ery. Not the impossible world of a psychotic seeking escape. He was a
rodeo cowboy as much for having to be as for wanting to be. Rodeo
served as a genuine inner demand.[14]

Bull rider Jerome Robinson's admonition to the students at his rodeo
school was, "Sometimes you get 'difficult' confused with 'fun.'"[15] It is
all in the perspective from which you look at it: the positive attitude,
making an impossible or near-impossible situation work. Today's professional rodeo cowboy consciously works at coming to terms with the
difficulties and dangers inherent in the sport. His degree of success in
that effort has enormous bearing on his victories in the arena. Six-time
all-around world champion Tom Ferguson expresses it tersely but simply: "If things go wrong, make them right."[16] Absolutely nothing must
be impossible to a winner or to one who wants to become a winner.

Aside from determination, skill, and an overwhelming desire to
win, there are other factors that account for a cowboy's monetary success. He must travel well over one hundred thousand miles a year and
enter up to five or six rodeos a week. As the sport grows, his mileage
must increase, as well as the number of rodeos at which he competes.
Many contestants today own airplanes or lease them, sometimes together with other cowboys. When Larry Mahan, one year, was not
winning often enough, he considered buying a Cessna, not just to enable him to travel to more rodeos but also because he felt that the financial obligation would be an incentive to try harder.[17]

Professional rodeo today is extremely hectic. Cowboys do not have
as much time to enjoy life as their earlier counterparts if they expect to
make a living competing. The constant traveling in every direction
fifty weeks a year has to a degree lessened the closeness and common
bond that contestants of earlier years enjoyed; although the contestant
of the 1980s may have a few close friends among his traveling companions, the schedule demanded by today's competition makes wider
friendships difficult to establish. The same group used to stay together
throughout the winter and early spring rodeos in the Southwest. Those
living in the Texas-Oklahoma area would see each other regularly at
rodeos in their region. By the time the summer contests started, everyone would travel north into Utah, Idaho, Nevada, Wyoming, and

western Montana and stay in that general area throughout the summer. They would meet at the big rodeos in Salt Lake City and Ogden, Utah, and in Cheyenne, Wyoming.[18] Then followed the contests in the Northwest in the early fall.

Labor Day is in a sense a small Fourth of July today for the professional contestant, and it also marks the end of the truly busy part of the season, with the San Francisco Cow Palace rodeo a notable interruption before the National Finals in December. By contrast, the cowboys of the 1940s and 1950s would disperse in late September, to reunite at the World's Championship rodeos in New York City and Boston, neither of which is held today. The year 1959 marked the end of an era for regular large East Coast contests. The difficulty of transporting stock to such a distant location has been cited as a major reason for discontinuing what had become truly a tradition in rodeo,[19] though a marked change in the sentiments and attitudes of the public was also important. The New York rodeo—on a smaller scale—was revived in 1969, continuing through 1973; Boston, however, saw its last contest in 1959.

At every rodeo, the announcer will introduce each cowboy as his turn comes up, including in the introduction various data about the contestant—and his hometown: "So-and-so from . . ." Or, announcers often use the clichés: "This cowboy hails from . . ."; "This cowboy calls N-town home."

But does the rodeo cowboy, who travels 350-or-so days a year, really have a hometown? He often loses it the very first time he goes down the road. From then on, he is *from* someplace.[20] He will likely return to that town between rodeos, but he will no longer *belong* there. Cam in *The Bronc Rider*, was of the opinion that the small towns from which the rodeo cowboy often came were "great places to live and be from—a hell of a long ways from."[21] Quite possibly, Cam, the composite of many cowboys from many places, expresses the majority's opinion.

Conversely, the town does not lose the cowboy. If he is successful, he is forever a hometown boy, a favorite son, to its citizens. They may even put up a sign at the city limits or at the fairgrounds, if the latter exists, proclaiming that this is, indeed, the home of their sometimes only claim to fame. In one case, a town even changed its name to honor its local celebrity: Berwyn, Oklahoma, became Gene Autry, Oklahoma, in 1942.[22] Although its namesake never actually competed in rodeos, he organized and toured with the Flying "A" Ranch Stampede, a wild-west show, and, as a CTA member, also performed at many Madison Square Garden rodeos, in addition to being a successful stock contractor.

The cowboy of twenty or thirty years ago who really wanted to compete was capable of making travel arrangements as complex as those made by today's active contestants. To a modern-day cowboy, it becomes even more important to cover a large territory in order to enter as many rodeos as possible. There are more men competing, and to stay either alive, on top, or both, it is essential to do an inordinate amount of traveling. Larry Mahan managed to enter five rodeos in Texas, Louisiana, and Arizona in a single forty-eight-hour time span. Doing so involved both flying and driving. When bad weather prevented him from catching a plane at one point, he bought a 1955 Pontiac from a car dealer for a hundred dollars; about a day and a half and many miles later, he managed to sell it back to the same dealer for sixty dollars. By then the weather had cleared, and he could fly to the next rodeo. It is no wonder that he called his airline credit card the greatest influence on his rodeo career.[23]

Ingenuity is nothing new to cowboys, especially when it concerns getting down the road. When Casey Tibbs started out in rodeo at age fourteen in 1943, he would lie across the highway to attract the attention of motoring passersby in order to get a ride.[24] Another story is told of a contestant who was late getting on his way to a contest one hundred miles away. He talked a man into flying him in his small plane, with the intention of landing right on the rodeo grounds. However, the area proved too small, and the pilot was forced to fly low over a nearby potato field, plowing up fifty yards of ground and potatoes in the process, and allowing the cowboy-passenger to step out over the side of the plane. Unconcerned, the cowboy proceeded to the rodeo and won his event.[25]

There is yet another element that determines the winnings, and this is one over which the contestant has absolutely no control: the draw—that is, the stock drawn for him to ride or rope in any given contest. There is very little a cowboy can do to dress up* a horse or a bull that performs badly, or to prevent a calf or steer from running along the fence or employing any other trick to keep from being caught.

---

*Making the animal appear to perform better than it would normally do.

Therefore, he is anxious to draw as difficult an animal as possible to allow him the opportunity to make the very best of the few seconds at his disposal. A low score or a no-time means no money at the pay window. If cheating is ever tried in rodeo, the draw is the only area where it could possibly happen. One of the very few scandals, if not the only one, that have ever shaken the sport occurred when, in September of 1963 at a rodeo in Memphis, Tennessee, the secretary, R. C. ("Judge") Tolbirt, held out a certain bareback horse for Paul Mayo, then the leader in that event. Although the cowboy denied any knowledge of the occurrence, both he and Mr. Tolbirt were suspended by the RCA and fined five hundred dollars each.[26] Mayo was apparently ignorant of Tolbirt's action; his suspension was lifted, and by 1965 he ranked second in the bareback standings. Tolbirt, too, was reinstated but remained an RCA member for only one year, resigning in November of 1965.[27] It is significant that nothing untoward has ever been reported concerning livestock in rodeo, as is so often the case in other sports involving animals.

For one who has chosen rodeo as his way of life, nothing is going to stop him from pursuing his career. The early cowboy had to work on ranches to save up enough money to get to a rodeo, especially if it was far away, such as New York City. Once there, if he did not fare too well, he might possibly have had to take a job on a dude ranch (a phenomenon that first appeared in the 1920s) in order to pay for his ticket home. Then there was more ranch work until the next big rodeo lured him to try his luck.[28] It is not to be wondered at, then, that rancher-employers found him undependable.

Today's contestant prefers to be his own boss in making his living, and rodeo is one of the few professions that offer that kind of freedom. Riding-event contestant Sandy Kirby, for example, when asked in the PRCA biographical questionnaire what he liked best about rodeo, replied, "You don't have any bosses."[29] If the professional rodeo cowboy is going to succeed, he needs to devote all his time, effort, and energy to the circuit.

With ever-rising travel costs, one way of alleviating the shortage of money has been to "rodeo on the thirds": with two companions, the contestant travels from one contest to the next, sharing expenses and dividing the winnings. (This was especially common in the 1940s and 1950s.)[30] Or a cowboy may be lucky enough to become the protégé of an already well-established contestant, who, for a share—often a sub-

Jim Like in a bull-riding scene from the early 1940s. Photograph by J. Homer Venters, courtesy the Carl Studer Papers, Southwest Collection, Texas Tech University, Lubbock

George Mills being thrown from a bull, early 1940s. Photograph by J. Homer Venters, courtesy the Carl Studer Papers, Southwest Collection, Texas Tech University, Lubbock

Charles Sampson, 1982 bull-riding world champion, the first black contestant to win such a title.

stantial one—of the winnings, will sponsor him until he can manage his own, a system known as hauling.[31] Mostly, however, it is learning to do without or do with very little until winnings start coming in. Even if he does not have the entry fee, the cowboy will try to find a solution.

Because of the high travel expenses, an annual income that would seem more than adequate in a regular profession can make it impossible for a cowboy to make ends meet. The cost of contesting in professional rodeos has doubled in the last few years; the overhead of today's contestant is estimated to be half of his winnings. However, rodeo cowboys are a cooperative lot in spite of competition. Bill Linderman, RCA president 1951–57, once said, "In rodeo, if a competitor's broke, we'll not only loan him transportation and entry [fee], we'll throw in a saddle. Besides, we'll tell him how the horse he draws bucks."[32] One newswriter described this difference between cowboys and other professional athletes as "frontier honesty."[33]

Despite today's mobility, which keeps the cowboys scattered, cooperation remains a large factor in their lives. It is reported that one bull rider travels with a toothbrush as his only baggage, expecting to borrow whatever else he needs. As most riders are pretty much the same size—on the small side—and a great number of ropers and steer wrestlers are of similar proportions (a little larger), this system works well. One cowboy borrowed a pair of jeans that contained five different laundry marks, none of them with the initials of the last wearer.[34] Whether or not the lender ever expects to get his belongings back no one knows. He no doubt figures that, at some point, he will be the borrower. The system works.

Lending horses is another form of the cowboy's generosity. However, here he expects part of the winnings if the borrower places. In fact, for the owner of a good roping or steer-wrestling horse, this can prove an extra and very substantial source of income. Willard Coombs' Baby Doll netted him $75,000 in 1957;[35] today it is possible for owners of top timed-event horses to average $20,000 or more per month by lending them to other competitors. If anyone should complain that these money-making animals are overworked, it must be remembered that a steer-wrestling horse is ridden about two seconds before its rider drops on the running steer. A roping horse has to last a few seconds longer and then assist its rider as the roped steer or calf is handled.

In the steer-wrestling contest there is also another form of coopera-

The famous steer-wrestling horse Baby Doll and her owner, Willard Combs. When Baby Doll died in 1961, many of the cowboys who had ridden her to victory in the arena attended her funeral in Checotah, Oklahoma. Photograph by DeVere

tion—hazing. That is, one cowboy will ride to the steer's right, while the steer wrestler himself rides on the left-hand side of the animal. It is the hazer's function to keep the steer in a straight line until the moment the contestant leaves his horse and takes hold of the steer's head. A cowboy will haze for another even if he is competing in the same event. However, he does expect a percentage of the prize money if, in fact, there is any. As for the riders, they will not only lend their gear to and share tips with fellow contestants but also help with the cinching and getting the cowboy properly positioned on the animal before the chute gate opens.

Larry Mahan once said, "When I can't reach down and pull up a bunch of want-to out of myself, I'll know it's time to quit."[36] There comes a time when any cowboy can no longer make a living rodeoing. What happens when the professional cowboy can no longer compete? To some, rodeo is a relatively short career. Those who work the riding events, for example, can expect to retire by age thirty-five, although there have been notable exceptions. (Curiously, an article in the *New Yorker* in 1940 remarked that "rodeo is not a young man's calling").[37] A riding-event contestant who does not start young has very little chance of reaching the top or getting anywhere near it. The participants in the less strenuous timed events, however, can compete successfully into their sixties or even later. That is not to say that these events do not require stamina and strength, but there is not nearly the strain and abuse on the body as in the bull and bronc riding.

To the early cowboy, ranch bred and ranch raised, the choice upon retirement was obvious. Ranch work was the only training he had. However, to some contestants who had seen the proverbial elephant and heard the owl hoot, who had been to the big cities and received the adulation of tens of thousands of spectators, ranch life probably seemed rather tame. Quite a few drifted toward California, where they worked as stuntmen in films, also a supplementary source of income during slow periods. In the days of silent movies, names like Tom Mix and Yakima Canutt became well known. In the heyday of the Western, first in feature films in the 1940s and then also in television in the 1950s, another generation of rodeo performers helped make the production more realistic. Some rose to other functions in the film industry and worked as technical advisors and second-unit directors; a few even became actors, notably Ben Johnson and Slim Pickens. There is showmanship and flair in rodeo and in its participants that can be adapted with advantage to other forms of entertainment.

Some performers stayed in rodeo, becoming stock contractors and producers. Cotton Rosser and Lex Connelly have already been mentioned; others are Jim Shoulders and team roper Andy Jauregui of Newhall, California. Rodeo cowboys today, however, are more prepared to enter the business world upon retirement. For one thing, they are better educated than their earlier counterparts, and many are trained to take up a conventional occupation when the time comes. Also, during their rodeo careers they more consciously prepare for the time when they can no longer compete. Even though rodeo, to the professional cowboy, is an end in itself, it is at the same time a means to another end; today's contestant does not hesitate to admit that the sport can lead him into another career and that he is using rodeo to further himself in another field. There is a great deal more foresight today.

The modern cowboy also is considerably more at ease in all kinds of situations as a result both of a better education and of a greater exposure to the world around him. His immediate associates in the sport itself represent a much wider variety of backgrounds than did the cowboys of a generation ago. Professional rodeo has become a means by which the cowboy can further himself not only in competition but in society as a whole.

Even during their active years in competition, many cowboys are often involved in various enterprises sometimes on a large scale, propelled by their fame in the sport as well as by their innate or acquired business acumen. Larry Mahan has been referred to as a tycoon, reportedly making millions of dollars a year from his line of cowboy boots alone.[38] Many a top contestant designs, manufactures, and sells rodeo equipment bearing his name; each article carries the stamp of some characteristic or improvement associated with that cowboy's particular riding or roping style. This is, of course, something in which he can remain active even after he is no longer competing.

The drive necessary to succeed in rodeo, the positive attitude required to make impossible situations possible, the pride and security in knowing himself, and the belief in free enterprise—professional rodeo being perhaps the freest of them all—that the sport has given him are the best tools a cowboy can bring with him when he decides to retire from rodeo. However, there is a negative side to it: the constant drive to win—winning as the propelling force, as a life-force—can be an impediment in a future career, especially to a rodeo star. The cowboy refuses to deal with failure. By accepting it, which, to him, has hitherto been impossible, he is being untrue to himself. It runs contrary to his way of life and his way of thinking. A champion wants to stay a champion for the rest of his life. Reconciling himself to the impossibility can often be the hardest task he ever faces.

As noted previously, today's cowboy is definitely in the sport for the money. Even though the aspects of a re-creation of the Old West have always been played up by rodeo publicity, the contestant did not for some time feel that he was an actor in that spectacle. To him, it was strictly a livelihood.[39] When he no longer could earn a living that way, he was prepared and willing to move on to another, more profitable field. However, in the last few years, parallels have been increasingly drawn between the modern rodeo contestant and the nineteenth-century working cowboy who took part in railhead contests and Fourth-of-July tournaments. Quite possibly, the sport has now reached a point where it feels it is time to look back and explore its place in American history.

The difficulties and strife at the beginning of organized rodeo are far enough into the past that they are no longer uncomfortable to face. The leaders of the early contestants are beginning to be regarded in perspective, and the roles they played are being analyzed in terms of what conditions at the time demanded. Although some of the tactics that were employed then would be totally inappropriate today, they were necessary at the time they were used. Those who by their often dictatorial and violent leadership methods guided the cowboys and their organization through several turbulent years are now proclaimed heroes of their era, while it is at the same time admitted that their means would not have worked on later occasions. However, then as now, the cowboy was adamant in his belief in free enterprise, and in that belief he has continued to represent the prototype of the American frontiersman.

9

Occupational Hazards

Rodeo has often been referred to as the suicide circuit and called "an athlete's crap game."[1] Some contend that the sport is so stacked against the cowboy that it can hardly even be called gambling.[2] It cannot be denied that injury is an inevitable risk of any sport, but in no other are the odds as heavy against the participant. Injury is an almost unavoidable component of the rodeo profession. To escape injury or, if injured, to accelerate recovery for a speedy return to the arena has become a prime concern of the cowboy. As competition has become stiffer over the years, more thought has had to be given to this important aspect of the game.

A cowboy who competes on a full-time basis may enter as many as 150 rodeos a year and may, whether he works the timed or the riding events, handle 450 or more animals within that year and compete for a total of only ninety minutes. However, during that brief time he has 450 chances of getting hurt, 450 chances of getting killed. The cowboy can become injured even after a successful ride or run.[3] The enormous strain on muscles, tendons, and bones can easily cause something to give or snap even if the cowboy makes the whistle or the calf is tied. The thought of injury, though, does not seem to deter the professional cowboy. The possibility of being injured is there, but if he allows it to bother him he might as well choose another profession.

Each event presents its own peculiar injuries. The force of the first jump of an animal out of the chute can be compared to that of whiplash in an average car accident. Once out of the chute, the contestants in the three riding events are subject to differing kinds of injuries. For the bull rider, it is the riding arm: strained ligaments, pulled muscles, bone chips in the elbow, and shoulder separations, to say nothing of what can happen after the ride is over and both the bull and the cowboy are on the ground. The bareback rider suffers bad knees from the awkward position of spurring the animal, sometimes lying almost flat with his back against that of the animal and his feet spurring its neck in rhythm with the jumps.[4] In addition, he will suffer what is known as hypertrophy of the ulna, an enlargement of the ulna bone in the forearm through the building up of calcium deposits. This can be quite painful.[5] To the saddle-bronc rider, the injury usually comes after he leaves the horse, especially if he lands hard on the back of his neck.[6] In all three of these events, the great risk of being "hung up" is ever-present: in saddle-bronc riding, in the stirrups; in bareback and bull riding, in the handhold and rope, respectively. The bull rider is the only one who runs the danger of being attacked by the animal. The bareback-bronc and saddle-bronc rider can accidentally be kicked by the horse, but the animal, as a rule, does not intentionally harm the man.

Contestants in the timed events are not spared from injury or accidents either. Ropers can easily lose a finger; steer wrestlers hurt their knees as they strike the ground at thirty-five miles an hour to reach for the running steer. Not even the hazer is free from danger: four-time calf-roping world champion Clyde Burk was accidentally killed in 1945 when his horse fell on him while he was hazing for fellow contestant Bill Hancock in the old Denver Coliseum.[7]

Today's cowboy is very much aware of this number-one occupational hazard. He was when he made the decision to become a professional rodeo contestant, and his determination then overrode all the fear and apprehension of those elements that could make his career a very short one indeed. Nevertheless, the possibility of injury will remain with him.

Contestants of earlier days seem to have had a greater disregard for the threat of injury, as well as their own way of coping with it. Lee Caldwell of Pendleton, Oregon, one of the greatest bronc riders of all time, broke his arm the day before the semifinals in the 1920 Round-Up.* When the cast was applied, an aperture was left in it to enable him to take a painkilling injection before the ride. Caldwell, however, refused the shot. The pain made him—in his words—"dad-burned mad,"[8] but that state, in turn, put him in such a frame of mind that he

---

*Semifinals are no longer held at the Pendleton Round-Up.

made the only qualified ride on the bronc Two Step that season.[9] Even after the ride, he again refused a shot: "I'm too mad to take it—I want to be a little mad—a man always rides better."[10] In a Grand Finals ride on Long Tom, Caldwell was thrown against the horn of the saddle* and broke his sternum, but he stayed with the bronc.[11] After successfully completing three more rides, he won the "Rough-Riding Championship of the World."[12]

One of the most amazing examples of the tenacity cowboys display after injuries was demonstrated by Bob Crosby ("Wild Horse Bob") of Roswell, New Mexico, a multi-event competitor in the 1920s, 1930s, and 1940s. During Crosby's career, every bone in his body, except his spine and left leg, was broken at least once.

When Crosby fractured his right leg for the fifth time, in 1930, it looked as if his career had come to a sudden end. Because of an overtight cast, he developed gangrene. He was taken to the Mayo Clinic, where an amputation was advised. Crosby refused, left the operating table, and went back home to New Mexico. His local doctor twice treated the injured leg. Finally, Crosby decided to try one of the many home remedies for which at least old-time cowboys were noted. By encasing the leg for two days in an inner tube packed with cow manure, he subdued the gangrene—or, as he put it, "the red centipedes plumb disappeared." It was only a few months before he was back in competition. However, he did make one concession after the fifth fracture: he gave up bronc riding and steer wrestling and concentrated on steer roping—not because he wanted to but because his insurance company had added a clause that would invalidate the policy if he were killed in either of those events.[13]

The *New Yorker* once referred to this kind of bravery or foolhardiness as "foolish heroisms"[14] and cited a few examples of such heroisms, among them cowboy Gene Ross's riding in Cheyenne with a recently broken leg and cowgirl Fox Hastings's making her escape from a New York hospital, where she was under observation for a concussion, to ride in all bronc-riding events at Madison Square Garden and finish in the money.[15] Ripley's *Believe It Or Not* once carried an item about steer wrestler Bob Henry, who, with casts on both arms, wrestled a steer at the San Francisco Cow Palace to split first and second money with another contestant.[16]

---

*Nowadays the saddle used in the saddle-bronc riding (the so-called committee saddle or association saddle) does not have a horn.

Roosevelt Trophy winner Bob Crosby of Kenna, New Mexico, on Pumpkin.

It stands to reason that physical fitness is an important ingredient in any athletic event. Hence, the modern cowboy is totally aware of the need to stay in shape. It was not too long ago, however, that rodeo contestants dismissed such a notion. In 1951, in a *Life* cover story, two-time all-around world champion Casey Tibbs, then twenty-two years old, denied the need for physical fitness in his sport. His reason was that a rodeo contestant has to last only a few seconds, whereas participants in other sports require more endurance.[17] At the time the article was written, Tibbs had not yet broken any or many of the thirty-nine bones that were to be fractured during his rodeo career. However, he did not dismiss the fact that riding required skill—sometimes—and could lead to a wreck* if that skill was not put to use. "When a bronc starts mixing up his tricks, you gotta know your business," he said. "If you don't, you'll either pop your gizzard or eat dirt."[18] Sooner or later, something will happen that will force the cowboy, even one with a once-nonchalant attitude, to revise his thinking somewhat. Two years after the *Life* magazine article, Tibbs reflected: "Twice in my life I thought about getting hurt as I came out of the chute. If I ever feel like that a third time, I'll quit."[19] Fortunately, if that third time ever occurred, he came to terms with it. He went on to win three more world championships and one more all-around, which, along with his flamboyant life-style and colorful personality, made him one of the legends of professional rodeo.

Although there has never been a way of actually avoiding injuries, the likelihood can be lessened to a large degree by the cowboy himself. In the last several years, possibly with the advent of the so-called new breed of cowboy, contestants have devised means of coping with fear of injury and death, and they are rationally dealing with their thoughts in this regard.

One of the most popular and common ways a cowboy, as well as a prospective contestant, can learn to prevent injury is to attend one of the ever-growing number of rodeo schools and seminars. (In one early-1983 issue of *Prorodeo Sports News*, for example, no less than thirty-seven sessions were listed to take place in fifteen states within a three-month period.)[20] One such school once billed itself, in a large advertisement that filled two-thirds of a page, as a "Bionic Bull Riding Clinic,"[21] which is probably as new-breed as you can get: turn your

---

*Rodeo term for accident in the arena.

body into a computer that will do whatever you make it do. The tuition for a one- to three-day session varies between $100 and $275, but that might be a small price to pay for learning how to save your life while improving your skills.

Cowboys have different ways of handling the fear of injury, a fear that no one denies is very real. Experience does not remove the element of fear—or of injury, for that matter. But it allows more time to learn to live with it.

Few would be better qualified to speak about this subject than Freckles Brown of Soper, Oklahoma. Brown has had an amazing career, which began in 1937. Thirty years later, at the age of forty-six and fifteen years beyond the normal retirement age for a bull rider, he was the first man to ride the notorious Jim Shoulders bull Tornado, at the 1967 National Finals Rodeo. This incredible feat earned him a five-minute standing ovation.[22] Steer roper Everett Shaw, one of the incorporators of the then RCA,[23] remarked that "Freckles could be elected governor of Oklahoma tonight."[24]

Brown explained his longevity in rodeo—and his survival: "I've been hurt a lot, but mental attitude and staying in physical shape, that's the two things I think that's helped me to ride as long as I have."[25] When asked whether he thought there was a fear of dying among contestants, especially in the bull-riding event, his reply was:

> I don't think there is a bit, on my part. I never think of gettin' hurt. I think of tryin' to do this and tryin' to ride real good and get the best out of a bull or buckin' horse, and I'm thinkin' about winnin'. It never crosses my mind that I might get hurt; I don't even think about that. I think it's part of this mental process. You'd defeat yourself if you even thought about that.[26]

Mental attitude and staying in good physical shape are, indeed, the keys to success for the professional rodeo cowboy. The fact that Freckles Brown believed in that philosophy despite a number of serious injuries, including a broken neck in 1962,* demonstrates how important and well tested this belief is. Today's contestants are very much in tune

---

*In spite of this debilitating injury, Freckles Brown won in that year his first world championship in the bull-riding event. By the time his accident occurred—at Portland, Oregon, in October—he was so far ahead in the standings that he was assured of the world title without the additional prize money he would have stood to win, had he been able to mount his eight bulls at the NFR.

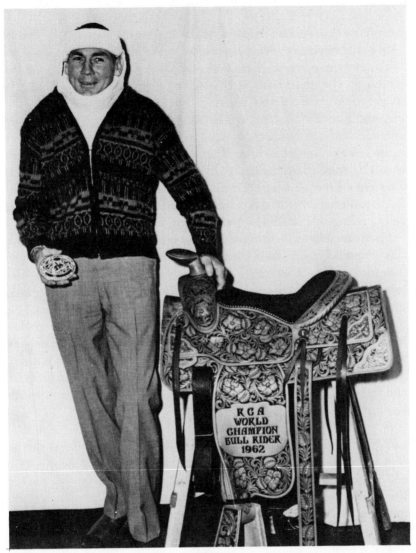

Freckles Brown, 1962 world-champion bull rider, who had accumulated enough points to win the title before suffering a broken neck that fall. Photograph by DeVere

with these concepts, whereas twenty-five or thirty years ago they probably would have dismissed Brown's philosophizing as nonsense.

On the whole, there is a greater consciousness of health today among
cowboys. The champions work out and make a point of staying in
shape: many have actively taken up other sports such as running, ski-
ing, and golf. Moderation, in fact, is the word that best describes the
attitude of the contemporary contestant, and the fact that he is regarded as and considers himself an athlete has something to do with
this. Dr. Frank Barrett, arena physician since the early 1950s at the
Cheyenne Frontier Days, sums it up: "These fellows have changed a
lot. I can remember when cowboys used to squat down and drink up
before riding. I treated a lot more injuries then."[27]

Sports medicine is taking a growing interest in rodeo-related injuries. *Prorodeo Sports News* carries a regular column on the subject by
orthopedic surgeon Bruce F. Claussen, M.D., of North Platte, Nebraska. Since 1981, through a grant from the Justin Boot Company,
Don Andrews (director of Sports Medicine Programs at the Rehabili-
tation/Sports Medicine Clinic of the Texas College of Osteopathic
Medicine at North Texas State University in Fort Worth) has been
retained by the PRCA. Known as the Justin Heeler, Andrews is director of the Justin Heeler/PRCA Prorodeo Sports Medicine Program
and served at twenty major rodeos in 1981 and at twenty-one the following year.

At the 1982 National Finals Rodeo, he introduced the first fully
equipped mobile medical center in sports history.[28] Andrews argues
that many physicians do not understand the nature of rodeo injuries
and, perhaps more important, the nature of the rodeo cowboy's work
situation.[29] However, the fact that cowboys submit to his presence and
ministrations is clear proof that they are realizing proper care is essential if they are to continue to make a living as professional athletes.

Today's cowboys refuse to think of what can happen and instead
concentrate on riding the animal or roping the calf or steer, going over
the process a hundred times in their minds until their reaction to anything that might happen is automatic and instantaneous. The expressions "riding by thinking" and "scientific rodeoing" have been used.[30]
It is necessary for them to defeat the animal in their own minds before
tackling it.[31] The knowledge that injury is likely to occur is there, but
to talk about it will not minimize the danger. The cowboys do not feel
sympathy for one another because it simply is not going to help.[32] Nor

Mobile Sports Medicine Center of the Justin Heeler program, a milestone not only in rodeo but in sports medicine as a whole. Courtesy Justin Boot Co., Fort Worth, Texas

Inside the Justin Heeler traveling rig is sophisticated medical equipment. Courtesy Justin Boot Co., Fort Worth, Texas

is much sympathy dispensed by rodeo officials. Once, when Larry Mahan, walking on crutches and needing help with the pedals on his Cessna, asked to turn out* his bareback horses at a large rodeo, he was suspected of doing so because the animals he had drawn were not of the caliber that would get him good scores.[33]

The cowboys program their mental computers for any eventuality to such a degree that the actual process leading up to the ride is far more exhausting than the ride itself. Larry Mahan spent four days preparing, or psyching himself up, to ride the bareback horse Necklace at the 1973 Cow Palace rodeo.[34]

One cowboy went so far as to admit: "Hell, I like to see a good wreck . . . but I sure don't want to see anybody get hurt. I like to see somebody pop up and get back in there again. . . . And as long as you walk away, it's okay. Just good, clean fun."[35] Maybe such a statement is proof that he had overcome the fear he felt compelled to conquer and was, indeed, in charge: man's triumph, not over beast but over himself. Another cowboy blamed failure—in this case, missing a horse out (by not having his spurs in the proper position over the animal's shoulders when the chute gate opened)—on "a weak heart."[36] He was apparently not prepared enough to want or dare to pursue the ride and gave up before even leaving the chute.

After a contestant has been injured, he loses no time in returning to competition, even against incredible odds. Here, also, he must apply psychocybernetics to overcome his temporary handicap in the same way he overcomes fear before a ride or a run.

A much-injured cowboy is saddle-bronc rider Shawn Davis, who in 1982 took over the presidency of the PRCA. In 1969 Davis broke his back. Thirteen months later he was placing in his event. Eight years after that he was still third in the standings. When asked what made him successful after his comeback and what even made him want to return to rodeo, he answered:

It's probably the same thing that started me rodeoin'. You know, they told me when I broke my back I'd never be able to ride again, especially

---

*"To turn out" means to pass on roping or riding an animal that has been drawn—whether because of injury, fear of a low mark or poor time, or just failure to show up. Quite often a cowboy will enter more rodeos than he can make, then have to "turn out" stock at those he cannot get to.

never a bronc, never even a saddle horse. Well, when I was about two, my mother and dad told me that I could never rodeo and that I could never ride, so it's probably the same thing.[37]

His answer oversimplified the situation, but no one would deny that he had what in rodeo is known as try, both as a two-year-old and later in life.

Cowboys have an obsession about shortening their recovery time to get back to rodeo, even if it means secretly escaping from the hospital or breaking a cast—or riding with it. This is nothing they brag about; it is part of what they prepare for. Recent advances in sports medicine have helped make the healing process an easier one. Also, the professional contestant today does not hesitate to seek the best possible medical assistance. Furthermore, the medical profession seems to have an attitude of greater cooperation with athletes who are injured in the pursuit of their sports.

There are even those who believe that injury is required really to emerge as a full-fledged contestant. One old-timer said, "To be really great, a guy's got to git over a couple of injuries and show what he can do when he's hurtin' bad."[38] This display of bravery is just part of playing the role of the professional rodeo contestant. It is not so much the loss of income in times of injury, although that probably has something to do with it; it is just that in rodeo there are certain things you have to do, and few cowboys, if any, can put their finger on the reason why or even exactly on what those things are. They prepare for problems that may occur and tackle them in the order they present themselves, whether they be injury, a streak of bad luck in competition, or any other adversity. The words *can't* and *don't* do not exist in the cowboy's lexicon,[39] or should not exist if he wants to be successful at his game. Strangely enough, having been injured can work to the cowboy's advantage. He likes to make an adverse circumstance work *for* him, not just to make the best of a not-so-good situation but actually to put it to use and benefit from it.

To be sure, the dangers a cowboy faces do not differ significantly from those encountered by the bronc buster and the other working cowboys out of whose work rodeo evolved. But the ways of preventing them from becoming a reality have changed, as well as the methods of coping with the threat they present.

Jim Shoulders off Harry Rowell's bull No. 18 at the California Rodeo, Salinas, California, 1950. Photograph by DeVere

Jim Shoulders, whose career as a contestant and as a stock contractor has spanned almost two generations, expressed it another way. Shoulders, who has been written up in articles with such titles as "The Suicide Circuit" and "Mr. Broken Bones,"[40] once broke his leg in five places. His comment was, "You can't stop something like this from hurtin', but you can damn well not let it bother you."[41]

To acquire that attitude and to abide by it are what the professional rodeo contestant is all about.

10

Man and Beast: The Western View

In 1978, the Sportswriters of America voted bull riding, one of the five standard events in rodeos sanctioned by the Professional Rodeo Cowboys Association, the most dangerous sports contest in this country—with respect to the contestant, not the bull. Throughout the existence of rodeo, however, the sport has come under attack by various humane groups, concerned with the welfare of the livestock. Over the years, intensified criticism has been directed at rodeo by various radical offshoots and splinter groups of animal-protection agencies and, at times, also by ad hoc groups of citizens and even single individuals. At times these protests against different events—and, for that matter, against the entire sport—have been rather vociferous and have resulted in public hearings, picketing, and attempts at legislation.

While some humane organizations would like to see rodeo eliminated altogether, others contend that such a drastic measure would be impossible without also doing away with all other sports where animals are ostensibly exploited for entertainment and profit, such as horse races, circuses, and horse, dog, and cat shows. At the same time, the rodeo interests have all along been making valiant attempts to demonstrate that the very events protested against are, in fact, carried out in a humane manner with concern for the animals' welfare.

According to statistics, the injury of livestock in PRCA rodeos is one-tenth of one percent. By comparison, the injury and death loss on an average farm or ranch is 1 to 3 percent.[1] In addition, it is estimated that 11 percent of the contesting cowboys will suffer some form of injury, although death is extremely infrequent. The philosophy of the PRCA as well as of the amateur International Rodeo Association (IRA) reflects the same concern and respect for animal welfare. More-

over, both organizations have humane rules, worked out in conjunction with the American Humane Association (AHA), and welcome
qualified humane officials to inspect livestock, equipment, and facili-
ties. This is definitely to rodeo's advantage and serves to offset the profusion of misinformation and rumors surrounding the sport.

Quite often, it appears, the humane groups are hasty in lodging
their protests and do so without first apprising themselves of the tech-
nicalities involved. Or, if some information does exist, it has at times
been distorted in order to illustrate a particular point that the organization wishes to make. Few appeals for support are as effective as those
using the suffering-animal tactic.

There is no denying that some criticism against various practices in
the early days was warranted. The cowboy listened, and is still listen-
ing. However, he resented then, and he resents now, unfounded complaints based on misinformation, ignorance, and misrepresentation of
facts. The cowboy knows, loves, and respects animals, or he would
not be a cowboy in the first place. Nevertheless, the humane movement has changed, shaped, and even improved the sport of rodeo over
the years. Before examining the role of the humane movement, a review of the western man's relationship with and attitude toward animals is warranted.

In 1860, it was estimated that there were 25,640,337 cattle in the
United States, nearly as many as humans (31,417,331). The number
of cattle, particularly in Texas, increased further during the Civil War.
They existed in such large numbers that, with the lack of money occa-
sioned by the conflict, they did not even bring a dollar a head at the
marketplace.[2]

It is quite understandable that anything so plentiful and low in
monetary value would be regarded as a downright nuisance. As such,
cattle did not even hold the low position in which some present moral
philosophers have placed animals since the beginning of the tech-
nological age; however, they occupy a place in that era, even if only as
victims, by furthering science, production, and the economy.[3]

Furthermore, at the time of the Civil War, humane ideas, originated in Great Britain, had not even begun to reach the East, let
alone penetrate to the frontiers, where day-to-day survival overshadowed any other considerations. The cattle belonged to whoever cared
to claim them. It took a substantial increase in the demand for cattle—
and, significantly, in their price—for the western man to begin to

treat them as more than expendable objects. They now constituted his livelihood, and so, again, economic objectives pointed his actions in a more humane direction.

On a cattle drive, each animal would become known to the drovers for its idiosyncrasies and habits. The cowboys would, in fact, mentally record these so as to be able to act quickly in an emergency.[4] (Similarly, rodeo cowboys today observe the quirks and peculiarities of the stock in order to be prepared to meet the challenge during the few seconds in the arena.)

Even though horses were undoubtedly the cowboy's prime tool in his work and daily existence, they were plentiful, cheap, and therefore also expendable. They were found in enormous herds and often had to be slaughtered by the hundreds in order to save the grass for the now more valuable cattle.[5] Once caught, some were broken for ranch work; others were gentled, to some extent, to be sold. The methods varied, with the horses to be kept as cow ponies perhaps receiving a somewhat kinder initiation to the work they were expected to perform. For those to be sold merely as gentled horses, there was no particular concern whether they were spoiled or not: they brought a price, and a price was better than no price. To ensure quick turnover, the faster these could be gentled, the better. Gentling was done by rough riding with generous applications of spurs and quirt, akin to the methods by which wild horses had earlier been broken.[6]

There is no question that the procedures and tools at times were cruel, not to injure the animal intentionally but for the sake of expediency and economy. The more resistance the horse gave, the rougher the treatment it received. Although the cowboys themselves often ended up with numerous injuries and broken bones, that fact has been ignored, just as the rodeo cowboys' injuries are often overlooked today. Both horse breaking and rodeo are activities in which enormous risks are taken by both man and beast.

It has been argued that man has the choice of participating, whereas the animal does not. However, when one stops to consider the sufferings the animal might be forced to endure in a natural state, maybe it is worth it to bear the moments of discomfort and fear when first handled by man for the protection and care it will stand to receive when put to use by humans. Certainly, rodeo bucking stock today would not even be alive were it nor for its usefulness in the arena.

These horses are misfits—humane-society claims to the contrary—for which there is no practical use outside the sport.

It must be remembered that there are ways in which animals are *not* capable of suffering, while humans are. A calf, for example, does not suffer from the knowledge that it is going to be slaughtered in a given period of time.[7] Likewise, a horse would not be concerned about the possibility of starvation, injury, or death if it were allowed to continue to roam free. Conversely, a pet dog or cat might be panic-stricken over a car ride to a veterinarian's office for treatment. Although the trip is undertaken solely for the welfare of that animal, it nevertheless produces great fear. However, the owner can in no way be considered to be cruel to his pet.

Some horses never submitted to any form of gentling, remaining "outlaws." These were eagerly sought by early-day rodeo promoters. Douglas Branch contended that, as the number of horses that by nature were outlaws declined, those of gentler disposition were deliberately "spoiled" by humans in order to fill the demands of the growing sport of rodeo.[8] The decrease of outlaws was presumably due to inbreeding with domestic strings. The same accusation as Branch's is made today by those unfamiliar with livestock and rodeo, who are given to elaborate with great imagination on how this spoiling is accomplished and how rodeo animals are induced to buck as the result of inhumane treatment. However, those who are familiar with horses and rodeo know that an animal either is or is not spoiled; no mechanical or human devices will change that state. On rare occasions, in fact, a gentle horse will decide on its own to give up its conventional status and join the rough string.

The horse breaker—or bronco buster,* as he has popularly been called—belonged in a highly specialized category of cowboys. He would travel from one ranch to another, breaking horses and receiving five dollars a head, a rate that remained constant well into the twentieth century in many locations. Economics again was a factor, as Lee Warren, a horse breaker from Montana, explained:

---

*The term *bronco buster* will be used here, since the professional man is called by that appellation in the literature of the time. Likewise, *bronco busting* will describe the action of his profession. The word *bronco* will sometimes be spelled *broncho* if that word was used in the account from which the information was taken.

If a buster was getting fifteen bones [dollars] a head instead of five, and all the time he needed for a bunch like this, horse fighting would be a heap safer for horses and men. . . . Bosses won't stand for a fifteen-dollar finish on a thirty-five-dollar horse.[9]

As noted above, cruelty in the handling of horses was not intentional but rather was sometimes incidental to the business. However, once a member of the string, a horse could occupy a true place of affection with his rider and receive consideration and treatment quite in proportion to the importance of the work it performed and the loyalty it displayed. Jim Christian, a cowboy on the JA Ranch in the Texas Panhandle, enjoyed his assignment as a line rider, despite the loneliness: "My comrade was my horse. A fellow could spend lots of time petting, currying and fooling with a horse."[10] Employers did not look kindly on men who mistreated their animals. Alexander Majors, who started freighting on the Santa Fe Trail in 1848, administered an oath to each of the men in his service: "While I am in the employ of Alexander Majors, I agree not to use profane language, not to get drunk, *not to treat animals cruelly*, and not to do anything else that is incompatible with the character of a gentleman. . . ." Apparently, no man ever broke the agreement. Had anyone done so, he would have been discharged without pay.[11]

One of the XIT Ranch's rules reflected humane concerns:

The abuse of horses, mules or cattle by any employee will not be tolerated; and any one who strikes his horse or mule over the head, or spurs it in the shoulder, or in any other manner abuses or neglects to care for it while in his charge, shall be dismissed from the Company's service.[12]

In spite of the severity of these regulations, it is a fact that no one was ever discharged from the XIT except for a violation on this rule.[13]

It appears, then, that, as the ranching industry took on a vital role in the economy of the West, more humane attitudes began to prevail. Unquestionably, however, monetary considerations won out over sentimentality, much as they do in the ranching business today. It is safe to assume that few, if any, of the anti-cruelty ideas that by the late 1860s had begun to take hold in the East were absorbed by the western man of the time because he had little time and patience for philosophy. Moreover, he held his bank account in higher regard than the welfare of his cattle until he learned that the two were dependent upon each other. As a result, he did not hesitate to overstock ranges with a view to larger profits the following year.

The danger inherent in this practice was beginning to be understood. In 1883, the *Mobeetie* (Texas) *Panhandle* warned, "An overstocked range must bleed when the blizzards sit in judgment." Similarly, the *Denver Field and Farm*, in its first year of publication in 1886, commented on the hundred thousand head of Texas and New Mexico cattle being brought to Colorado ranges that summer:

> Turned loose to rustle on a chewed-out range and die in winter, we suppose? Oh, Humanity, thy name does not dwell in the lodge of the rangemen and thy precious office is to them unknown.[14]

It took a near disaster, however, to bring about the change.

The terrible blizzards of the winter of 1886–87 drove many cattlemen out of business. Those who managed to remain finally came to realize that cattle raising no longer brought automatic profits, as it had in its infancy. It had grown into an industry that required the same care and attention as other businesses in order to produce dividends. Besides, here they were dealing with the unpredictable combination of live creatures and the elements of nature.

Rodeo comprises those same ingredients. The animals represent large investments to their owners. Like the cattle industry before it, the sport has grown into a business. Those involved in it have learned to act accordingly.

As discussed earlier, in the early days of the range-cattle industry, the cowboys would, for their own amusement and as a test of skill, often compete with each other or with cowboys of neighboring outfits in horsemanship, roping, and other feats indigenous to their line of work, as men involved in other vocations have often done. This contest could take place at the ranch itself or, often, at the end of a cattle drive, on the outskirts of town. When such an exhibition was held, particularly near a settlement, it quite naturally attracted curious spectators—and a rodeo of sorts was in progress.

In the early 1870s, the citizens of Cheyenne, Wyoming Territory, were twice treated to such a spectacle. The Fourth of July of 1872 was celebrated by the Texas cowboys, just arrived, with an exhibition of steer riding.[15] Presumably, at the end of the trail, all the horses that had taken part in the drive from Texas had been gentled enough not to offer any challenge to the sporting punchers. However, the following year, the townspeople were regaled with a show of bronco busting on Sixteenth Street. In those days, bronc riding was far different from the eight-second event it is today: the horse was riden until it, or the rider, gave out, a process that could take fifteen minutes or more.

Both incidents were criticized by the editor of the *Cheyenne Daily Leader*. It is believed that he was an easterner, unaccustomed to the manner in which cowboys amused themselves;[16] it is possible that, before coming to Cheyenne, he had learned of the humane ideas that by then had infiltrated the East. In any event, he had doubtless grasped the theory of the anti-cruelty movement, if not necessarily its application to conditions in Wyoming Territory. Although that movement did not include rodeo in its platform, the editor brought the principles of animal-welfare teachings to bear on a situation with which he was not familiar. His might possibly be the first voiced protest against the sport, a protest that was to grow in the next hundred years.

About a decade later, William F. Cody (Buffalo Bill) staged the 1882 Independence Day celebration in his hometown of North Platte, Nebraska. Appropriately termed the Old Glory Blow-Out,[17] it included roping, riding, and bronco breaking. No fewer than one thousand cowboys entered these events to compete for prizes—an amazing figure, considering that the richest rodeo in the United States, the Cheyenne Frontier Days, in 1982 attracted more than eleven hundred contestants.[18] The North Platte celebration in 1882 is considered the beginning both of the wild-west show and of rodeo.[19]

The following year, Buffalo Bill brought an even larger spectacle to his home state in the form of the Rocky Mountain and Prairie Exhibition, performed at the Omaha Fair Grounds.[20] This was a pageant, "strictly in accordance with reality," comprising the various acts that were to become standard in subsequent wild-west shows, where the "Cow-boys' Fun" was only a small part of the entertainment and was sandwiched in among various and sundry other acts. However, it was the part that would survive and develop into rodeo as it is known today. At Omaha, the "Cow-boys' Fun" or "Cow-boys' Frolic" occupied the ninth, tenth, and eleventh positions on the twelve-feature program. An introduction of "Bucking and Kicking Ponies" was followed by "Roping, Tying, and Riding the Wild Texas Steers" and, as a final event, "Lassoing and Riding the Wild Bison of the Plains."[21]

Scheduled to open on Thursday, May 17, the show was postponed for two days because of rain. No criticism of the affair has been recorded but rather a great deal of enthusiasm for and local pride in the undertaking, much as rodeo today is a community effort. Of the eight thousand and nine thousand specatators who viewed, respectively, the Saturday and Sunday performances, an estimated two thousand had flocked to Omaha from other Nebraska towns. The *Omaha Daily Herald* noted that the postponement had caused much disappointment in the crowds (the delay was even recorded by the *New York Dramatic Mirror*). Once the celebration was underway, however, the *Herald* seems to have covered the events in minute detail and with justifiable civic pride. The May 20 edition quoted Buffalo Bill's well-received closing speech, in which he announced his intention of taking the exhibition on the road, making it "a thoroughbred Nebraska show in which they should hold the mirror up to nature."[22]

This exhibition went on tour to various cities in Illinois and on the East Coast, always playing in outdoor arenas in afternoon performances so as to avoid the problem of illumination. The affair was a success and spawned many imitators.[23] By 1885, more than fifty wild-west shows were touring the country, with varying degrees of success, dictated by the vicissitudes of outdoor entertainment.[24]

When Buffalo Bill's troupe performed at Staten Island, New York, in 1886, a complaint of cruelty to animals reached Henry Bergh, the founder and president of the American Society for the Prevention of Cruelty to Animals (ASPCA). Bergh went in person to investigate the charge. However, not even the father of American humane work could find anything untoward in the treatment of the show's livestock, and he reported to the *New York Herald* his pleasure with the "interesting and instructive" show. He went on: "I never saw so many Indians together in my life. They ride with great spirit and are very careful of their horses and other animals."[25] Although cowboys and cowboy sports were always a part of the performances, Bergh apparently found nothing about which to be concerned.

Obviously, it was in the interest of the organizers of the show to keep the animals well and in good condition. The exhibition was a dazzling one in feats and costumes, and an animal that looked less than healthy would detract from the spectacle and quality of the performance. Then, as now, an unwell or ill-treated animal would not perform to advantage or present a good appearance in the arena. Cer-

Eng.ᵈ by Geo E Perine N York

Henry Bergh (1811–88), founder and first president of the American Society for the Prevention of Cruelty to Animals. Courtesy the American Humane Association, Denver, Colorado

tainly other protests would have been lodged if the eastern audiences had found reason to do so. This is not necessarily to say that everything was also handled properly in the smaller, imitative shows, however, which often had to struggle to survive the competition from the big names in wild-west entertainment and the growing popularity of the circus. Today, a similar situation arises in connection with smaller, nonprofessional rodeos arranged by amateur groups, roping clubs, and the like, where it is difficult, if not impossible, to inspect and police every single location where animals are used for sport, entertainment, and, to a degree, exploitation. It is without question what the public sees at these functions that gives a bad name to all of rodeo. Even though the sport is an extremely popular one today, and becoming more so every year, the majority of audiences does not—it would appear—distinguish between professional and amateur contests to nearly the same degree as in other sports, where there is a clear distinction between the two levels of competition.

A few years later, Nebraska came up with another way in which its cowboys could exhibit their skill and that also came under the scrutiny of humane interests. A company was organized, in 1892, to race on horseback the approximately one thousand miles between Chadron, Nebraska, and Chicago, where the World's Fair was to be held the following year. The finish line was the Nebraska Pavilion, and a prize of $1,000 and a gold medal for the winner were added inducement. That this was the beginning of the end of the horse-and-buggy days is indicated by the fact that two men on a tandem bicycle challenged the horsemen, with a large premium offered should they arrive at the goal before the riders. The world-champion cyclist, John S. Prince, trained specifically to make this race one that would, once and for all, usher in the machine age in transportation.

However, as day dawned on Tuesday, May 15, 1893, only ten riders appeared at the starting line for what was believed to be the greatest race ever undertaken, the rest having been discouraged from participating by threats made by the humane society. What the press referred to as a "rather suspicious telegram" cited the reason for the poor attendance as the failure of the contestants to pay the entry fees.

All the horses used in the race were cow ponies; proponents of trotting races turned their backs on the contest as it was considered too strenuous for their breed. One of the rules was that the animals had to be in fairly good condition upon reaching the finish line in order for the riders to be entitled to the prizes.[26] This was a stipulation laid down by the organizers of the race, but whether or not it was at the prompting of the humane society the contemporary newspaper accounts do not indicate.

Nevertheless, a representative of that society accompanied the riders. The *Denver Field and Farm*, however, which gave weekly accounts of the progress of the race, reported that the official had found no reason to intervene as of five days before the destination was reached and that he was not expected to have occasion to, unless the finish was a close one. Furthermore, humane functionaries examined all the horses upon their arrival at the World's Fair on June 27 and 28 and found them all to be in good condition, including the brown broncho stallion that the winner, John Berry, had ridden 150 miles the previous day. This, *Field and Farm* asserted, demonstrated

> not only that western bronchos are possessed of remarkable endurance, but also that cowboys know how to handle them humanely while still working them to the limit of their powers. The people who have been harping on the inevitable brutality of the race have nothing left to say. There has been no brutality, although better time than expected has been made.[27]

Rodeos had been held with increasing frequency throughout the 1880s in Texas, Colorado, and Montana and in the New Mexico and Arizona territories, but this was probably the first time that officials of a humane society had actually supervised a cowboy function and subsequently examined the animals used. The participation of the society's representatives also marked the beginning of future humane-society involvement in cowboy sports.

The next recorded incident occurred two years later, in connection with the Festival of Mountain and Plain at the Denver Wheel Club Park. Although this was before actual rodeo events were included in the celebration, which was still more on the order of a wild-west show, the spectators were given a showing of what cowboy sports were like. Arizona Charlie (Charles Meadows), a wild-west-show and circus performer who billed himself as a "grand specimen of the real cowboy," gave an exhibition of the lassoing and throwing of bulls.[28] From the description in the *Rocky Mountain News*, it appears that what Arizona

Charlie demonstrated was very close to what today is steer roping, something that has long been an issue of controversy.

While apparently the audience of two thousand appreciated his efforts and the newspaper wrote flatteringly about the performance, Secretary Thomson of the Humane Society thought otherwise. It was quite apparent, also, that this gentleman had been forewarned about the event, for he appeared in the arena, determined, carrying what was referred to as "his trusty cane," which he used to theatrical advantage. It was equally apparent that the star performer, Arizona Charlie, had ancitipated the trouble that ensued. After the first of his two arrests during the performance, the fact that a bondsman was present received some comment in the *News*. Taking advantage of this opportunity, Charlie proceeded with his performance, the bond thus secured.

What followed was not so much a show as a contest of patience between Charlie and Thomson. After a second arrest, Meadows, his brother, and a third performer were released on bond. An effort on Charlie's part to swear out a warrant against Thomson for his interference with the show was postponed. That day's evening performance was abandoned and further exhibitions closed down indefinitely.[29] However, bets were being taken whether or not a bull fight would be demonstrated before Charlie left the city for other parts.[30]

The incident in Denver, coupled with an earlier bull-fighting episode of Charlie's in Gillett, Colorado,* soon became a national issue. A protest had reached the president of the American Humane Association, along with a request that a resolution be passed to censure Governor McIntire of Colorado for "timidity and indifference." Efforts were made to stop Charlie's future performances in other locations in the state, with varying degrees of success.[31] Humane-society officials throughout the state were kept on guard through a network of information as to his whereabouts and activities, disseminated by the society.[32]

In the case of Arizona Charlie, it was primarily what would become steer roping that was under attack. To this day, this is the one event to receive the most criticism. Steer roping is currently permitted in five states: Arizona, Oklahoma, Oregon, Utah, and Wyoming. Although it does take place elsewhere as well, it is never a part of professional

---

*Gillett, a gold-mining community four miles north of Cripple Creek, ceased to exist in 1913.

Charles Meadows, known as Arizona Charlie, had one of the first animal acts in rodeo to attract the attention of American humane officials. Courtesy Jean E. King, Granada Hills, California

Steer roping has come under attack more than any other rodeo event. This picture from the Cheyenne Frontier Days in 1907 shows a man named Wills roping a steer. Photograph by J. L. Stimson, courtesy Stimson Collection, Wyoming State Archives, Museums and Historical Department

rodeo in the rest of the nation. However, because of increased safety measures and stringent rules of competition for the sake of protecting the steer, the popularity of the event is now growing and more states allow it than before.[33]

In earlier years, though, it was under constant attack, the next time at the 1907 Cheyenne Frontier Days celebration, then in its eleventh year. The July 27 edition of the *Wyoming Tribune* contained a humane-society protest headlined "Steer Busting. State Agent Gough Gives Reason for Action of Wyoming Humane Society. Says Throwing and Tying of Steers is no Longer Characteristic of the Cattle Range and is not permitted by Western Stock Growers."[34] The organization felt steer busting* was not representative of range-work procedures of the time, especially when performed by contestants "not in regular practice." An order to stop it from being included was issued.[35]

Wyoming is one of the states where the enforcement of anti-cruelty laws is the responsibility of the state government.[36] Dr. Pflaeging, state veterinarian as well as humane-society representative, was present at the 1907 Frontier Days. He is said to have given warnings to the riders on several occasions but, at the same time, is credited with being fair in his actions. It was believed that his presence minimized incidents of possible cruelty while not detracting from the excitement of the contests.[37] This is an early example of how cooperation between rodeo and humane factions can work to a definite advantage, as long as they understand and appreciate each other's objectives.

In 1909, steer roping again came under attack at Cheyenne. The humane society and the rodeo committee could not agree on the rules for the event. (This was before there were any official rules that governed all professional rodeo contests.) It was called off on the last day of the celebration. The range cowboys who took part, however, not only did not consider the event cruel but in fact felt it was representative of their work in the days before ranches had pens, corrals, and chutes.[38] In this connection, they were directly in opposition to the stand the cattlemen, supported by the humane society, had taken two years previously.

It should be borne in mind that those who participated in the contests were actually working cowboys, many of whom had been present at the time when a transition to more efficient methods of cattle rais-

---

*Another term for steer roping, used in earlier times. The steer is said to be "busted" by the manner in which it is thrown.

ing had taken place. On the other hand, as has been discussed, the majority of today's rodeo cowboys do not have a ranching background but are strictly athletes. More important, many do not feel they are a part of the tradition that dates back to the time when the working and the rodeo cowboy were one and the same person.[39]

Although most rodeo events have evolved from the range work of another era (some contests, notably bareback-bronc riding and bull riding, are later additions), it may be that the showmanship of modern rodeo, the businesslike manner in which it is conducted, and the commercialism that surrounds it somehow conceal its Old West beginnings. In any case, humane groups have focused on the Old West aspect, characterizing it as the disguise under which purported exploitation of and cruelty to animals are allowed to flourish. Thus, although rodeo continues to be represented and promoted as a re-creation of scenes from the Old West, it has engendered a great deal of controversy, coming most strongly from animal-welfare interests.

11

Lessons in Cooperation

The early contests in connection with the Cheyenne Frontier Days were not the only ones to come under humane-society attack. Contemporaneously, protests were going on elsewhere, although at this early stage there were few established rodeos that recurred on a regular basis. One of these, the Calgary Stampede, had its beginning in 1912. On the program were both steer roping and steer wrestling. According to Clifford P. Westermeier, the rodeo's first year is of "historical significance because the contests of bulldogging and steer roping were outlawed after that show.[1] However, there is contradictory information regarding these events and their survival as part of the Stampede.

There were, indeed, protests, but as far as can be determined they were only with regard to the steer-wrestling event. One was made by a woman named Genevieve Lipsett-Skinner, who apparently had appointed herself spokesman for "every woman," in an article in the *Calgary Daily Herald*; her report on the pageantry of the first Stampede is interspersed with dramatic outcries against "the appalling cruelty to the steers chosen to illustrate the prowess of the cowboys in the manly art of 'bulldogging.'"[2]

Lipsett-Skinner's article includes descriptions of how the horn was torn off by the steer wrestler. It would hardly be possible, however, for a man, with his bare hands, to break the horns of a steer in a way that would be painful—that is, to tear them off the animal's skull, as in the dehorning process. Even the breaking of a horn partway is extremely rare; should this occur, it can be compared to a human's breaking a fingernail. In a report prepared by the IRA's Humane Activities Office, it is explained as generally happening

FOX-WILSON
...Y WOMAN BULL DOGG... IN THE WOR...

Through the 1930s, female contestants competed in events they do not now usually enter in professional rodeo. Fox Hastings Wilson, one of the prominent early cowgirls, is here competing in steer wrestling, circa 1925.

when both the cowboy and steer turn a somersault together. This is not considered by veterinarians as a major serious injury and if it happens, the steer is merely dehorned, as the rest of the herd will be when they are retired from rodeo, and fattened for beef purposes.[3]

In other words, it is an experience that cattle, whether of the rodeo or the commercial variety, have to go through at some point in their lives.

Protests notwithstanding, the events were, in fact, on the program again at the next Calgary Stampede. This did not take place until 1919, financial difficulties having made it impossible to include the rodeo contests in the Calgary Exhibition in the intervening years. Subsequently, difficulties once more beset the Stampede, and for three years none was held; it returned in 1923. Yet, though the show has remained an annual event ever since, there were no steer-wrestling and steer-roping contests at Calgary for about forty years.

There are at least two reasons for their elimination. First, in 1922, the year prior to the resumption of the Stampede, the Calgary Humane Society was incorporated as a charity organization,[4] giving the protesters a united voice. Second, although there were reports, which proved to be false, that there had been petitions to outlaw the two events in question, it turned out that the real reason for the protests was the opposition of cattlemen in the United States. They had called on the government to make steer wrestling a punishable offense because of the damage done to their herds by cowboys who practiced on their cattle.[5] (The damage was in the weight loss the cattle sustained from being run excessively.) Thus, when rodeo contests were again included in the Stampede in 1923, the two events under criticism were not among them—but, significantly, not for reasons of cruelty to animals.

The 1923 Stampede did see two new contests to add to the excitement: the chuck-wagon race and the wild-horse race. In 1927, steer decorating* was introduced, to take the place of steer wrestling. However, in the mid-1960s steer wrestling was reinstated at Canadian professional rodeos, including the Calgary Stampede. The Canadian Professional Rodeo Association [CPRA] was anxious to effect this change so that points in the event could be won uniformly by members of that

---

*Instead of wrestling the steer to the ground, the cowboy places a ribbon, attached to a rubber band, around its nose or on one of its horns.

organization, as well as of the PRCA, competing in the two countries. The Canadian Society for the Prevention of Cruelty to Animals was informed of the inclusion, and no complaint was registered with the CPRA or the Calgary Stampede officials.[6]

The period from about 1915 to the end of the 1920s was a time during which rodeos, the Frontier Days and Pioneer Days celebrations, and the declining wild-west shows everywhere were subject to much protest and even court action, brought on not just by humane societies but also by women's clubs and other similar organizations.[7] Now, half a century later, the events of those days can be regarded in perspective. This leads the observer to speculate whether some of the protests may not have been aimed more at the cowboy himself and the unorganized, itinerant rodeos of the day. The rodeo cowboy of that time was, for example, described as a "bum" rather than as a man engaged in a legitimate professional sport. By exploiting the cruelty angle, those who did not want cowboys around were more likely to be heard, since the humane movement had already gained momentum.

One exception to the rule was the Pendleton Round-Up, held at Pendleton, Oregon, which had its beginning in 1910. This show received early praise for the manner in which the livestock was treated. One author took pains to emphasize the point, declaring: "And let this be clear: there is no cruelty to animals. The broken bones—and necks too—are the loss of the two-legged contestants."[8]

During the period under discussion, 1926 seemed to be a year in which humane agitation reached a particularly intense level. At the national convention of humane organizations in Portland, Oregon, a discussion of rodeo was held,[9] possibly the first time there had been a consolidated attempt on the part of animal-welfare agencies to combat or at least modify rodeo. Walter E. Osborn, secretary of the Oakland, California, SPCA, felt that rodeos were "here to stay as long as there are competent cattlemen to support them and make them successful and an enthusiastic public to attend."[10] (This was an interesting observation in view of the relative newness of the sport, especially as public entertainment, and the turbulent times it was experiencing.) Osborn, who believed that cruel incidents had already been removed from the contests, offered a suggestion that proved to be a very sensible one, namely "that the humane organizations get together with rodeo committees and gradually eliminate objectionable features."[11] This is the philosophy of the American Humane Association today. Other dele-

Mike Stewart on the saddle bronc Bill McAdoo, Pendleton Round-Up, Pendleton, Oregon, 1926. Photograph by Pendleton Drug Co.

Tex Crockett on the saddle bronc South Dakota, Cheyenne Frontier Days, Cheyenne, Wyoming, 1919. Photograph by R. R. Doubleday, courtesy Wyoming State Archives, Museums and Historical Department

gates to the convention, however, apparently hoped that elimination
of what they deemed cruel features, purportedly still existing, would
result in financial failure of the sport.[12] At any rate, when the Washington State Humane Society was formed, also in 1926, its president,
taking a much firmer stand, declared, "Complete abolition [of rodeos]
is our objective." It was believed that enforcement of already existing
laws would accomplish that aim.[13]

Contests that did not belong to the RAA or that preceded that
organization wrote their own rules of competition. It is significant,
therefore, that, without exception, they included the humane treatment of livestock in these rules, which were published in prize list and
rules booklets prior to each rodeo. For example, the Prescott, Arizona,
Frontier Days Celebration—one of the country's oldest rodeos, dating
from 1888—included, before there was an RAA, the following in its
"General Rules":

> The Management reserves the right to withdraw any contestant's name
> and entry and refuse to allow his stock used for any of the following
> reasons, to-wit: . . . ABUSING STOCK. . . .[14]

The 1932 Denver National Western Stock Show and Rodeo (in its second year and at the time not yet an RAA member show) gave a similar
warning under "General Rules of the Rodeo":

> Any contestant, who mistreats or in any way enacts cruelty to any ani-
> mal, automatically disqualifies himself in all events, and forfeits any
> money due him. The manager positively will not permit cruelty of any
> nature to any animal. It will be the judges' duty to enforce this rule.[15]

It became the RAA's function, among many others, to standardize
rules of competition. Then, as now with the PRCA and formerly with
the IRA, these rules were written in such a way as to give the animal
every advantage over the contestant. That fact should dispel the often-
held notions that the cowboy inflicts cruelty on the animal upon which
he competes and that the animal's conduct is a result of this abuse. A
calf being roped in a rodeo contest is subjected to no more mental an-
guish or pain than one captured on the range for the purpose of brand-
ing, doctoring, or whatever ministration.

Nevertheless, in spite of all the efforts to make the public aware of
rodeo's concern for livestock, the protests continued. Westermeier

places the blame on newspaper and magazine writers who covered the sport without having any background in or knowledge of it.[16] To that category could be added the majority of the protesters of many humane groups through the years. It is, therefore, in a sense a testimony to its strength that, during nearly four decades, rodeo continued to grow despite the intense debate over the sport and attempts at legislation to outlaw it.

The attitude of the humane movement toward rodeo is well illustrated by its position on the use of spurs, which has long come under attack. Humane groups like to have the public believe that spurs cause the horse to perform the action of bucking, which is instead natural and instinctive for American range-bred horses. Today's cowboy uses spurs with very blunt rowels, about the same as for riding a regular saddle horse. Furthermore, the PRCA rules for saddle-bronc riding state that a contestant will be disqualified for "riding with locked rowels or rowels that will lock on spurs." Locked rowels are also not permitted in the bareback-riding event. In addition, judges will examine spurs (and other equipment) to ascertain whether a "foreign substance" has been applied, an infraction that also results in disqualification and imposes besides a thirty-day ineligibility to compete. (An exception is made "if local rules make it necessary for the covering of spur rowels.") Similarly, the rules of the International Rodeo Association, for the same events, set forth that one of the grounds for disqualification is "riding with locked rowels or rowels that will lock during ride."[17] The fact that the horses often will continue bucking after the cowboy has been unseated, as well as after removal of the flank strap, should be convincing enough evidence that spurs do not make the horses buck.

Another example of humane groups' efforts to restrict rodeo activities is a bill (SB-476) introduced in 1937 by Sen. Dan E. Williams (R) in the California Senate. Aimed primarily at the motion-picture industry, it attempted to ban the so-called Running W device, used in horse falls.[18] If passed, it could have been expanded to take in the roping events in rodeos as well.

In California, the rodeo promoters had always made a particular point of conforming to the demands of the state's humane societies. In Los Angeles, for instance, they worked actively with the animal-welfare agency and encouraged it to deal directly with each individual rodeo in cases involving possible violation of rules instead of making a public attack.[19] Reflecting his association's satisfaction with the results, a representative of the RAA declared, "We have found, in California, that by working with the Humane Societies, the rodeos have been much better off than when there was open warfare."[20] Possibly the reason why the system worked so well in that state is that the RAA's national headquarters were located in the city of Salinas, California.

Although the bill banning the Running W device originally passed the state senate by a 22-7 majority, the united effort of the managements of California rodeos led to a vote for reconsideration. The result was a decision by the senators to table the bill.[21] By continuing the methods already favored by the RAA, rodeo in California would constructively carry on the work of building up the sport's reputation, which, at that time, badly needed a boost.

This incident was the first of numerous occasions when rodeo interests had to rally to the defense of the sport in state legislatures throughout the country, in most cases successfully. As Henry Bergh said in 1866, "Politics have no more to do with it [humane concerns] than astronomy. . . ."

Rodeo was by this time being written about regularly in major magazines. A *Saturday Evening Post* article for example, defended the treatment of livestock at the larger shows:

> Naturally, representing considerable investment, the contractor's animals are given the best of treatment. And, incidentally, though there may be accidents, there is no cruelty in rodeo run under the auspices of the R.A.A. Outlaw shows, where they sometimes put high-test gas in the ears of the neighborhood plow horse, are something else again.[22]

Today, there are countless of these smaller so-called rodeos, some without much advertising, and thus it is practically impossible for humane societies to inspect them all. Unfortunately, however, what complaints are made—based on observations at these rodeos—have an adverse effect on professional rodeo as well. Apparently, many people do not distinguish between professional and amateur contests to nearly the same degree as in other sports, where there is a clear distinction between the two levels of competition.

Even though protests were going on the entire time, not one of the forty-seven magazine articles on rodeo published in the late 1950s or the forty-four articles that appeared in the 1960s contains anything derogatory about rodeo. However, rodeo in the 1960s was not in the least spared criticism in the state legislatures. This is in large measure attributable to the activities of various anti-cruelty organizations operating outside the already long-established American Humane Association.

The two most notable anti-rodeo measures of the decade originated in the California and Ohio legislatures, respectively. In the former, Assembly Bill No. 888 was introduced in 1967 by Assemblyman Leon Ralph (D) of Los Angeles. Aimed specifically at rodeos, it would, if passed, have prevented the use of hotshots. Ironically, the text of the bill was such that its coverage would have been extended to the cattle industry as well. Moreover, the sponsors of the bill intended, upon passage, to amend it to include also the elimination of the use of flank straps on horses and bulls.

The hotshot, or electric prod, has long been a controversial piece of equipment. However, until the invention of this device, whips and clubs were used to move cattle through the chutes. About the prod, a veterinarian, Dr. Robert M. Miller, says, "I cannot think of a more humane device." [23] It works on three to ten flashlight batteries, with three being the most common for use in handling rodeo stock. With only one-millionth of an ampere produced, the prod causes no burning. The only thing it does is create the effect of a mild shock, [24] which is certainly better than a blow of the club or the whip, more effective, and, most important, more humane.

The California prod bill, as it was popularly called, was referred to the Committee on Criminal Procedure and enjoyed a public hearing in May of 1967. At this, however, it became evident that the measure was opposed even by the state humane association, which called AB 888 "a retrogressive piece of legislation." Shortly thereafter, the bill was killed in committee. [25]

In Ohio, House Bill No. 541, introduced in the 1965–66 session of the legislature, was supported by various humane groups, in particular by those which wished to see an end to all sports and entertainment activities involving animals. Its text, as introduced, was so ambiguous that the state's attorney general had to rule on its meaning. In his opinion, it applied to work horses, not rodeo horses. [26] Nevertheless, when it passed on July 1, 1965, [27] this legislation had been amended to extend not only to rodeo and work horses but to practically any animal owned by Ohio residents. Specifically, it became unlawful for an individual to take his horse in a trailer to participate in any kind of competition.[28] The result was that, for two years, rodeo was virtually nonexistent in the state of Ohio.

During the 1967–68 session, a repealer bill, HB 260, was introduced in the Ohio House of Representatives by Rep. Robert E. Stockdale (R). In preparing the text, Representative Stockdale had used the RCA's rules to ensure humane treatment of livestock. With the backing of RCA director Clem McSpadden, who played an important role in preventing anti-rodeo legislation during these years and was present at a hearing,[29] the bill passed out of the Agriculture Committee in April. At a final hearing, all five veterinarians called to testify were in favor of the passage of the bill, which would amend the existing law to allow competition to resume and, implicitly, the use of flank straps. The Ohio Department of Agriculture concurred with the veterinarians.[30]

HB 260 was clearly destined for passage. In the meantime, however, an interesting development occurred. The Honorable Rex Weaver, judge of the Municipal Court of Miamisburg, Ohio, declared that the law that HB 260 was designed to amend—section 959.20 of the Ohio Revised Code—was unconstitutional, holding that it violated not only the Fourteenth Amendment to the United States Constitution but also sections 1, 2, and 16 of article 1 of the constitution of the State of Ohio.[31] (Evidently, one of the privileges of Americans, protected under the Constitution, is the freedom to carry on activities involving animals for a variety of purposes. In connection with the conduct of these, opinions differ as to the extent to which the participants should be entrusted with responsibility for the treatment of such animals without interference of law.)

Similar legislative activity went on in Connecticut, Illinois, New York, Pennsylvania, Wisconsin, and other states. In virtually every case, passage would have meant total abolition, not only of rodeo but also of any event in which animals played a part. Throughout this period of agitation, representatives of the RCA and other interested parties participated in hearings and gave testimony. To many outsiders it must have been an eye-opener to discover the importance their active involvement had: the anti-rodeo bills were universally tabled or defeated. The victory was due in no small measure to the efforts of Clem McSpadden, whose appeal the *Hartford Courant* acknowledged on the front page after McSpadden's fifteen-minute speech concluded a 1967 debate in the Connecticut House Agriculture Committee: "Tall, articulate and tanned, McSpadden drew a standing ovation when he completed his talk and a couple of people asked him if he would like to run for governor of Connecticut."[32]

The lack of success encountered by every anti-rodeo bill of the 1960s should, it would seem, have indicated that any future efforts would fail. Far from it: the decade had been merely a training period for protesters.

12

A Decade of Protest

During the 1960s, protesting had become a way of life for many; in fact, it may be the feature with which that decade will continue to be most readily identified. By the time the 1970s began, it had become fashionable to be against, in particular, established institutions. What better to turn against, then, than rodeo, which represented strength and—to some—violence, as well as time-honored practice. Consequently, the early part of the decade was a time of unprecedented anti-rodeo agitation.

Simultaneously, there was a decline in rodeo coverage in magazines. The articles that did appear often took a stand for or against the sport, or at least brought out arguments of both pro- and anti-rodeo factions; earlier, very little, if anything, had been mentioned about the controversy. The furor against rodeo that characterized the decade may be seen in the chapter in Gerald Carson's book *Men, Beasts, and Gods*, entitled "Rodeo: Cruelty Packaged as Americana." In it the author went so far as to term the sport "our modern recreational equivalent of the public hanging."[1] Indeed, Carson placed the word *sport* within quotation marks, which is the way the word appears in much humane-society literature.

It was in the 1970s that the efforts of the Humane Society of the United States (HSUS) began to make themselves felt. Although that society had come into existence in 1954 as a splinter group of the American Humane Association, it had devoted its first fifteen-or-so years primarily to agitation for humane-slaughter legislation, federal laws to protect laboratory animals, and amendments to laws—on all government levels—with respect to animal cruelty and animal regulation.[2] At the beginning of the 1970s, however, it directed its activities toward rodeo. In its current policy statement on the subject, the HSUS declares that its objective is "to work to eliminate all rodeo events in which there is danger of injury, pain, torture, fear, or harassment to the participating animals and to seek an end to the use of the devices which, through pain or discomfort, induce rodeo animals to react violently."[3] This organization goes a step farther than most anti-cruelty groups by professing that rodeo is "psychologically damaging" to children, who, it believes, are taught "tolerance of inhumane treatment of animals in the name of competition."[4]

Rather than the advocating of strict protection of animals for the sake of humaneness, the position of the HSUS implies a concern—genuine or not—for their sentience, and for their rights as sentient creatures. This feeling has become more prevalent in recent decades, although it is also reflected in writings of the latter part of the nineteenth century, such as in the philosophy of Henry S. Salt.[5]

The initial battle waged against rodeo by the HSUS, in 1971, which was financed by the allotment of one million dollars, was designed to do away with the sport once and for all. Considering that all humane organizations, except those that are part of a state governmental agency, depend solely on private donations for their survival, this was a rather staggering sum.

The failure that anti-rodeo legislation had suffered in many state legislatures did not deter the HSUS. This was possibly the most extensive crusade it had ever undertaken. In making this all-out effort, the HSUS had conceived a strategic plan, with two objectives. The first was to achieve a ban on rodeo advertising and rodeo broadcasting—in other words, to suppress every means by which rodeo got its publicity. It was hoped that, through lobbying in Washington, D.C., rulings effecting such a ban could be obtained from the Federal Trade Commission and the Federal Communications Commission.

The second objective was, regardless of the outcome of the encounter with the two commissions, to close down the Madison Square Garden rodeo in New York City (held that year June 24–27 and June 29–July 4). The HSUS protest organizers were convinced that picketing the event would force the management to cancel the show; that accomplishment could then be used as ammunition for further lobbying and for closing future rodeos everywhere.

Hired pickets marched in front of the Garden, distributing literature printed by the HSUS. In a countermove, the RCA had its leaflets
denying the HSUS's accusations passed out by the cowboys and cowgirls and by other rodeo adherents.[6] In addition, to reinforce further its
claim that rodeo was, in intent, a humane sport, the RCA staged an
educational demonstration through its public-relations firm, Ruder
and Finn of New York. In the RCA's opinion, it was largely through
protests stemming from the East that the issue had come to such a dramatic head.

In spite of the RCA demonstration, the eastern press apparently remained "bent on seeing it the way it prefers."[7] Nevertheless, that
effort put an end to the HSUS's campaign, which had been conceived
and begun on a grand scale but which had, after all, concluded in
defeat.

In correspondence with the author, the HSUS argues that "pain
and suffering do occur."[8] However, it objects specifically only to the
flank strap, which it describes elsewhere as a "tormenting device."[9]
Veterinarians, even those who have no vested interest in rodeo, deny
that it is. Dr. Donald Delahanty, professor of veterinary surgery at
Cornell University, states: "The flank strap is an annoyance. It cannot
cause physical harm. Pain is not an issue."[10] Dr. Robert M. Miller of
Thousand Oaks, California, a practicing veterinarian since 1954 who
specializes in equine medicine, echoes Dr. Delahanty's sentiments:

> Bucking and flanking straps are not painful devices. They serve to in-
> crease the bucking animal's action and to cause him to kick higher. If
> pulled too tight the animal cannot buck. In fact he will be unable to
> stand. We veterinarians commonly cast cattle for the [sic] treatment by
> simply pulling a rope tight around the body in the same place that the
> bucking strap fits.

Dr. Miller further illustrates the latter point by saying that he has himself, single-handedly, cast a bull, for the purpose of treatment, by applying a cincture around the area described.[11]

As most attentive observers of rodeo will have noticed, an animal is
likely to continue bucking in the arena even after the flanking strap
has been removed. Moreover, even gentle saddle horses that have

never in their lives felt the touch of a flank strap will buck, especially on chilly mornings or whenever they feel the need to "get the kinks out."

Of those humane groups that would like to see rodeo totally abolished, the HSUS is by far the most active. This is presumably because of adequate funding and a national organization broken down into seven regional offices and one Humane Education Center.

Another organizaton of the abolitionist faction is the Society for Animal Rights, Inc. Its original name, the National Catholic Society for Animal Welfare (NCSAW), itself caused controversy: the group was accused of misleading the public by the word *Catholic*, which implied that, through affiliation with the Catholic Church, its crusade carried some sanction. However, the "Catholic" in its name meant simply "all-inclusive," a definition that probably did not occur to most listeners on first hearing the word.

The tactics of this group were exposed during the hearing on repealer bill HB 260 in the Ohio legislature in 1967. The NCSAW had distributed a pamphlet, both nationally and to the Agriculture Committee of the legislature. Its most controversial aspect was a picture of a horse with someone holding its tongue extended from the left side of the mouth. The tongue was cut in two at least two-thirds across, about four inches from the tip. The brochure claimed that the injury had occurred at a rodeo and, moreover, that it was a common occurrence.[12] This totally misrepresented the situation, however, for bucking horses in rodeo have nothing in their mouths, and there is nothing used in the riding events that can cut the animals' tongues. The society's current brochure decrying rodeo contains rather agitated language, designed to appeal to people's emotionalism—and purses. Here, too, the illustrations appear to be deceptive.

Still another anti-rodeo group is Friends of Animals, Inc. At first devoted to actions for humane slaughter of livestock and the ending of the seal harvest,[13] this group, claiming that its members are "the arch-enemies of all men who cruelly exploit helpless animals everywhere," has jumped on the anti-rodeo bandwagon. In the evaluation of the Humane Activities Office of the International Rodeo Association, the organization's objective is "to abolish every animal event they do not understand."[14] In its own brochure, Friends of Animals purports to "tell the true facts" (with the admonition, "Read them like [sic] they are"), again in overemotional language—for example, animals described as being in a "crazed state of pain and fear;" flank straps "tightened unbearably, to provoke tame horses to go 'loco' in excruciating agony"; and calves and steers presented as "the pain-racked, horror-ridden animals unfortunate enough to be Rodeo 'stars.'"[15]

However, the activities of the Society for Animal Rights and Friends of Animals are eclipsed by those of the HSUS. Undaunted by its two defeats in 1971 (the FTC and FCC lobbying and the Madison Square Garden demonstrations), the society in that year commenced an investigation of rodeo, under the direction of "a veterinarian." The report issued at the conclusion of the study did not mention, however, that it was the veterinarian retained and salaried by HSUS, Dr. Robert C. Bay, and that he, at the outset, had been given the assignment to "prove" that rodeo was cruel to animals.[16]

The investigators spent two years attending rodeos in Montana, Wyoming, and Colorado. Technical data and assistance for the study were given by personnel who, by their credentials in veterinary medicine and animal husbandry, may well have possessed knowledge of livestock; however, the methodology employed by the HSUS and its researchers made the study appear rather unreliable to those with knowledge of rodeo events. Nevertheless, when the findings were presented to the general public, the impact of the report was powerful. Curiously, the only rodeo event that did not come under direct attack was steer wrestling. In all others, the investigators found that some kind of injury had occurred.

The results were published widely at the conclusion of the investigation. The HSUS itself issued a six-page, illustrated *Special Report on Rodeos*. It was reprinted verbatim in *The Ark*, the bulletin of the Catholic Study Circle for Animal Welfare, London, affiliated with the Catholic Church in Great Britain. Furthermore, an Associated Press article about the study, with the headline, "Animal Lovers Spur Drive to Outlaw Rodeo," appeared in many newspapers across the country.[17]

Before the results of the study were even made public, they were used, by the HSUS, to give testimony in favor of anti-rodeo bills SB 384 and SB 385, which were introduced in the Colorado state legislature by Sen. Ted Strickland (R) in the spring of 1973. These bills, aimed specifically at the calf-roping and team-roping events, were designed to outlaw roping and busting of any animal in rodeos.

The subsequent failure on the two bills was blamed by the HSUS on the "overwhelming presence of rodeo supporters" at the hearing on April 30. Fourteen individuals from every level of rodeo, Little Britches to professional, were given an opportunity to speak before the legislature. However, it was the testimony by two noted Colorado veterinarians, Dr. O. R. Adams of Colorado State University, Fort Collins, and Dr. Marvin Beeman of the Littleton Large Animal Clinic, exposing the errors in and inconclusiveness of the HSUS's two-year study, that convinced the legislators to table this legislation.[18]

The year after HSUS's study was concluded, the Professional Rodeo Cowboys Association initiated its own investigation, specifically to study the stress placed on calves in roping. No scientific information existed before that time. The study was prompted by the growing number of protests by humane associations, particularly against the roping events (in spite of the failure of Senator Strickland's bills the previous year). In order to be able to answer the accusations made by these groups, it was necessary to obtain data, in the form of percentages, weights, and time, gathered under rodeo conditions, although these were simulated for the purpose of the study.

Undertaken by students at California Polytechnic State University, San Luis Obispo, and at the University of California, Davis, the investigation began with the formulation of the following question: "Do rodeo calves which are roped during rodeos undergo a significant amount of stress as compared to calves which are not roped?" Stress, by dictionary definition, is "force exerted upon a body that tends to strain or deform its shape" or "mental or physical tension or strain." If stress does occur, it will consequently interfere with vital functions, such as respiration, digestion, temperature, and so forth, and render the animal incapable of leading the same kind of life as one that is not subjected to this stress. The control group consisted of calves that were never roped for the twenty-six-day duration of the investigation. Three other segments were the subjects of the test: Group One, roped once a day; Group Two, twice a day; and Group Three, three times a day. The physical conditions of a rodeo were re-created, while seven different areas of function and condition were tested: temperature, pulse, respiration, three types of blood values—plasma protein, white-blood-cell count, and hematocrit—and weight.

With 95 percent confidence, considered a very high accuracy percentage, the study concluded that there is no significant amount of

It is scenes like this that have given rise to the criticisms of rodeo by advocates of animal rights. Two-time team-roping world champion Dale Smith dismounts in the calf-roping event at the 1961 La Fiesta de los Vaqueros Rodeo, Tucson, Arizona. Photograph by DeVere

roping stress suffered by calves during a rodeo. Much of the only slight variation in values between the three active groups and the control group was due to the absence of physical exercise in the latter. Although, by comparison with normal cattle, the roped cattle exhibited a small increase in blood levels, indicating some damage to muscles in the neck and back areas, it was impossible to establish a pattern because of the low number of calves tested.[19] In addition, it could not be determined with any certainty that the damage, if any, was permanent or even temporarily debilitating; in fact, the more extensive tests would lead one to believe that, even if some injury did occur in some of the animals (and there were wide variations in the readings), it did not interfere with vital functions or with weight gain, as determined by the main investigation.

Simultaneously, a twenty-nine-day test using bucking horses and bulls was undertaken, also at California Polytechnic State University. The bulls and horses, each numbering eight, with a control group of three, were ridden on nine test days. In addition to the same observations made on the roping calves, photographs were taken at close range of those parts of the animals' anatomy where injury from equipment could possibly occur (flank, heart, girth, and shoulder areas)—in other words, those regions where humane societies have claimed that animals are hurt during the events. In neither the bulls nor the horses was any significant variation measured as compared to the control group, except, again, in respiration and pulse, because of the increased physical activity of the animals ridden. Equally important, none of the photographs showed any cuts or bruises caused by equipment used either on the animals or by the riders. As with the preliminary test involving roping calves, the investigators hesitated to draw firm conclusions based on the low number of animals tested.[20]

To people in rodeo, the sport has always been a humane activity. The stock contractors, who own the animals, and the cowboys themselves have no intention of inflicting injury on what provides their livelihood. Cruelty has been made an issue by outsiders, many of whom do not possess enough information justifiably to make the charges that are, in fact, made. Rodeo today, however, realizes the necessity for a solid collection of facts to present in its defense against attacks by animal-welfare organizations. The line between use and exploitation is the one being debated; abuse, although an extreme, is unfortunately often equated with use. It is the method of use and the quality of the user himself that are the determinants of cruelty.

Accidents do occur, as in any sport, and the rodeo associations do not in any way deny this, although they have been accused of doing so. By comparison, the incidence of injury in horse racing, although often suppressed, is far greater than in rodeo; yet, because of the large amounts of money involved in horse racing, it has long been virtually immune from attack. Moreover, the injuries in rodeo are not intentional—as they are in bullfighting and boxing, where injury is the desired result.

Cowboys have great respect and admiration for rodeo animals. Six-time all-around world champion Larry Mahan says:

> A cowboy looks at a great bucking animal the way he would a great athlete. Sometimes a horse will be saddle broke until he's ten years old, and then all the sudden [sic] he'll start throwing everybody. He just got tired of people sitting on his back. So he could be a good bucking horse until he's twenty or twenty-five years old. A lot more cowboys get hurt than animals.[21]

The American Humane Association (AHA), which used to campaign directly against the sport through anti-rodeo literature and other means, found over the years that earlier methods were not the answer to the problem it believed existed. Instead, the organization changed its strategy, after a decision was made that it was better to work with rodeo than against it. The new approach, which began in the 1950s, resulted in the establishment of rules to ensure humane treatment of livestock, developed in collaboration with the RCA. These rules, twenty in number, are part of the PRCA rule book. Similar regulations were also worked out with the IRA.

Officials of the AHA believe that the problem of animal exploitation begins "when you start mixing animals, people and money together." Since these elements are present in many activities, it is not just rodeo that comes under the scrutiny and criticism of the AHA; nor does the organization feel that it is possible to eliminate one area where animals are used while excluding others from such a ban. The improvement that the AHA feels has taken place in the past fifteen-or-so years is ascribed partially to a change in people's attitude in general and partially to the city and college background of the modern-day rodeo contestants.

The AHA's greatest concern today is the nonsanctioned smaller, weekend rodeos, where the treatment of animals seriously affects the reputation of the professionally sanctioned contests. The AHA maintains close supervision of professional rodeo as well, keeping informed about rule changes and negotiating about these, if need be, with the PRCA and the International Rodeo Association, to ensure that the animals receive proper protection. The association is particularly opposed to all timed events, not because of the actual roping or wrestling of the animal but because of the race against the clock. It is believed that the rules of competition are designed in such a way as not to make the animal arena-wise but to turn it into a machine.[22]

One moral philosopher, Peter Singer, has attacked humane societies, the AHA in particular, for their active collaboration "with those responsible for cruelty," thereby lending an air of respectability to the alleged cruelties in rodeo.[23] However, the AHA asserts that the cooperation with rodeo is not done for exploitative purposes. While those groups which use more aggressive techniques in fighting rodeo have not accomplished a great deal, the AHA has succeeded in bringing about improvements and, perhaps more important, in making people more aware. The difference between the radical groups and the AHA is, in the association's opinion, that it studies the problems before attacking. The AHA believes that other organizations instead plan their activities according to season: when the rodeo season starts, so does the campaign to raise funds at the sport's expense.[24]

Executive Vice President Bob Eidson of the Professional Rodeo Cowboys Association concurs with AHA officials in their true concern for animals, while calling the methods of operation of the more radical groups "a big rip -off."[25]

It is the efforts of these last-mentioned organizations that have seriously hurt rodeo. But they are at the same time, through their tactics, the ones most readily influencing the public, which is swept along by anti-cruelty tirades and misrepresentation of facts. By appealing to sentimentality and emotionalism, the so-called anti-cruelists have been able to raise millions, making possible their continued crusade.

Even if rodeo is the last stronghold of individualism, its tremendous growth has made it necessary for it to take into account a great number of outside considerations. In this regard, the humane agitation, although often unfair, has probably served to stimulate an awareness of those considerations, and as such has served a purpose. However, rodeo has managed to grow and improve in spite of these attacks, and that testifies to its inherent strength. That it has succeeded in doing so while still retaining essentially its original character is even more remarkable.

13

"The Money Is Here, Cowboys; It Is Yours If You Can Win It!"

Thus reads the invitation in the booklet of contest rules and local rules for the 1934 Sheridan-Wyo Rodeo.[1] But winning the money did not necessarily mean a living for the cowboy. In fact, as one writer observed in a 1946 article for *Collier's*, most cowboys still "never get rich on what they win."[2]

The cowboy has been referred to, by outsiders, as "a professional in a strange amateur sort of way."[3] Although rodeo is, indeed, a professional sport, it differs from most other professional athletics in two signifcant respects. One, to compete, the cowboy has to pay anywhere from $25 to $350 in entry fees per event at each rodeo. Two, his income is strictly in accordance with his ability to win—and, in no small measure, with his luck in the draw (i.e., the drawing of animals on which to compete). Besides, he has to pay his own way from one rodeo to the next as well as all expenses in connection with his stay. There is no traveling by chartered planes as the ball teams do, nor contracts guaranteeing an annual income. In fact, if he is injured and unable to work, or has a bad streak of luck in competition, there may be no income at all, although in recent years, a program of disability insurance has been worked out.

It may seem strange to the uninitiated that anyone should choose such an uncertain line of work as an occupation. The cowboy's answer might very well be that he has chosen rodeo precisely because of the factors just discussed, as these offer him the kind of freedom he desires. It has even been claimed that it is not the cowboy who chooses rodeo but rather rodeo that chooses the cowboy.[4] That statement may be true in that rodeo offers the environment in which a free-spirited and independent individual, such as the cowboy, can best function and express himself.

Professional rodeo today can for certain provide a good living for the contestant, but only for a relatively small number of the 5,461 members and 4,105 permit holders* of the Professional Rodeo Cowboys Association is it a *total* living. To be sure, as rodeo has grown in popularity and scope, so has the money that could be won at the contests. But, even more important, in recent years another factor has made the sport more profitable for the participant, and that is the support it receives from a variety of businesses and manufacturers on a national level.

From early on, rodeo—or the cowboy contest and cowboy tournament—was a community affair, and it was only natural that a local firm should contribute a prize to the winner at the annual rodeo. However, now large national concerns, not necessarily associated with merchandise or services related to the sport, are providing considerable sums of money and special prizes on all levels of competition. This has enabled the cowboy to maintain the independence and freedom so vital to his existence. The important factor to be borne in mind is that, no matter what the source of the prize money, it still has to be *won*. In order to evaluate how these added bonuses have served to change and develop the sport, it is necessary first to examine the economic situation of the rodeo cowboy through the years.

Men chose the rodeo long before it was possible to make a living at it. In the early days, there was really no such thing as a rodeo cowboy. The man who competed in rodeos was also a working cowboy, since, as there were scarcely many regularly scheduled contests, rodeo was a rather uncertain form of supplementary income. For a steadier kind of work, many cowboys hired out to the wild-west shows. Some made quite a name for themselves in these shows and went on to become heroes in the nascent motion-picture industry, among them Tom Mix and Hoot Gibson. That industry, ironically, spelled the doom for wild-west shows, as films could be played in far more places at the same time and at lower ticket prices than the traveling, live shows. However, the rodeo elements of that entertainment form somehow survived.

In the days when riding and roping contests were just a diversion and a test of skill for the working cowboys, it is doubtful that the contestants gave much thought to prizes and awards. Merely winning and

*Figures as of December 31, 1982.

being named champion provided enough glory. There were no spectators except from among the cowboys themselves, and, as a result, few early chroniclers made mention of the events.

Nevertheless, the idea of some form of reward for the best cowboy—as an extra incentive—did occur from time to time. One of the very earliest recorded competitions was a bronco-busting contest held at Deer Trail, Colorado Territory, on July 4, 1869. Cowboys from several ranches took part. The prize was a suit of clothes; from an account of the event, written thirty years later, it appears that it was furnished by the cattlemen whose cowboys participated in the match. The suit was awarded to an Englishman, Emilnie Gardenshire, a cowboy from the Milliron Ranch, for his fifteen-minute ride* on the renowned Montana Blizzard, a bay horse belonging to the Hashknife Ranch. In addition to the prize, Gardenshire won the title "Champion Bronco Buster of the Plains."[5]

At the Texas State Fair held in Austin in 1882 a silver-trimmed saddle valued at three hundred dollars was given to the cowboy who roped, threw, and tied a steer in the fastest time. Ten cowboys competed for this trophy.[6] Likewise, at the cowboy tournament in connection with the 1886 fair in Albuquerque, New Mexico Territory, the winning steer roper received "an elegant saddle," although this one was worth a mere seventy-five dollars.[7] (That was about the going rate for saddles at that time, so it was probably more functional than elegant.) It is interesting to note that, although riding events were included in these contests, the winners in those events apparently received no special prizes. Perhaps it was felt that being a roper required more skill than being a bronco buster, although that reasoning would deny the traditional position of the horse breaker or bronco buster among the elite of cowboys. Conditions have changed in just the last few years, but it has consistently been the contestants in the riding events who have won the most money.

In the early days, the first order of business at a contest was to take up a collection to serve as prize money for the winner, at least at the smaller, more informal contests.[8]

The cowboy tournament was a more organized and public variety of the roping and riding contests. Its evolution into such a form occurred

---

* In the early days, bronc riding was judged on the rider's ability to stay on the horse the longest, in the tradition of the horse *breaker*. Today, both saddle-bronc and bareback-bronc riding are eight-second events.

after the growth and changes of the livestock industry had made the cowboys less peripatetic and placed them in proximity to settled communities.[9] Such a cowboy tournament was announced in connection with the Denver Exposition, held at River Front Park in the fall of 1887. It was heralded as one of the fair's greatest attractions and was expected to provide a novel spectacle to the local citizens and in particular to visitors from the East.[10] Not only was the competition itself a novelty, but it boasted besides a published prize list. In addition to cash prizes of from thirty to fifty dollars in four of the six "classes" (events), two of the categories offered special prizes: the winner in "foot-roping of cattle on horseback" would receive a "fine silver water set," valued at forty dollars and offered by Denver jeweler Henry Bohm, while the man winning the event described as "picking up twenty single potatoes by a rider going at a pace not slower than a lope" would be the recipient of a silver-inlaid bit, offered by Range Journal Publishing and valued at thirty dollars.[11] This is with little doubt the first time in rodeo history that business supported the sport by providing prizes for the winners.

At another cowboy tournament, held in the Broadway Athletic Park in Denver in 1890, the cash prizes were substantially higher. Not only were the amounts larger, ranging from fifty to two hundred dollars, but the man who placed second also received a share of the money, not only in the roping and riding of bronchos (in which the men worked in teams of two) but also in the steer roping and another game on horseback.[12] Until that time, only the winner in each event had received recognition. This marked the beginning of the development that was to take in and benefit an ever-larger segment of the contestants. Prize money derived from entry fees had by then become an expected part of cowboy contests, as well as, not infrequently, additional money and special prizes provided by private citizens and local business firms.

In 1893, the horse race heralded as the greatest one ever seen (see chapter 10) took place between Chadron, Nebraska, and the Nebraska Pavilion at the Chicago World's Fair. It was an event for cowboys riding "ponies" over the thousand-mile course. For the undertaking, no less than two purses were offered: the Cowboy Prize of $1,000 contributed by the citizens of Chadron, and Buffalo Bill's Wild West Purse of $500. In addition, the entrance fees, estimated at several thousand dollars, were to be paid out in the form of prize money. The Cowboy

Prize was divided among seven men, the Buffalo Bill Purse among eight. More significant for the purposes here, a saddle offered by Montgomery Ward and Company was presented to the winner. This is quite likely the first time a major concern supported cowboy sports. (The recipient was John Berry, who was also awarded $175 of the prize money. The most money in the contest—$275—was taken by a C. W. Smith, who received a portion of both purses). The *Denver Republican* reported that a Colt revolver was awarded to one of the runners-up, but the newspaper did not mention who contributed the weapon.[13]

That same year, at the midsummer fair at Calgary, Alberta (June 21–24), two companies each provided a seventy-five-dollar saddle to be presented to the best steer roper and the winner of the cowboy race, respectively, while second prizes were also awarded to the first runners-up in these events.[14]

By the turn of the century, cowboy tournaments and contests were common throughout the western states, especially in conjunction with Fourth of July, Frontier Days, and Pioneer Days celebrations but also as a special attraction at conventions. Perhaps the most famous demonstration before such a gathering was in June of 1905, when the 101 Ranch's cowboys and cowgirls performed for the convention of the National Editorial Association, held at Guthrie, Oklahoma Territory.[15] However, contests were not held so frequently that the participants could depend on regular winnings, even as income supplementing that of their ordinary occupations.

As the years progressed in the new century, prize money, as well as the number of rodeos, increased. In 1919, purses of over two thousand and five thousand dollars, respectively, are reported to have been shared by contestants at two Colorado stampedes.[16] By that time, rodeo had become quite a popular sport, and the promotion of contests was itself beginning to develop into something profitable—though at first often clearly more for the promoter than for the cowboy.

By 1931, rodeo was referred to, from time to time, as "a national institution" and "big business."[17] At this point, it was possible to make rodeo a full-time career and to derive from it—with luck—a decent livelihood. It was reported that Bob Crosby of Kenna, New Mexico, made fifteen to twenty thousand dollars a year, after his banker had suggested rodeo as a way out of the financial difficulties in which his ranch had been placed.[18] Such a high income from contesting was, however, very rare in this period.

As a result of its growth in scope and popularity, rodeo was no longer limited to the western states. Easterners had witnessed contests on visits to the West, especially in connection with the growing phenomenon of dude ranches. The attraction the sport held was recognized by Col. William T. Johnson, producer of the World's Championship rodeos in New York City and Boston.[19] New Yorkers had been exposed to rodeo as early as 1916, at Sheepshead Bay, Brooklyn, where at least one year Theodore Roosevelt and his family attended the show and were seated in special bleachers above the bucking chutes. However, it was not until Colonel Johnson brought his production to Madison Square Garden that the sport became a regular feature on the East Coast.[20] The event was conducted for several days each fall both in New York City and at Boston Garden. The New York show was sometimes referred to as the World's Series Rodeo,[21] although, as *News Week* noted in 1933,

> it is said that the cowboys and cowgirls . . . are not as well cared for financially as tennis players. Presumably they have to pay their own board and rent. They borrow money and spend their last cent hoping to win prize money. First place in most of the major events at this rodeo will earn over $6,000.[22]

Conditions continued to improve as the Depression waned. In 1936, it was reported that an "expert cowboy" could earn an annual income of twelve to fifteen thousand dollars,[23] and before the new decade began rodeo was recognized by *Time* as "a big-time U.S. sport."[24] This attracted, during the early 1940s, many of the cowboys whose names are now legendary. The sport grew through the war years, and by mid-decade, rodeo attendance was reported as second only to that of baseball. Total prize money for the year 1946 was estimated at over $2 million.[25]

When the Cowboys Turtle Association reorganized in 1945 and became the Rodeo Cowboys Association, nine purposes were stated in the second article of the articles of association. Some merely reiterated goals set by the CTA; others set forth new steps that were to be taken to ensure the sport's continued growth and its services both to participants and to the ticket-buying public.[26]

The RCA, starting in its first year, began keeping records of money won by the cowboys in each event and at the end of the year published these in the form of standings. The top money winner in each event was named world champion for the year; in addition, beginning in 1947, there was named an all-around world champion—that is, the cowboy who had won the most money in any two events. There are no extant records of the amounts won by any one cowboy in the lists of champions prior to 1945. However, from that year on, as the RCA took over the record keeping, the lists show a very slow but steady increase each year. By the mid-1970s, the prize money earned by contestants began to reflect the growing commercial sponsorship as well as the larger public patronage of the sport.

It would seem that, with the improved conditions and the possibilities for higher earnings that began to be more prevalent after the 1945 reorganization, there should have been little reason for discontent among the cowboys. However, the conditions might vary at the different rodeos, especially since, for several years to come, contests were held under the purview of one or both of the existing organizations, the RCA and the IRA. Hence, contestants were still on guard to make sure that they received what was rightfully due them, for they were not yet taken quite seriously, as if in the game just for the fun and not necessarily for profit.

An incident happened at the Reno, Nevada, rodeo in 1949, held July 2–4. The purse was advertised as fifteen hundred dollars in each of the five major events. However, four local gambling clubs had contributed a total of four thousand dollars, designated as an addition to the purses, which made the purse for each event twenty-three hundred dollars. The rodeo officials argued, nevertheless, that the donated amount was not to be distributed as an addition to the purses, as advertised, but that it had already been included in them.

A strike was threatened as the negotiations delayed the last day's performance by half an hour. What made the directors finally accede to the cowboys' demands was that a strike, brought on by the contestants' refusal to compete, would have made it necessary to refund twenty thousand dollars to the ticket-buying audience. Therefore, the four thousand dollars was added to the purses, but reportedly under strong protests.[27] Some of the top cowboys of the day participated and were said to have "put on a high grade exhibition" before the eight thousand spectators. The committee, however, was disillusioned with professional rodeo; several members threatened to resign, and a return to amateur contests was considered for 1950. In response, the *Nevada*

State Journal took an editorial stand in favor of professional rodeo at Reno, a tradition since 1936, urging the committee to "carry on."[28]

Although a few successful cowboys amassed winnings in excess of twenty thousand dollars in 1948 and 1949, there were many, even among the top five in each event, who made only a few thousand dollars in prize money for the entire year. Thus, for the great majority of contestants, the economic situation was still rather bleak. This may have prompted a 1950 article in *Nation*, entitled "The Cowpoke Is Always Broke," in which the author, quite erroneously, asserted that, "because a cowpoke is always broke, he doesn't care whether the purse money is high or low."[29]

Clearly, the cowboy did care, and he also tried to do something about it for two reasons. First, it was estimated that a top rider in 1950 paid two thousand dollars in entry fees during the year. Second, although a record high of over thirty thousand dollars was won by that year's all-around world champion, Bill Linderman, and though a number of contestants earned anywhere from seven thousand to twenty-seven thousand dollars, a great many more made only a few thousand. Thus, even if the average cowpoke was always broke, it is highy doubtful that he did not care about the purses. In fact, the sport had to face the issue that same year during a dispute at the Cheyenne Frontier Days. The RCA, speaking in the cowboys' behalf, insisted that the prize money per event per day be raised from five hundred to six hundred fifty dollars. A compromise was finally reached, fixing the daily prize money per event at six hundred dollars.

Some felt in this period that the RCA was demanding too much. It was a new concept to have a business organization of some power and prestige working solely for the weal of the cowboys. The author of the article in *Nation* commented:

> Perhaps the greatest deterrent to its [the RCA's] success is a sort of emotional displacement. We have a nostalgia for the early West and our minds are filled with stereotypes. We like the reckless, individualistic cowhand who believed in going to hell as he damned well pleased, who wrote hot checks and tasted hot gin. We find it difficult to associate his lineal descendant with collective bargaining, even though such a method is the only one open to him in his attempt to raise his standard of living. We forget that the rodeo rider has been forced to organize.[30]

A way in which the cowboy could conceivably increase his winnings was to contest more at rodeos, which in turn, of course, meant greater expenses. It was therefore a gamble then, as it is now, to see whether the added travel costs and entry fees would bring in proportionately greater earnings. In 1947, it was estimated that the average professional cowboy went to thirty rodeos a year;[31] today's high-ranked contestant will have to compete at well over a hundred in order to stay on top. There are also considerably more sanctioned rodeos today. In 1938, ninety-six RAA-approved contests were held; by 1953, the number of RCA-sanctioned shows had risen to 578, and an all-time high was reached in 1982 with 651.[32]

For a long time it was the riding-event contestants who stood to earn the largest sums in any one year, while those competing in the timed events trailed in the money department. However, that pattern is gradually changing. Having to bring their horses along naturally slows down travel for timed-event contestants. Consequently, cowboys, have always willingly lent their roping horses to competing colleagues, thus enabling those who, for one reason or another, could not or did not bring their mounts. With the increased competition and cost of rodeoing in recent years, however, it is more and more common for a contestant to have horses stationed at strategic points. In this way, he can travel by air and have the horse closest to the location of a particular rodeo brought by someone using ground transportation.

That team ropers never reach the sums that contestants in other events attain is simply attributable to the fact that team roping is not included, and is not required to be included, in every rodeo program. In 1982, 301 of the 651 PRCA-sanctioned rodeos carried the event.[33] Steer wrestlers fall somewhere in between calf ropers and team ropers in regard to winnings. There is more than one explanation for this. The steer wrestlers themselves claim their event is strictly a drawing contest. In the average herd, only 25 percent of the steers run in such a way that the cowboys can make a placing run. Furthermore, if a steer starts out as a poor contest animal, it will in time only get worse, while good steers will get better. In the other timed events, many factors can be controlled, regardless of the caliber of the stock: the horse plays an important part in aiding its rider and continues its assistance after the cowboy has actually roped the calf or the steer. Also, the roper has two to three times longer to complete his run than does the steer wrestler,

Leo Camarillo heading, and his cousin Reg Camarillo heeling, in the team-roping event, National Finals Rodeo, 1974. Photograph by Al Long

Chris Lybbert, 1982 all-around champion, shown here in the steer-wrestling event. He also enters team roping and calf roping.

and the extra seconds work to his advantage. Another important aspect to consider is that, at most rodeos, steer wrestling is a one-head contest, because of the proportionately larger number of cowboys entering the event. The reason for this is that it is by far more common in steer wrestling than in the roping events to use another cowboy's horse, and consequently steer wrestling attracts large numbers of contestants. As a result, time and the availability of stock allow these to compete on only one animal—that is, give them one chance to win.[34]

Entry fees have always been an important consideration for the cowboy. Often, winning enough to pay the entry fees for the next rodeo is to him the most critical aspect of his profession. To be sure, these have increased, along with the number of contests. Statistics in this area are available from 1953 on. In that year, the 3,001 members of the RCA paid an average of $335 in such fees, whereas the same figure for 1982 was $1,485.* The total prize money in the former year was $2,491,856, while in 1982 it had increased to a record high of just over $13 million.[35]

---

*The average is based on full PRCA members only. Total entry fees paid in 1982 amounted to $8,109,354.

14

The Making of the Cowboy Plutocrat

I can envision . . . a coming race of plutocratic cowboys whose earnings, as a result of their prowess in sticking on wild horses, throwing the lasso and wrestling with the steer, will rival those of Hollywood, and far eclipse the emoluments of such worthies as Babe Ruth.

Those words were written in 1924 by John L. Balderston, London staff correspondent to the *New York World.*[1] Mr. Balderston's prediction about a coming race of cowboy capitalists is, even by today's standards, slightly exaggerated, although not too far from reality.

It was not until 1976 that a cowboy—Tom Ferguson of Miami, Oklahoma, competing in all four timed events—became the first to exceed $100,000 in winnings for one year, with total earnings of $114,110.[2] In 1982 two other records were set with respect to the $100,000 mark: that year's all-around world champion, Chris Lybbert of Coyote, California, was the first cowboy to surpass that amount in regular arena earnings ($101,351) *before* the National Finals Rodeo, and bareback-bronc rider Bruce Ford of Kersey, Colorado, became the first contestant to reach $100,000 in a single event, winning $113,655 and the world championship.[3] However, even with incomes in that category becoming more prevalent, the majority of rodeo contestants still lag far behind participants in other professional sports.

However, the purse, plus entry fees, is not necessarily the only financial reward the professional cowboy can receive. Over the years, as has been discussed, any number of firms and individuals have donated merchandise, money, and trophies. It has not always been easy to find a sponsor or a trophy donor. In the late 1930s and early 1940s, when

Chris Lybbert, calf roping, 1982.

Bruce Ford, world-champion bareback-bronc rider in 1982 and 1983. In 1982 Ford became the first cowboy to earn over $100,000 in one event in a single year.

rodeo had become well established, with both a rodeo-management organization and a cowboy association that, by then, worked well together, the RAA on more than one occasion had to advertise for donors. One was sought for the 1939 world-champion bareback rider: "Who will give $100 as a prize in this event?"[4]

Two years later, after two additional events (team tying and single steer tying [steer roping]) had been recognized by the RAA, the following appeal was issued:

> At this time there are no trophy donors for these events. Any organization wishing to offer trophies for first and second place for these events should immediately notify the Secretary's office of their desire to do so. The Association is anxious that the winners of these events be awarded on a basis comparable to the winners in other events. Who will be the first to come forward with their trophy for these new events.[5]

Even when trophy donors were available, it used to be the case that the recipient always had to be a winner or a champion to benefit from the prizes, while the great number of contestants had to go without awards. In this regard, conditions have changed, and programs have been established to enable a larger portion of contestants to enjoy a share of the prizes.

Commercial sponsorship of rodeo is now a highly involved business in itself. For the year 1982, a number of corporations all over the country contributed $2 million in prize money alone* to professional rodeo.[6] As a result of the large amounts offered by national concerns, the PRCA was, in that year, able to eliminate the share of monetary compensation it had always guaranteed the world champions.[7]

As an all-around champion has to have won money in two or more events in order to earn his title, he stands the chance of also receiving anything from more money to more pairs of boots, belt buckles, saddles, a paid vacation, an oil painting of himself, a horse trailer, a belt, a camper top, a year's supply of horse feed, a pair of chaps, free stud service, a set of tires, various tack, a watch, a diamond ring, a pickup truck, or any combination of these. The list could go on and on, and it would vary from year to year. To give an overview of the amount of extra benefits a successful professional rodeo contestant can reap, Ap-

---

*The total contribution by corporations in 1982, including promotional activities and sponsorship of rodeo television broadcasts, amounted to $8.3 million.

pendix A illustrates what the all-around world champion received in four different years over a thirty-year period.

Although anyone—a company or an individual—can of course donate prizes to be distributed to the top cowboys,[8] there are some among the donors who have been particularly instrumental in shaping the sport through their consistent participation and support. The three major manufacturers of blue jeans—H. D. Lee and Company, Shawnee Mission, Kansas; Levi Strauss and Company, San Francisco, California; and Blue Bell, Inc., Greensboro, North Carolina (maker of the Wrangler Brand)—were donors from the early days of organized professional rodeo.[9] With the increased participation by Blue Bell, which has propelled Wrangler to the forefront of rodeo sponsors, the other two manufacturers have now withdrawn from the professional rodeo scene.

Wrangler's Pro Officials System, to which Blue Bell contributed $200,000 in 1982, has already been discussed. In addition, to recognize bull fighters and barrelmen, the long-overlooked rodeo clowns who are such essential performers in the rodeo contest, Blue Bell since 1979 has sponsored the Wrangler Bullfighter Contests, in which clowns especially selected by the top thirty bull riders, the stock contractors, and the previous year's NFR clowns compete in bull-rider protection, bull-fighting skill, and showmanship. The winners receive cash awards contributed by Blue Bell. In the twenty-three contests held in 1982, $172,000 was distributed, with a substantial increase budgeted for 1983.[10]

The Justin Boot Company, Fort Worth, Texas, has been a continuous donor since 1952, and even earlier contributed awards to rodeo champions. It is now also the exclusive manufacturer of the official boot and belt line of the Professional Rodeo Cowboys Association. A selected few western apparel and equipment firms have been chosen to receive the PRCA stamp of approval for their products, in return for which they pay a 5–10 percent licensing fee to the subsidiary PRCA Properties, Inc. The Justin Heeler program, discussed above, will expand in 1983, with the mobile medical center scheduled to appear at more than twenty-five PRCA rodeos during the year.[11]

Denver-based Frontier Airlines first sponsored an award in 1973: the $1,250 saddle given to the bareback champion of that year. In 1974, Frontier was designated "Official Airline of the Rodeo Cowboys Association." That year, it served 225 RCA-sanctioned rodeos in eighteen

Bullfighter Miles Hare of Fort Worth, Texas, in the Beauty and the Beast contest, National Finals Rodeo, 1982. Photograph © 1982 by James Fain

All products that have been licensed by PRCA Properties, Inc., bear this label.

states, out of the total of 590 rodeos. The designation came about partly because of the loyal support the cowboys had given the airline in the past and partly because of the exposure Frontier would receive by this designation. Having an official airline facilitates planning for today's much-traveling cowboys. By identifying themselves as "code 7 travelers," they receive special reservation service when calling Frontier's central number. In 1975, as part of its Superstars Program, the airline paid the entry fees and lodging for top contestants at selected rodeos.

After contributing a saddle in 1973, as mentioned, and again in 1975 (then to the top rookie saddle-bronc rider), the airline in 1976 became the donor of all eight of the world-championship saddles (seven events and all-around). In addition, in 1977 and 1978, Frontier joined with Ford dealers in the Oklahoma and Texas panhandle region to cosponsor the awarding of two heavy-duty vehicles each year to top contestants at the National Finals Rodeo. As part of its efforts to gain more exposure through rodeo, the company also assists local committees in promoting their contests and contributes prize-money assistance within its market area. A result of these joint efforts has been, the airline reports, "a marked upswing in public enthusiasm for this traditional American sport."[12]

Recent trends have indicated that many trophy and money donors who previously favored only the top winners now wish to see their generosity shared by a larger number of contestants. Frontier Airlines, for example, has a program, begun in 1979, whereby each one of the National Finals Rodeo qualifiers receives a commemorative silver ring; the world champions are given championship rings. Another area in which Frontier shows its overall support of professional rodeo is by providing the printed documents and forms, used by the association and rodeo-committee secretaries, on which the records of the contests are kept. In 1981, Frontier instituted yet another prize: unlimited air travel on the airline was given to each event champion and the all-around world champion. The total value of this prize is estimated at $150,000.[13]

What was termed "the biggest single boost ever given professional rodeo" took place in October, 1971. The R. J. Reynolds Tobacco Company, Winston-Salem, North Carolina, announced that, for the following year, it would contribute no less than $105,000 in cash prizes to the sport.

The program came about as a result of the ban on advertising of tobacco products on television. R. J. Reynolds was searching for other areas of exposure to reach both old and prospective customers. It began looking into sporting events, specifically those conducted in large arenas before a substantial number of spectators, where banner advertising and plugs from the announcers could recapture segments of the population lost through the electronic-advertising ban. A year or two before zeroing in on rodeo, the firm began supporting stock-car and drag racing. Rodeo was another sport that met the criteria set down. Reynolds's first team manager for the Winston Rodeo Awards was Richard L. Dilworth, a New Mexican who was quite knowledgeable about the sport and instrumental in the program's establishment. Regardless of his expertise and familiarity, it appeared the RCA was rather skeptical when an amount as large as $105,000 was suggested, unaccustomed as it was to such a generous offer. The company chose to work most closely with one of the association's directors, stock contractor Harry Knight, whom it deemed by far the most business oriented at the time. Nevertheless, Winston Rodeo Team Manager J. Kelly Riley states that it was not until the first payoff in 1972 was a fact that the RCA and the cowboys fully believed in the intentions of the Reynolds company.[14]

The Winston Championship Awards were designed to enable a number of cowboys to profit from the generous program. This was to be accomplished by paying out the prizes in three stages during the year. On July 4, the top five cowboys in each of the six standard events would share $30,000, as follows: No. 1, $2,000 (40 percent); No. 2, $1,500 (30 percent); No. 3, $750 (15 percent); No. 4, $500 (10 percent); No. 5, $250 (5 percent). Then the tabulation started all over again for the second half of the year, thus giving more contestants a chance to reap the benefits of the second $30,000. The third phase— the remaining $45,000—combined the entire season. Each of the six event champions received $5,000, the all-around champion won $10,000, and the top five money winners in steer roping (who were not part of the first and second phases) shared $5,000.

By 1973, while the total amount remained the same, the semiannual distribution benefited the top seven cowboys in each event. In the program's third year, 1974, the prize money was increased to $120,000, and from that year on the top ten contestants shared in the twice-a-year allotments.

Three times more in this awards structure Winston added to the total yearly sum, which was $135,000 in 1975, $150,000 in 1976 and 1977, and $175,000 in 1978 and 1979.[15] Although the year-end presentation remained the same from the inception of the program ($10,000 to the all-around world champion and $5,000 to the world champion in each event), 120 cowboys now had the chance of sharing the larger portion of the money twice a year. To be sure, one who wins money in the first half can also win in the second period and, for that matter, can also be the all-around and/or an event champion. However, at the outset of each half, any 120 cowboys stood to benefit, and that is what made the Winston Championship Awards unique and such an improvement in the rodeo cowboys' economic situation. Appendix B lists the first-place winners in the program through the years, as well as their respective winnings and positions in the regular standings.

Early in 1980, the R. J. Reynolds Tobacco Company revised its awards program in an effort to reach an even larger number of contestants. Through the Winston Rodeo Series, a cowboy can earn points, in the average, toward a total of $168,000 to be distributed annually to point winners at designated Winston Series Rodeos (seventy rodeos in 1980, seventy-three in 1981, and seventy-five in 1982). In addition, the next nine places receive checks of between $1,000 and $7,000. Furthermore, $45,000 is distributed to the world champions at the end of the season, while $15,000 is contributed to the top contestants in women's barrel racing. Winston also spends about half a million dollars a year on promotional activities in connection with the Winston Series Rodeos, which are selected on the basis of drawing power, market area, and each committee's cooperation in terms of exposure with series officials.[16]

Another way in which the company serves professional rodeo, while also making itself highly visible, is through the Winston Scoreboards. Until 1977, the only source of information a spectator had available as to time, points, and place of a contestant was the rodeo announcer. As the events move quite rapidly, it can often be difficult—especially for the uninitiated—to follow all the action in the arena and at the same time keep track of the statistics. An electronic scoreboard invented by electronics specialist E. L. (Buck) Sutherland of Grand Junction, Colorado, allows the spectators at the Winston Series Rodeos (and, before their inception, at about an equal annual number of non-series contests) to follow the performances better. For the 1983 sea-

The sophisticated Winston electronic scoreboard, in use here at a rodeo in Oakdale, California. Courtesy R. J. Reynolds Tobacco Company, Winston-Salem, North Carolina

son, new scoreboards are being designed, each valued at $100,000. As it travels from rodeo to rodeo, each board is transported on specially built gooseneck trailers, pulled by pickup trucks. The colors of these conveyances are, like the Winston packet, two panels of red with a panel of white in between. Each outfit is accompanied by a member of the Winston Scoreboard Team, composed of rodeo contestants.

Although an electronic scoreboard of Mr. Sutherland's design was used as early as 1958, it was not until the inventor's collaboration with Winston, in 1972, that the idea became successful and adapted to widespread use. This association coincided with the company's Rodeo Awards program, and the scoreboards provided a way of promoting the company, while offering service to the committees and the public. The trade name was added to the design, and Winston took over the sponsorship of the scoreboard, at no cost to the rodeos at which they are installed.

The scoreboards are intricately designed, with eleven miles of wire and more than a thousand diodes and transistors in each. Improvements are being made constantly.[17] It is difficult to measure the degree of contribution made by these scoreboards (there are usually two of them placed at each contest; one at each end of the arena). It is reasonable to assume, however, that an addition such as this can take a good amount of credit for the popularity and growth of the sport. The presence of the scoreboards cannot help but add an aura of big league to the proceedings, for, in spite of its size and popularity, rodeo is still trying to acquire an image on the order of other professional sports.

Winston's contribution benefits the cowboy, the sport, and the public. Yet, although the Winston money can now be enjoyed by a great many more cowboys than most other sponsored awards, the system nevertheless requires the contestants to travel quite extensively and to compete at numerous rodeos every year in order even to amass the points necessary. However, in 1975, a program came along to make it possible for those who, for whatever reason, can travel only within a limited area to compete. That program was the Circuit System, and its purpose was to give the cowboys "identity on their local level." By dividing the country into twelve (originally thirteen) regions, using state lines as boundaries, the circuits were established, including all forty-eight states in the continental United States. Each circuit has its own standings, with only cowboys and cowgirls living in that specific area eligible to accumulate points in those standings.[18] Contestants from outside the circuit may compete and win money within another circuit, but those points will be counted in the national standings only. This innovation has brought about a whole new area for sponsorship on both the national and local levels.

The major and overall sponsor of the Circuit System was, at the onset, the Jos. Schlitz Brewing Company, Milwaukee, Wisconsin. The firm became interested in rodeo after successful area support of the sport by wholesalers in Colorado and Wyoming. Following a presentation by the PRCA staff, the brewery decided, at first, to develop a program for the western states. It was not long before it was realized that a plan that was national in scope would be even better suited to the company's purposes. Richard B. Barron, Supervisor, Brand Projects, Schlitz and Schlitz Malt Liquor, discussed the company's reasoning:

> Our objective was to reach the rodeo participant and fan, down at the local or grass roots level continuously versus recognition of the top several performers each year. We decided that an awards program in the Circuit System was the best way to accomplish this—to recognize the cowboy or cowgirl who will probably never make it to the national finals [sic] but is a proven top performer in his or her circuit. In doing so, we hoped to make some loyal friends for our Brand along the way.[19]

Schlitz's participation in the Circuit System began in 1976, although no awards sponsored by the brewery are listed among that year's PRCA and world championship awards. In 1977, Schlitz awarded the PRCA Rookie of the Year $1,500 and a belt buckle.[20] By 1978, it had established its sponsorship on a nationwide basis, contributing $32,000 to each of the twelve circuits, which was distributed among the top three finishers in each event. The contestants placing first also received a trophy belt buckle, while the all-around cowboy was awarded a trophy saddle. Also, the top stock contractor in each circuit was given a cash prize as well as a trophy belt buckle. As part of Schlitz's plan to involve them in the rodeo program, wholesalers were given the option of making an award to the all-around cowboy at their respective local rodeos. This served the purpose of drawing each individual dealer into the sport as a sponsor, which provided him with favorable publicity in his trade area. In addition, the wholesalers were given merchandising pieces to be used to promote rodeos within their respective circuits.[21]

Any number of local sponsors would also honor the top cowboys with awards of anywhere from twenty-five to several thousand dollars. In March of 1980, professional rodeo terminated its liaison with Schlitz, which in its five years of participation had given the sport in excess of $400,000.[22]

For several years, negotiations had been conducted with the Adolph Coors Company, Golden, Colorado. The results were announced in the spring of 1980 and consisted of the brewery's underwriting of two separate programs. These were designed to contribute a total of one million dollars over a twenty-one-month period, concluding, under that particular structure, at the end of 1981. In 1982, Coors's monetary contribution of awards alone amounted to approximately half a million dollars.[23]

The company had actually entered the rodeo scene a year before the million-dollar announcement was made. As one of the sponsors of the Blair/Prorodeo Network telecasts since their inception in 1979, with its especially produced High Country rodeo commercials, Coors had already had an opportunity to study the mutual benefits that could be derived from further involvement. The reason behind the company's entry into actual contest sponsorship was threefold: one, as would be natural with any manufacturer, Coors anticipated increased sales of its products; two, it considered rodeo the most exciting sport in the United States and the world; and, three, it expected that its association with the people in rodeo would be the additional magic ingredient in the combination.[24] Coors's sponsorship of the circuits, taken over from its competitor Schlitz, amounted to $277,000 over the first two years of involvement.[25] This money was given out in the form of finals money and awards in each circuit. In addition, Coors offered promotional support in a variety of ways to local committees, placing its name in very visible areas.

However, that part of the brewery's participation in rodeo sponsorship to which the larger portion of the budget is now devoted is in the Coors Chute-Out concept, which also began in 1980. Although originally devised in a more complicated fashion than most awards patterns, it nevertheless benefits any number of contestants rather than just the champions. During its first two years, this was accomplished as follows. The 1979 champions in the standard events, plus team roping and women's barrel racing, were provided with $32,500 each in special bank accounts. For the next year's champions that figure increased to $51,000, to be used in 1981. At especially selected Coors Chute-Out rodeos* (twenty-five in 1980 and thirty in 1981) contestants challenged the champions. Should the challenger win, he (or she) received $1,000 from the champion's Coors account; the champion received $300, regardless of how he fared. If the champion retained his position, he was entitled to a full $1,300 check from the bonus money. At the end of the season, each champion was assured $7,500, provided he had not turned out stock. In 1981, the second year of the Chute-Out concept, $250 in day money was added per event at each rodeo, as well as a bonus amounting to $150, paid to the stock contractor by each champion. The idea of the challenge brought back into the contest an element that was essential to the very creation of the sport. Nevertheless, mainly because of the complicated bookkeeping, the format was changed for the seventy-seven Chute-Out rodeos in 1982. The champion was automatically awarded a $500 bonus. Another important category of participants was included, as rodeo announcers also began reaping the financial benefits of large-scale commercial underwriting of the sport.[26]

Prior to Schlitz's awarding cash prizes and belt buckles to stock contractors, these important men of rodeo had been little recognized. From 1956 through 1972, Rodeo Sports News presented a silver halter to the top saddle bronc of the year, as voted by the cowboys. For this, of course, its owner, too, could take credit. Beginning in 1973, also the top bareback bronc and bull of the year were selected.[27]

Early in 1978, however, the "8 Seconds with Velvet" program came into being. It was developed with Black Velvet Spirits, a product of the Heublein Corporation, Hartford, Connecticut, in conjunction with PRCA Properties. Characterized as a "multi-element promotion," this program awarded annually the Black Velvet Trophy and $2,000 to the stock contractors whose animals were selected "Bucking [i.e., saddle-bronc] Horse of the Year," "Bareback Horse of the Year," and "Bull of the Year." Furthermore, a $20,000 "incentive program" was carried out throughout the year, whereby stock contractors were motivated to locate and buy additional high-caliber rough stock.

The concern had, prior to its awards program, already advertised Black Velvet in rodeo publications, with the advertisements, featur-

---

*The first Coors Chute-Out Rodeo was held, appropriately, at Golden, Colorado, May 30–June 1, 1980.

ing a young lady in black western attire, carrying out the color of the product's label. As part of the "8 Seconds with Velvet" campaign, the company began a search for "Miss Black Velvet—Rodeo" to promote the sport and appear in the corporation's rodeo-theme advertising beginning in 1979.[28]

In that year Heublein increased its contribution to the sport to a total of $50,000. In keeping with the trend to allow a greater number of individuals a share in the money, the Black Velvet Stock Contractor Awards were established. At the beginning of every year, each PRCA stock contractor nominates, from his own string, one saddle bronc, one bareback bronc, and, from 1980 on, one bull, which he believes has the potential for being the top animal in its event. At the same time, the animal is renamed with a name containing the word "Velvet," such as Smokin' Velvet, Velvet Raider, or Shot of Velvet. Each time during the year that that animal is bucked out, the owner receives $25; if the animal is selected to go to the National Finals Rodeo, he collects another $250.

The task of selecting the top animals in the riding events is entrusted to the thirty leading contestants in each of these contests. The owners of the winning stock receive $3,000 and a silver-and-gold belt buckle.[29] If, at the beginning of the year, the contractor has succeeded in naming the animal that also garners the most votes by the thirty cowboys at the end of the season, he is entitled to an additional $5,000 in bonus money, while the top animal receives $500.

In 1980, the amount of the Black Velvet Stock Contractor Awards grew to $80,000. The distribution remained the same as in 1979, with the addition of a $300 award to Black Velvet–nominated stock at each of the twelve circuit finals. Like some of the other sponsors, the distillery also works with local rodeo committees and advertises by means of billboards and in newspapers to promote the various contests.[30] The money allotted to this program has increased each year, reaching $172,000 in 1982.[31]

The Nestea Division of the Nestlé Company underwrote the sport on a large scale and in a variety of ways for four years, beginning in 1979. Nestea became involved in rodeo because the company believed in it as a wholesome family entertainment. The objective was to reach, in particular, young people in rodeo, allowing these to benefit from the promotional dollars the company had to spend. In its four years of rodeo participation, Nestea distributed nearly $600,000. A good third of that amount was earmarked for scholarships to the winners in the Nestea Teenage Top Hand Challenge contests, held in conjunction with several PRCA rodeos throughout the year, with the finals coming during the National Finals Rodeo in December. At those rodeos where the Challenge took place, Nestea provided an increase in the purses for the professional cowboy as well.[32]

The days when the RAA had to plead for a sponsor and the association questioned the intentions of an awards proposal have been left far behind. The PRCA has demonstrated an increased astuteness in soliciting corporations that can both support and promote rodeo on a large and effective scale. Its staff is capable of writing proposals and programs that appeal to concerns seeking other or additional avenues of commercial involvement.

One of the most intrepid ventures to date was the establishment, early in 1982, of PRCA Productions, created to produce, market, and distribute its own television broadcasts, "Rodeo ProTour USA," an especially devised new concept. (Previously, the PRCA had produced television coverage of selected rodeos in a joint venture with John Blair and Company of New York City, begun in 1979. Because of creative and financial differences, however, the PRCA chose to end that partnership after three years.) Several of the companies already committed to rodeo sponsorship rallied to support the new broadcast project, along with additional corporations that were canvassed. This generated, in the first year, an additional $300,000 in prize money, a Dodge pickup truck to each of the eight Rodeo ProTour "Finals I" champions, and an average 38 percent ratings share for the six telecasts, seen on one hundred television stations in twenty-two states from June to November in 1982.[33]

The National Finals Rodeo has been telecast in one manner or another since its first year in 1959, either in a special broadcast or as part of the television networks' weekly sports features. In 1974, the Hesston Corporation, manufacturer of farm equipment, began sponsoring broadcasts of the next to the last go-round, and since 1976 it has been the exclusive sponsor of the telecast of the final performance. By 1982, the ninth year of Hesston sponsorship, the telecast was seen on a total of 208 stations in thirty-eight states and three Canadian provinces. In many areas same-day coverage was possible. More than half of the telecast rights fee (which in 1982 amounted to $115,000) was, as usual, added to the payoff.[34]

The list of sponsors of professional rodeo grows each year. And, with few exceptions, those who remain supporters invariably increase their contributions and scope of participation over the years. As noted above, the overall trend has been to make it possible for an ever-larger number of rodeo participants to benefit from the various donor programs. The inclusion of other segments, such as stock contractors, clowns, announcers, and future contestants, has further broadened the base for the distribution of awards. Prizes and glory are no longer reserved for the select few. A world champion is still a champion and regarded as one, but professional rodeo in the 1980s can be a good and profitable place to be for many. Bruce Ford, 1982 bareback-bronc-riding world champion and runner-up for the all-around title, expressed the opinion of many of today's contestants when questioned about possible retirement during that year's National Finals Rodeo telecast: "It's hard to back out of a business that's paying so much money." [35]

Self-reliance has always been the most prominent trait in the American frontiersman, personified by the cowboy. The manner in which he has handled the development and growth of his sport—rodeo—demonstrates that this characteristic has been perpetuated and that the American cowboy has, indeed, succeeded in creating for himself a continuation of that frontier which once was his birthplace and domain.

Appendixes

Appendix A.

BONUS PRIZES TO ALL-AROUND WORLD CHAMPIONS, VARIOUS YEARS, 1951–81

1951	1959	1969	1981
$1,500 cash (Levi Strauss & Co., San Francisco)	$1,500 cash (Levi Strauss & Co.)	$1,500 cash (RCA: received in part from H. D. Lee & Co., Shawnee Mission, Kans.; Blue Bell, Inc., Greensboro, N.C.; Tony Lama Co., El Paso; Geo. S. Bailey Hat Co., Los Angeles; Fenton Sports, Inc., Denver)	$2,000 cash (PRCA)
$100 gold and silver belt buckle (Levi Strauss & Co.)	Special gold and silver belt buckle (Levi Strauss & Co.)	$1,500 cash (Levi Strauss & Co.)	PRCA western felt hat (Bailey Hat Co.)
$100 Dobbs Rancher Hat (Roy D. Barnes—Race, Rodeo & Western Suppliers, Denver)	$450 pair of specially made boots (Justin Boot Co., Fort Worth)	Gold and silver belt buckle (Levi Strauss & Co.)	Pair of boots (Tony Lama Boot Co.)
	Trophy spurs (Les Garcia Mfg. Co., Reno)	Saddle (Adolph Coors Co., Denver)	$1,500 cash (H. D. Lee & Co.)
	Free rent during Fort Worth Rodeo, 1/29–2/7, 1960 (Westmoor Court, Fort Worth)	Six pairs of boots (Justin Boot Co.)	Gear bag and flight bag (Morgan Horse Products, Ellsworth, Neb.)
	Donohoy hat (Donohoy Hats, Los Angeles)	Trophy spurs (Les Garcia Mfg. Co., Reno)	Unlimited air travel to $25,000 (Frontier Airlines, Denver)
	Jacket (Trego's Westwear, Woodward, Okla.)	Photo album (Carol Pinckney Enos, Nice, Calif.)	Trophy saddle (PRCA)
	Pair of boots (Tony Lama Co., El Paso)		
	Hand-tooled suitcase (Dell's Leather Shop, Riverton, Wyo.)		

SOURCES: "1951 Donors for Point Award Winners," *The Buckboard*, 7, no. 8 (January, 1952): 4; "Championship Donors for 1959," *Rodeo Sports News*, Championship Edition, 8, no. 4 (1960): 69; "Awards Pledged for 1969 Rodeo Cowboys Association Champions," *Rodeo Sports News*, Championship Edition, 18, no. 3 (1970): 115; "1981 PRCA Championship Awards," *Prorodeo Sports News*, Championship Edition, 30, no. 4 (1982): 121.

Appendix B.
WINSTON RODEO AWARDS, 1972–79

Year	Total Bonus Money[a]	Saddlebronc	Bareback Bronc	Bull Riding	Calf Roping	Steer Wrestling	Team Roping	All-Around
1972	$105,000 Top 5 + All-Around							Phil Lyne $60,852 #1
1st Half: $30,000		J. C. Bonine $24,925 #2	Gary Tucker $21,120 #4	Larry Mahan $18,480 #3	Dean Oliver $25,358 #3	Roy Duvall	Gary Gist $13,598 #1	
2nd Half: $30,000		Mel Hyland $26,812 #1	Joe Alexander $32,126 #1	Gary Leffew $17,629 #4	Phil Lyne $32,216 #1	Roy Duvall $24,327 #1	Leo Camarillo $17,587 #1	
1973	$105,000 Top 7 + All-Around							Larry Mahan $64,447 #1
1st Half: $32,500		Shawn Davis $16,077 #8	Joe Alexander	Don Gay $26,889 #2	Ernie Taylor	Tom Ferguson $23,604 #3	Leo Camarillo	
2nd Half: $32,500		John McBeth $21,868 #4	Joe Alexander $37,021 #1	Bobby Steiner $28,099 #1	Ernie Taylor $38,773 #1	Bob Marshall $31,817 #1	Leo Camarillo $20,693 #1	

							All-Around
1974 $120,000 Top 10 + All-Around							Tom Ferguson $66,929 #1
1st Half: $40,000	John McBeth	Joe Alexander	John Davis $24,720 #2	Tom Ferguson $40,839 #1	Frank Shepperson $24,554 #4	H. P. Evetts	
2nd Half: $40,000	John McBeth $36,918 #4	Joe Alexander $36,073 #1	Don Gay $32,917 #1	Dean Oliver $23,697 #2	Tommy Puryear $26,253 #1	H. P. Evetts $23,018 #1	
1975 $135,000 Top 10 + All-Around							Leo Camarillo $50,831 #1
1st Half: $47,550	Monty Henson	Rusty Riddle $38,767 #2	Don Gay	Junior Garrison $24,057 #3	Frank Shepperson	Leo Camarillo	
2nd Half: $47,550	Monty Henson $29,788 #1	Joe Alexander $41,184 #1	Don Gay $34,850 #1	Jeff Copenhaver $34,628 #1	Frank Shepperson $34,863 #1	Leo Camarillo $28,102 #1	

Year	Total Bonus Money	Saddlebronc	Bareback Bronc	Bull Riding	Calf Roping	Steer Wrestling	Team Roping	All-Around
1976[b]	$150,000 Top 10 + All-Around							Tom Ferguson $87,908 #1
1st Half: $55,000		Monty Henson	Joe Alexander	Don Gay	Tom Ferguson $35,691 #2	Bob Marshall $40,359 #2	Leo Camarillo	
2nd Half: $55,000		Monty Henson $34,383 #1	Joe Alexander $48,156 #1	Don Gay $33,316 #1	Roy Cooper $37,370 #1	Tom Ferguson $48,854 #1	Leo Camarillo $30,761 #1	
1977[c]	$150,000 Top 10 + All-Around							Tom Ferguson $76,730 #1
1st Half: $55,000		Monty Henson $28,226 #2	Joe Alexander	Butch Kirby $38,124 #2	Roy Cooper	Bob Marshall $23,854 #7	Jerold Camarillo	
2nd Half: $55,000		Bobby Berger $27,765 #1	Joe Alexander $46,213 #1	Don Gay $41,574 #1	Roy Cooper $51,446 #1	Bob Christopherson $26,407 #2	Jerold Camarillo $21,413 #1	

1978[d]	$175,000 Top 10 + All-Around							Tom Ferguson $83,734 #1
1st Half: $62,550		Joe Marvel $35,200 #1	Bruce Ford	Don Gay $38,275 #1	Roy Cooper	Byron Walker $40,881 #1	Doyle Gellerman/ Walt Woodward $21,104 #1/#2 split	
2nd Half: $62,550		Bud Monroe $32,281 #2	Bruce Ford $46,541 #1	Denny Flynn $37,992 #2	Roy Cooper $67,153 #1	Tom Ferguson $40,070 #2	Julio Moreno $18,624 #3	
1979[e]	$175,000 Top 10 + All-Around							Paul Tierney $92,201 #1
1st Half: $62,550		Mel Coleman $29,632 #11	Bruce Ford $80,260 #1	Don Gay	Tom Ferguson $59,106 #2	Stan Williamson $44,865 #1	Kent Winterton/ Don Kimble $20,508 #7/#8 split	
2nd Half: $62,550		Bobby Berger $41,709 #1	Sam Perkins $57,039 #2	Don Gay $59,999 #1	Paul Tierney $59,294 #1	Jack Hannum $38,818 #3	Julio Moreno/ Dennis Watkins $22,698 #5/#6 split	

SOURCES: "Winston Rodeo Awards," *Rodeo Sports News*, championship editions, 1973–78, *Prorodeo Sports News*, championship editions, 1979–80.

Note: The amount and number under each contestant's name are his regular winnings and his place within his event for the year indicated.

[a] In 1972 through 1975 first place in each event for each half of the season was worth $2,000 and the All-Around title worth $10,000. In 1973 through 1979 first place each event each half-season was worth $2,500 and the All-Around title worth $10,000.

[b] First year of "sudden-death" format—PRCA titles went to the cowboy winning the most money at the National Finals Rodeo instead of the one winning the most money for the year. Totals for 1976–78 do not include NFR money.

[c] In 1977 there was no average in the rough-stock events; all prize money was divided into day monies only. The timed events figured both day monies and the average.

[d] Averages were used in all events plus bonus points from first through sixth place, with 300 points available in the timed events and 200 points in the riding events. The cowboy in each event with the highest number of percentage points became the World Champion for that event.

[e] In 1979 there was a reversion to the old formula, by which World Champions were determined by their winnings throughout the year added to those at the National Finals Rodeo.

Notes

INTRODUCTION

1. L. P. McCann, "Ride 'em Cowboy!" *Sunset* 59 (September, 1927): 18.
2. Max Kegley, *Rodeo—The Sport of the Cow Country*, p. 7.
3. Fred Schnell, *Rodeo! The Suicide Circuit*, p. 34.
4. Ramon F. Adams, *The Old-Time Cowhand*, p. 19.
5. Johnie Fain and Learah Cooper Morgan, "The Cowboy and the Rodeo," *Arizona Highways* 36, no. 2 (February, 1960): 30.
6. Ibid.
7. Gerald Carson, "The Late, Late Frontier," *American Heritage* 23 (April, 1972): 75.
8. McCann, p. 20. Leivas' medal has disappeared—by theft or loss—from the Sharlot Hall Museum in Prescott, where it was preserved for many years.
9. "Upcoming Rodeos," *Prorodeo Sports News*, June 30, 1982, p. 12.
10. "Cowboys and Wild Horses," *Denver Republican*, October 15, 1887, p. 1.
11. "The Humane Society," *Denver Republican*, October 15, 1887, p. 1.

CHAPTER I

1. A. Britt, "Ride 'im, Cowboy!" *Outlook*, September 26, 1923, pp. 136–39; L. P. McCann, "Ride 'em Cowboy!" *Sunset* 59 (September, 1927): 18–20; G. W. Earle, "Ride 'im, Cowboy!" *Popular Mechanics* 53 (June, 1930): 906–11; E. W. Gage, "Ride 'im Cowboy!" *Travel* 65 (June, 1935): 33–35 ff.; "Ride 'em Cowboy!" *Popular Mechanics* 72 (October, 1939): 497–504 ff.; R. Garis, "Ride 'im Cowboy!" *New York Times Magazine*, October 8, 1950, pp. 20 ff.
2. H. H. Smith, "New Wild West," *Outlook*, October 28, 1931, pp. 272–73 ff.; "Rodeo: Riders Bring Wild West Thrills to Jaded Easterners," *News Week* [later *Newsweek*], October 21, 1933, p. 17; "Out of the Wild West They Came," *Literary Digest*, October 19, 1935, p. 34; "The Wild West in New York City," *Literary Digest*, October 24, 1936, pp. 44–46; "Shades of the Old West . . . ," *Literary Digest*, November 25, 1933, p. 25.

3. Ulrich Calvosa, "Cowboys Are Crazy," *Collier's*, October 5, 1946, pp. 22–24; P. Friggens, "Rip-Roarin', R'arin' Rodeo," *Reader's Digest* 51 (October, 1947): 111–14; J. A. Burkhart, "The Cowpoke Is Always Broke," *Nation*, September 9, 1950, pp. 224–25; R. Froman, "Ornery Critters Are His Fortune," *Nation's Business* 40 (May, 1952): 56 ff.

4. *Readers' Guide to Periodical Literature*, vol. 11, July, 1937–June, 1939, ed. Alice M. Dougan, Bertha Joel, and Jeanette Moore-Smith, p. 1561.

5. Ibid., vol. 21, *March, 1957–February, 1959*, ed. Sarita Robinson, p. 1665.

6. H. Glafcke, editorial, *Cheyenne Daily Leader*, July 6, 1872, p. 4: "The most exciting and laughable part of the programme was the riding of a wild Texan steer by 'Whitcomb's Sam,' the most accomplished horse jockey in this Territory. He retained his seat with great skill and dexterity, and accomplished the mile in 1:16."

7. Examples of recent articles include Patricia Goldstone, "Rodeo Cowgirls on the Horns of a Dilemma," *Los Angeles Times*, November 7, 1980, pt. 5, pp. 12–14, and Tabitha Chance, "There's Mindy's Dad on the Trombone," *TV Guide*, November 29, 1980, pp. 14–16.

8. John Baumann, "On a Western Ranche," *Fortnightly Review*, April 1, 1887, p. 516.

9. Edward Everett Dale, *Cow Country*, p. 133.

10. Julian Ralph, "A Talk with a Cowboy," *Harper's Weekly*, April 16, 1892, p. 379.

11. Joseph Nimmo, Jr., "The American Cow-Boy," *Harper's New Monthly Magazine* 73 (November, 1886): 884.

12. Thomas Holme, "A Cowboy's Life," *Chatauquan* 19 (September, 1894): 731.

13. Ibid., pp. 731–32.

14. John Baumann, "Experiences of a Cow-Boy," *Lippincott's Magazine* 38 (August, 1886): 314.

15. Arthur Chapman, "The Cowboy of Today," *World's Work* 8 (September, 1904): 5772.

16. Harry P. Stegner, "Photographing the Cowboy as He Disappears," *World's Work* 17 (January, 1909): 11117.

17. Clifford P. Westermeier, *Trailing the Cowboy*, p. 342.

18. Don Russell, *The Wild West: A History of the Wild West Shows*, p. 1.

19. Robert West Howard and Oren Arnold, *Rodeo: Last Frontier of the Old West*, p. 33.

20. Dale, p. 233.

21. Russell, p. 7.

22. Willard H. Porter, *Roping and Riding: Fast Horses and Short Ropes*, p. 170; idem, "American Rodeo: Sport and Spectacle," *American West* 8, no. 4 (July, 1971): 45.

23. Clifford P. Westermeier, *Man, Beast, Dust—The Story of Rodeo*, p. 40.

24. Arthur Chapman, "Rodeo Dollars," *World's Work* 60 (July, 1931): 29.

25. Tom C. Brody, "The Roughest Rides to Richest," *Sports Illustrated*, December 18, 1967, p. 22.

26. "The Cowboys of the Western Plains and Their Horses," reprint from *Providence Journal* in *Cheyenne Daily Leader*, October 3, 1882, p. 4.

27. "The Cowboy, Like the Indian, Has Passed His Hey-Day of Life Here," *Calgary Daily Herald*, September 4, 1912, p. 7.
28. Mody C. Boatright, "The American Rodeo," *American Quarterly* 16, no. 2 (Summer, 1964): 200; Leo Cremer et al., "Rodeos of Today," *Hoofs and Horns* 9, no. 1 (July, 1939): 5; Westermeier, *Man, Beast, Dust*, p. 96.
29. Westermeier, *Man, Beast, Dust*, pp. 96–97.
30. Burkhart, p. 224.
31. Westermeier, *Man, Beast, Dust*, p. 97.
32. Charles Wellington Furlong, *Let 'Er Buck: A Story of the Passing of the Old West*, pp. 11, 172, 192.
33. Ibid., p. 99.
34. Fred Gipson, *Fabulous Empire: Colonel Zack Miller's Story*, p. 239.
35. James Cox et al., *Historical and Biographical Record of the Cattle Industry and the Cattlemen of Texas and Adjacent Territory*, p. 171; Eugene F. Kinkead, "Cowboy Business," *New Yorker*, October 26, 1940, pp. 16, 46.

CHAPTER 2

1. Don Russell, *The Wild West: A History of the Wild West Shows*, pp. 63, 55, 40, 72.
2. Colin Lofting, "How to Get Rich on a Horse," *Saturday Evening Post*, August 25, 1956, p. 85.
3. Foghorn (Fred M.) Clancy, "Cowboy Sports and Frontier Contests," *Billboard*, March 17, 1923, pp. 10, 246; John E. Hartwig, "Is Rodeo History Repeating Itself?" *Billboard*, March 28, 1931, p. 17.
4. Rodeo Association of America, *Constitution and By-Laws and Rules of the Rodeo Association of America*, 1941, p. 3.
5. Clifford P. Westermeier, *Man, Beast, Dust—The Story of Rodeo*, pp. 183–84. It is now known that organizational meetings for the establishment of the Rodeo Association of America were held as early as late 1926, initiated by Maxwell McNutt, a member of the San Francisco judiciary and chairman of the California Rodeo, Salinas. He subsequently became president of the RAA.
6. Rodeo Association of America, pp. 5–6.
7. Ibid.; Westermeier, *Man, Beast, Dust*, p. 184.
8. Tex Sherman, "Rodeo News," *Hoofs and Horns* 3, no. 9 (February, 1934): 13.
9. Westermeier, *Man, Beast, Dust*, pp. 185–86.
10. Ibid., pp. 97–98.
11. "Champion Cowboy," *Time*, March 8, 1954, p. 55; Westermeier, *Man, Beast, Dust*, p. 187.
12. "Rodeo Performers Agree to Settle Labor Disputes," *Denver Post*, January 8, 1938, p. 8.
13. "Trial of Herbert Frizzell, Rodeo Cowboy, Switched from Big Spring to Midland, Texas," *Buckboard* 5, no. 7 (January, 1950): 10; Edmund Christopher, "World's Roughest Sport," *Holiday* 19 (June, 1956): 95.
14. "PRCA Approves Pro Judging System," *Rodeo Sports News*, October 19, 1977, pp. 1, 6.

15. Interview with Hugh Chambliss, director of Pro Officials, Professional Rodeo Cowboys Association, at Colorado Springs, Colo., March 8, 1983; "Program 'Most Comprehensive' for Wrangler," *Prorodeo Sports News*, February 10, 1982, p. 6; "Pro Official Staff to Increase in 1983," *Prorodeo Sports News*, November 17, 1982, p. 1.

16. Professional Rodeo Cowboys Association, *Articles of Incorporation, By-laws and Rules*, 1983, p. 50.

17. Clifford P. Westermeier, *Trailing the Cowboy*, p. 131; Lewis Atherton, *The Cattle Kings*, p. 182.

18. Westermeier, *Trailing the Cowboy*, p. 132; idem, *Man, Beast, Dust*, p. 96.

19. Foghorn (Fred M.) Clancy, *My Fifty Years in Rodeo*, p. 46.

20. Gib Potter, "Trailering 40 Years Ago—Texas to Calgary," *Western Horseman* 33, no. 7 (July, 1968): 46–47, 93–97.

21. "The Broncho Busters' Union," *Denver Republican*, September 10, 1910, p. 6.

22. Ibid.

23. Fay Ward, "Organization," *Wild Bunch*, May, 1916, p. 8.

24. "First 'Cowboy Union' Ever Organized Will Form in Denver," *Denver Post*, January 18, 1932, p. 5.

25. "Cowpokes Form Union to Improve Standards," *Denver Post*, January 20, 1932, p. 8.

26. Ibid.

27. "First 'Cowboy Union,'" p. 5; "Cowpokes Form Union," p. 8.

28. Interview with Charles "Sharkey" Irwin at Colorado Springs, Colo., May 4, 1982; "Buster Champion Injured at Big Rodeo in Springs," *Rocky Mountain News*, August 17, 1922, p. 3.

29. Reprint from *Denver News* in *Fort Collins Courier*, April 12, 1883, p. 2.

30. Westermeier, *Trailing the Cowboy*, pp. 130–31.

31. "Field and Farm," *Denver Field and Farm*, May 15, 1886, p. 8.

32. Max Kegley, *Rodeo—The Sport of the Cow Country*, p. 8; Willard H. Porter, *Roping and Riding: Fast Horses and Short Ropes*, p. 110.

CHAPTER 3

1. *Official Program, Colonel W. T. Johnson's Sixth Annual World's Championship Rodeo*, Boston Garden, Boston, Mass., November 2–11, 1936, p. 15.

2. "Lorena Trickey Bids World in General 'Good Morning,'" *Colorado Springs Gazette*, August 13, 1922, sec. 2C, p. 1; *Official Program, Cheyenne Frontier Days*, Cheyenne, Wyo., July 27–31, 1926, inside front cover.

3. *Official Program, Colonel W. T. Johnson's Sixth Annual World's Championship Rodeo*, 1936, p. 15.

4. Gene Pruett, "Cowboys Turtle Association to Big Time Corporation," *Persimmon Hill* 4, no. 1 (Summer, 1973): 7.

5. Ethel A. Hopkins, "Editorial Comment," *Hoofs and Horns* 5, no. 10 (March, 1936): 10.

6. "Walked Out of Rodeo because of Money," *Boston Daily Record*, final ed., November 3, 1936, p. 7; *Prize List*, World's Championship Rodeo, Madison Square Garden, New York, N.Y., October 7–25, 1936.

7. *Official Program*, 40th Annual Frontier Days Rodeo, Cheyenne, Wyo., July 22–25, 1936.

8. "Walked Out of Rodeo," p. 7.

9. "Broadway Cowboys," *Time*, October 21, 1935, p. 52; "Broadway Rodeo," *Time*, October 18, 1937, p. 57.

10. Editors of Time-Life Books, *This Fabulous Century*, vol. 4, *1930–1940*, p. 53.

11. "Broadway Cowboys," p. 53.

12. Pruett, p. 7.

13. Reproduction of original document, Archives, Prorodeo Hall of Champions, Colorado Springs, Colo.

14. "Empty Saddles," *Wild Bunch* 2, no. 2 (May, 1980): 8 (Richard Merchant obituary).

15. Robert West Howard and Oren Arnold, *Rodeo: Last Frontier of the Old West*, p. 103.

16. "Strike at Rodeo in Boston Ends, Men Re-employed," *Boston Evening Transcript*, November 3, 1936, p. 4.

17. Gene Lamb, *Rodeo Back of the Chutes*, p. 41.

18. "Strike at Rodeo in Boston Ends," p. 4; Howard and Arnold, p. 104.

19. *Contestants Entry Blank*, Col. W. T. Johnson's World's Championship Rodeo, Boston Garden, Boston, Mass., November 2–11, 1936.

20. "Cowboys Turtle Association," *Hoofs and Horns* 6, no. 7 (December, 1936): 24.

21. Pruett, pp. 7–8.

22. Howard and Arnold, p. 104.

23. Lamb, p. 42.

24. Ibid., p. 43.

25. "Cowboys Turtle Association," p. 24.

26. Ibid.

27. Clifford A. Westermeier, *Man, Beast, Dust—The Story of Rodeo*, pp. 101–103.

28. Ibid., p. 101 (reproduction of original document).

29. Ibid., pp. 101–103; Pruett, p. 6.

30. Westermeier, *Man, Beast, Dust*, pp. 104–105.

31. "Cooperation with Cowboys," *Hoofs and Horns* 6, no. 11 (May, 1937): 19; "Secretary's Message," *RAA Bulletin*, n.s. 1, no. 9 (September, 1937), in *Hoofs and Horns* 7, no. 4 (October, 1937): 19.

32. Westermeier, *Man, Beast, Dust*, pp. 107–11; *Tucson, Official Rodeo Program*, La Fiesta de los Vaqueros, Tucson, Ariz., February 21–23, 1936.

33. "Secretary's Message," p. 19.

34. Westermeier, *Man, Beast, Dust*, p. 112.

35. "Secretary's Message," p. 19; Westermeier, *Man, Beast, Dust*, pp. 112–13.

36. "Greatest Show in Nearly 20 Years Attracts 25,000," *East Oregonian*, September 18, 1937, p. 1.

37. Westermeier, *Man, Beast, Dust*, p. 113.

38. Advertisement (World's Championship Rodeo, Madison Square Garden, New York, N.Y.), *Hoofs and Horns* 7, no. 2 (August, 1937): 21; "Broadway Rodeo," p. 57.
39. Westermeier, *Man, Beast, Dust*, p. 113.
40. Ibid., p. 119.
41. Ibid., pp. 113–14, 116–17.
42. Ibid., p. 119.
43. Interview with Wanden (M. LaFarge) Kane at Fountain, Colo., February 9, 1983; Wanden M. LaFarge, "No Turtles Need Apply," *Saturday Evening Post*, July 9, 1938, pp. 18–19, 46–47; Westermeier, *Man, Beast, Dust*, p. 119.
44. Westermeier, *Man, Beast, Dust*, p. 119.
45. "Parade in Ogden Will Open Pioneer Celebration Today," *Salt Lake Tribune*, July 21, 1939, clipping in scrapbook, Everett Bowman Collection, Prorodeo Hall of Champions.
46. "Cowboy Union Fines Fifty in Ogden Show," *Salt Lake Tribune*, July 22, 1939, p. 17.
47. "Rodeo Riders' Association Head Resigns," *Salt Lake Tribune*, July 23, 1939, pp. 1, 4.
48. Guy Weadick, "What Are Rodeos Doing?" *Hoofs and Horns* 7, no. 7 (January, 1938): 14.
49. Ibid., pp. 14–15.
50. Westermeier, *Man, Beast, Dust*, p. 125.
51. J. Evetts Haley, *Charles Goodnight—Cowman and Plainsman*, p. 351.
52. J. Evetts Haley, *The XIT Ranch of Texas and the Early Days of the Llano Estacado*, p. 243; Cordia Sloan Duke and Joe B. Frantz, *6000 Miles of Fence—Life on the XIT Ranch of Texas*, p. 214.

CHAPTER 4

1. Sam Savitt, *Rodeo—Cowboys, Bulls and Broncos*, p. 11.
2. *RAA Bulletin*, n.s. 8, no. 2 (February, 1944), reprinted in *Hoofs and Horns* 13, no. 9 (March, 1944): 18.
3. Horace V. Stewart, "Happy-Go-Lucky Band of Cowboys Are Real Men, Says Show Chief," *Denver Post*, January 24, 1931, p. 3.
4. "Stock Show Will Have Many Added Attractions This Year," *Denver Post*, January 11, 1931, p. 13.
5. B. Beckner, "Rodeo," *Popular Mechanics* 46 (August, 1926): 190–200; "Rodeo: Riders Bring Wild West Thrills to Jaded Easterners," *Newsweek*, October 21, 1933, p. 17; "Broadway Cowboys," *Time*, October 21, 1935, p. 52.
6. *RAA Bulletin*, n.s. 1, no. 3 (March, 1936), reprinted in *Hoofs and Horns*, 5, no. 11 (April, 1936): 18.
7. "Cowboys Turtle Association," *Hoofs and Horns* 7, no. 10 (April, 1938): 12.
8. "New Service Offered," *Hoofs and Horns* 6, no. 10 (April, 1937): 3 (misprinted on issue as vol. 11, no. 10.)

9. *Western Horseman* 13, no. 4. (July–August, 1948): 2.

10. *Western Horseman* 39, no. 7 (July, 1974): front cover.

11. Herbert S. Maddy, "Eastern Rodeos," *Hoofs and Horns* 4, no. 10 (March, 1935): 16.

12. Ibid.

13. Herbert S. Maddy, "Eastern Rodeos," *Hoofs and Horns* 4, no. 12 (May, 1935): 14.

14. "Notice," *Hoofs and Horns* 4, no. 7 (December, 1934): 8.

15. New York Public Library to author, February 18, 1981.

16. Bruce Clinton, "Rodeos—The New Big-Time Business and Sport," *Hoofs and Horns* 6, no. 2 (July, 1936): 17.

17. Ibid.

18. George Williams, "Ike Rude—Rodeo's Iron Man," *Persimmon Hill* 5, no. 4 (Spring, 1976): 49.

19. E. W. Thistlethwaite, "Cowboys—Old and Modern," *Hoofs and Horns* 6, no. 10 (April, 1937): 13.

20. Ibid.

21. Bruce Clinton, "Modern Cowboy Contestants," *Western Horseman* 5, no. 4 (July–August, 1940): 12.

22. Bruce Clinton, "Are Cowboys Athletes?" *Hoofs and Horns* 8, no. 9 (March, 1939): 19.

23. Ibid.

24. *RAA Bulletin* 4, no. 5 (May, 1940), reprinted in *Hoofs and Horns* 9, no. 12 (June, 1940): 15. Progress in this regard is still very slight. The *World Almanac and Book of Facts 1983* lists, under the heading "Pro Rodeo Championship Standings," those for the year 1981. In addition, the all-around champions for the years 1963–81 are enumerated (p. 870). The book, however, devotes ninety-six pages to sports, while only a portion of one page is allotted to rodeo.

25. *RAA Bulletin*, n.s. 6, no. 8 (August, 1942), reprinted in *Hoofs and Horns* 12, no. 3 (September, 1942): 14.

26. *RAA Bulletin*, n.s. 6, no. 12 (December, 1942), reprinted in *Hoofs and Horns*, 12, no. 7 (January, 1943): 8.

27. "Editor's Page," *Western Horseman* 3, no. 5 (September–October, 1938): 3.

28. Foghorn (Fred M.) Clancy, "Rodeo Fans of America Proposed," *Hoofs and Horns* 10 (April, 1941): 11; Roy Cuddy, "Rodeo Fans of America," *Hoofs and Horns* 10, no. 12 (June, 1941): 10.

29. Cuddy, p. 10.

30. Guy Weadick, "What Are Rodeos Doing?" *Hoofs and Horns* 7, no. 7 (January, 1938): 14.

31. Ibid.; Leo Cremer et al., "Rodeos of Today," *Hoofs and Horns* 9, no. 1 (July, 1939): 4–5.

32. Weadick, p. 15.

33. "Non-Pro Rodeo Has No Future, Gardner Says," *Hoofs and Horns* 9, no. 2 (August, 1939): 16.

34. *RAA Bulletin*, n.s. 3, no. 8 (August, 1939), reprinted in *Hoofs and Horns*, 9, no. 3 (September, 1939): 14.

35. *RAA Bulletin*, n.s. 4, no. 4 (April, 1940), reprinted in *Hoofs and Horns* 9, no. 11 (May, 1940): 21.
36. Ibid.
37. *RAA Bulletin*, n.s. 5, no. 2 (February, 1941), reprinted in *Hoofs and Horns* 10, no. 9 (March, 1941): 24.
38. "Cowboys Turtle Association," *Hoofs and Horns* 9, no. 8 (February, 1940): 12.
39. "Cowboys Turtle Association," *Hoofs and Horns* 10, no. 2 (August, 1940): 15.
40. "Cowboys Turtle Association," *Hoofs and Horns* 9, no. 11 (May, 1940): 15.
41. J. D. McCormick, Council Grove, Kans., to Hugh Bennett (CTA secretary-treasurer 1936–40), December 14, 1939, reprinted in *Hoofs and Horns* 9, no. 8 (February, 1940): 12.
42. "From the Secretary" (CTA), *Hoofs and Horns* 10, no. 12 (June, 1941): 12.
43. Bruce Clinton, "Rodeo Conscious," *Hoofs and Horns* 10, no. 8 (February, 1941): 13.

CHAPTER 5

1. C. M. Black, "Suicide Circuit," *Collier's*, October 26, 1940, p. 41; Eugene F. Kinkead, "Cowboy Business," *New Yorker*, October 26, 1940, p. 48.
2. P. Friggens, "Rip-Roarin', R'arin' Rodeo," *Reader's Digest* 51 (October, 1947): 113.
3. "From the Secretary" (RAA), *RAA Bulletin* n.s. 5, no. 8 (September, 1941) in *Hoofs and Horns* 11, no. 4 (October, 1941): 14.
4. "Cowboys Turtle Association," *Hoofs and Horns* 12, no. 1 (July, 1942): 14.
5. Cecil Wright, "California News Items," *Hoofs and Horns* 11, no. 8 (February, 1942): 3; "Soldier Gene Autry," *Hoofs and Horns* 12, no. 2 (August, 1942): 9. Fritz Truan was the world-champion saddle-bronc rider for the years 1939 and 1940. He died on Iwo Jima on February 28, 1945.
6. "This and That," *Hoofs and Horns* 12, no. 6 (December, 1942): 2 (letter from John "Buck" Taylor, training in Corsicana, Tex.).
7. "This and That," *Hoofs and Horns* 12, no. 2 (August, 1942): 2.
8. Chuck Martin, "The Place of Rodeos in National Defense," *Hoofs and Horns* 11, no. 9 (March, 1942): 4.
9. Ibid.
10. "West Watches First Stock Show since Wartime in Denver," *Denver Post*, January 7, 1942, p. 13.
11. "Denver Stock Show to Stress Role of Ranchers in National Defense," *Denver Post*, January 5, 1942, p. 8; "Fast Action Features Rodeo Opener," *Denver Post*, January 11, 1942, p. 2.
12. "Champions 'Crowned' as Rodeo Ends with Thrill Packed Show," *Denver Post*, January 18, 1942, p. 10.
13. *RAA Bulletin*, n.s. 6, no. 2 (February, 1942) reprinted in *Hoofs and Horns* 11, no. 9 (March, 1942): 21.
14. "All Soldier Rodeo," *Hoofs and Horns* 12, no. 5 (November, 1942): 10; *RAA Bulletin*, n.s. 7, no. 6 (June, 1943), reprinted in *Hoofs and Horns* 13, no. 1 (July, 1943): 17.

15. *RAA Bulletin*, June, 1943, p. 17.
16. "Army Rodeos," *Hoofs and Horns* 15, no. 4 (October, 1945): 10.
17. "Rodeo in France," *Hoofs and Horns* 15, no. 4 (October, 1945): 14.
18. "Buckaroos 'Down Under,'" *Western Horseman* 9, no. 1 (January–February, 1944): 27; Sgt. "Red" Bouvee, "Rodeo in Italy," *Western Horseman* 9, no. 5 (September–October, 1944): 16; "Bronc-Busting in Gandhi-land," *Western Horseman* 10, no. 2 (March–April, 1945): 4–5.
19. "A Generous Gift," *Hoofs and Horns* 13, no. 8 (February, 1944): 2.
20. "Rodeos Curtailed along Coast," *Western Horseman* 7, no. 2 (March–April, 1942): 44; "The Japs Take Over," *Western Horseman* 7, no. 3 (May–June, 1942): 38.
21. Don Grant, "Curtailment of Horse Events," *Western Horseman* 7, no. 3 (May–June, 1942): 24, 56.
22. "Rodeos Curtailed along Coast," p. 44.
23. Jerry Armstrong, "The Collegiate Cowboy's Column," *Western Horseman* 7, no. 4 (July–August, 1942): 15.
24. Jerry Armstrong, "The Collegiate Cowboy's Column," *Western Horseman* 7, no. 5 (September–October, 1942): 16–17, 22 passim; Barbara Roberts, "Sale at Baker [Oregon] Is a Huge Success," *Western Horseman* 9, no. 5 (September–October, 1944): 18–19.
25. Tex Garland, "Chuck Wagon Chatter," *Rodeo Fans* 3, no. 3 (March, 1944): 3.
26. "Turtle Notes," *Hoofs and Horns* 11, no. 10 (April, 1942): 9.
27. "Report of Activities under New Business Manager to Be Made Soon," *Hoofs and Horns* 15, no. 1 (July, 1945): 16; "Report of First Three Months['] Activities under New Manager," *Buckboard* 1, no. 1 (July, 1945): 3.
28. "Real Job Lies Ahead for Rodeo Profession," *RAA Bulletin*, n.s. 6, no. 3 (March, 1942), reprinted in *Hoofs and Horns* 11, no. 10 (April, 1942): 12.
29. Ibid.
30. "Wartime Status of Rodeos," *RAA Bulletin*, n.s. 6, no. 4 (April, 1942), reprinted in *Hoofs and Horns* 11, no. 11 (May, 1942): 18.
31. "Rodeo Picture Shaping Up Better," *RAA Bulletin*, n.s. 6, no. 6 (June, 1942), reprinted in *Hoofs and Horns* 12, no. 1 (July, 1942): 16.
32. Grant, pp. 24, 57.
33. Cecil Wright, "California News Items," *Hoofs and Horns* 11, no. 10 (April, 1942): 4.
34. "Haircuts for Army Horses Pay Big Dividends," *Western Horseman* 7, no. 4 (July–August, 1942): 13.
35. *RAA Bulletin*, n.s. 7, no. 2 (February, 1943), reprinted in *Hoofs and Horns* 12, no. 9 (March, 1943): 15.
36. "Discussion of Some Rodeo Questions," *RAA Bulletin*, n.s. 7, no. 3 (March, 1943), reprinted in *Hoofs and Horns* 12, no. 10 (April, 1943): 10.
37. *RAA Bulletin*, n.s. 6, no. 3 (March, 1942), reprinted in *Hoofs and Horns* 11, no. 10 (April, 1942): 12; ibid., n.s. 7, no. 3 (March, 1943), reprinted in *Hoofs and Horns* 12, no. 10 (April, 1943): 10.
38. "There's a Difference in Rodeos," *Denver Daily Record Stockman*, Stock Show ed., January 30, 1943, p. 112.

39. Walt Coburn, "Rodeos Don't Die," *Hoofs and Horns* 13, no. 9 (March, 1944): 5.
40. Garland, p. 3.
41. Jerry Armstrong, "The Collegiate Cowboy's Column," *Western Horseman* 9, no. 3 (May–June, 1944): 17; ibid., 9, no. 4 (July–August, 1944): 14.
42. Jerry Armstrong, "The Collegiate Cowboy's Column," *Western Horseman* 10, no. 1 (January–February, 1945): 14.

CHAPTER 6

1. Clifford P. Westermeier, *Man, Beast, Dust—The Story of Rodeo*, pp. 339–42.
2. "From the Secretary" (RAA), *RAA Bulletin*, n.s. 9, no. 4 (April, 1945), in *Hoofs and Horns* 14, no. 11 (May, 1945): 17.
3. "RCA—Cowboy Organization Makes Changes," *Hoofs and Horns* 14, no. 11 (May, 1945): 16.
4. Herman Linder, Cardston, Alberta, Canada, to author, March 19, 1981.
5. "C.T.A. Headquarters Moved," *Hoofs and Horns* 11, no. 9 (March, 1942): 20. The location was 733 West McDowell Road, Phoenix, Ariz.
6. Interview with Earl Lindsey, conducted by telephone by David Stout, August 7, 1982; "RCA—Cowboy Organization Makes Changes," p. 16 (letter from directors at Fort Worth meeting to Hugh Bennett, CTA secretary-treasurer 1936–40, and King Merritt, CTA steer-roping–team-tying director 1941–45, March 15, 1945).
7. "RCA—Cowboy Organization Makes Changes," p. 16.
8. "Fannye Lovelady Resigns," *Hoofs and Horns* 14, no. 11 (May, 1945): 14.
9. "RCA—Cowboy Organization Makes Changes," p. 16.
10. Cowboys Turtle Association, *Articles of Association, By-laws and Rules*, 1944, p. 6 (emphasis added).
11. "Statement from Everett Bowman," *Hoofs and Horns* 14, no. 12 (June, 1945): 13.
12. "RCA Point Awarding Sytem," *Hoofs and Horns* 14, no. 11 (May, 1945): 16.
13. Gene Lamb, *Rodeo Back of the Chutes*, p. 45.
14. Jerry Armstrong, "The Collegiate Cowboy's Column," *Western Horseman* 10, no. 4 (July–August, 1945): 15.
15. "From the Secretary" (RAA), p. 17; "RCA—Negotiations Still Pending Regarding Consolidation of IRA, NRA and RCA Point Awarding Systems," *Hoofs and Horns* 14, no. 12 (June, 1945): 16.
16. Jerry Armstrong, "The Collegiate Cowboy's Column," *Western Horseman* 11, no. 2 (March–April, 1946): 15; Jerry Armstrong, "Picked Up in the Rodeo Arena," *Western Horseman* 14, no. 3 (March, 1949): 10.
17. Jerry Armstrong, "The Collegiate Cowboy's Column," *Western Horseman* 12, no. 1 (January–February, 1947): 40.
18. Jerry Armstrong, "The Collegiate Cowboy's Column," *Western Horseman* 12, no. 3 (May–June, 1947): 10.
19. Jerry Armstrong, "Picked Up in the Rodeo Arena," *Western Horseman* 13, no. 3 (May–June, 1948): 37.

20. Jerry Armstrong, "Picked Up in the Rodeo Arena," March, 1949, p. 10.
21. *International Rodeo Association's 1947 Championship Rodeo in Conjunction with the Grand National Livestock Exposition and Horse Show*, San Francisco, Calif., November 1–9, 1947.
22. Jerry Armstrong, "Picked Up in the Rodeo Arena," *Western Horseman* 14, no. 5 (May, 1949): 12, 42–44.
23. Jerry Armstrong, "Picked Up in the Rodeo Arena," *Western Horseman* 16, no. 7 (July, 1951): 19.
24. Jerry Armstrong, "Picked Up in the Rodeo Arena," *Western Horseman* 17, no. 1 (January, 1952): 16.
25. Jerry Armstrong, "Picked Up in the Rodeo Arena," *Western Horseman* 20, no. 7 (July, 1955): 20.
26. "Rodeo's Point-Award System—How to Become a Champion," *Rodeo Sports News*, July 1, 1955, p. 1.
27. Eddie G. Cole, "From the I.R.A. Office," *Hoofs and Horns* 26, no. 8 (March, 1957): 8; David Stout, "PRCA's Growing Years," *Prorodeo Sports News*, August 25, 1982, p. 16-A.
28. Interview with Lex Connelly at Studio City, Calif., March 20, 1978.
29. P. Friggens, "Rip-Roarin', R'arin' Rodeo," *Reader's Digest* 51 (October, 1947): 114.
30. Interview with Lex Connelly, March 20, 1978.
31. "Event Winners at Larger Rodeos," *Rodeo Sports News*, Championship Edition, 1969, p. 99.
32. Eugene F. Kinkead, "Cowboy Business," *New Yorker*, October 26, 1940, p. 47; Professional Rodeo Cowboys Association, Inc., *President's Year-End Report to Membership*, February 1, 1983, p. 1.
33. Jean Muir, "Cowboys on the Campus," *Saturday Evening Post*, February 10, 1951, p. 37.
34. "College Rodeo," *Time*, May 21, 1951, p. 75.
35. Muir, p. 139.
36. Interview with Lex Connelly, March 20, 1978.

CHAPTER 7

1. Mike Swift, "The Rodeo Information Commission," *Rodeo Sports News*, Championship Edition, 1958, p. 120.
2. Mike Swift, "The Rodeo Information Commission," *Rodeo Sports News*, Championship Edition, 1959, p. 43.
3. John Van Cronkhite, "What the National Finals Will Mean to the Sport," *Rodeo Sports News*, Championship Edition, 1959, p. 39.
4. Swift, 1959, p. 43.
5. "TV, War Threat Making It Tough for Rodeo Hands," *Rocky Mountain News*, January 8, 1951, p. 6.
6. "Two a Year," *Rodeo Sports News*, Championship Edition, 1959, p. 17.
7. "Two National Telecasts," *Rodeo Sports News*, Championship Edition, 1959, p. 37.

8. "First Finals Rodeo in '59," *Rodeo Sports News*, Championship Edition, 1959, p. 38.

9. Ibid., p. 103.

10. Lex Connelly, "Founding and First Years of National Finals Rodeo," *Persimmon Hill* 4, no. 1 (Summer, 1973): 15.

11. Ibid.

12. "National Finals: A Growth Industry," *Rodeo Sports News*, January 25, 1978, p. 4.

13. Connelly, p. 15.

14. Red Smith, "Home, Home on the Range, New Jersey," *New York Times*, July 23, 1977, p. 13: "NFR and World Champions," *Rodeo Sports News*, May 1, 1976, p. 20.

15. "Myriad New Site . . . Sudden Death Out," *Prorodeo Sports News*, February 7, 1979, p. 2.

16. Ibid., p. 1.

17. Skipper Rigdon, "Rodeo Foundation," *Rodeo Sports News*, Championship Edition, 1960, p. 109.

18. Ibid.

19. "Rodeo Foundation," *Rodeo Sports News*, Championship Edition, 1962, p. 61.

20. "Rodeo Information Commission," *Rodeo Sports News*, Championship Edition, 1968, p. 81.

21. "Rodeo News Bureau," *Rodeo Sports News*, Championship Edition, 1974, p. 16.

22. "PRCA Pro Rodeo 1977," *Prorodeo Sports News*, Championship Edition, 1978, p. 4; "Stemler Joins PRCA in New Position," *Rodeo Sports News*, February 1, 1977, p. 2.

CHAPTER 8

1. "New Bronco Breed: Rodeo Cowboys," *Time*, September 2, 1974, p. 85.

2. "He Wants to Be a Cowboy," *Stock Grower and Farmer* (Las Vegas, N.M.T.), July 4, 1891, p. 10.

3. Ellsworth Collings and Alma Miller England, *The 101 Ranch*, p. 158.

4. "Shades of the Old West," *Literary Digest*, November 25, 1933, p. 25.

5. Willard H. Porter, *Roping and Riding, Fast Horses and Short Ropes*, p. 64.

6. Bruce Clinton, "Modern Cowboy Contestants," *Western Horseman* 5, no. 4 (July–August, 1940): 12.

7. Willard H. Porter, "Readin', Writin' and Ropin'," *Western Horseman* 21, no. 7, (July, 1956): 20.

8. Red Smith, "Rodeo School Has Finishing Touch," *Philadelphia Inquirer*, February 10, 1963.

9. Interview with John McBeth at Onida, S. Dak., June 4, 1975.

10. Ibid.

11. Jane Prattle, "A Thinking Man's Game," *Prorodeo Sports News*, May 31, 1978, p. 4.

12. Douglas Kent Hall, *Let 'Er Buck!* pp. 19, 98.

13. Ibid., p. 158.

14. William Crawford, *The Bronc Rider*, pp. 146–47.
15. Recollections of lecture at Rodeo School, Sutton Ranches, Onida, S. Dak., June 4, 1975.
16. Charlotte Moser, "At $100,000 a Year, He's America's Top Cowboy," *Us*, April 18, 1978, p. 65.
17. Giles Tippette, *The Brave Men*, p. 81.
18. Interview with Lex Connelly at Studio City, Calif., March 20, 1978.
19. Interview with David Stout at Colorado Springs, Colo., August 31, 1984.
20. Hall, pp. 11, 14.
21. Crawford, p. 217.
22. John W. Morris, *Ghost Towns of Oklahoma*, p. 91.
23. J. Stewart-Gordon, "Winningest Cowboy in the World," *Saturday Evening Post* 243 (Fall, 1971): 22.
24. Interviews with Casey Tibbs, various dates, 1967–69.
25. R. Froman, "Ornery Critters Are His Fortune," *Nation's Business* 40 (May, 1952): 60.
26. Red Smith, "Scandal," *New York Herald Tribune*, November 7, 1963.
27. "Paul Mayo and Judge Tolbirt Re-instated," *Rodeo Sports News*, June 15, 1964, p. 16; membership records, Membership Department, Professional Rodeo Cowboys Association, Inc., Colorado Springs, Colo.
28. Eugene F. Kinkead, "Cowboy Business," *New Yorker*, October 26, 1940, p. 48.
29. Red Smith, "Home, Home on the Range, New Jersey," *New York Times*, July 23, 1977, p. 13.
30. Tippette, p. 189; interview with Bob Eidson, executive vice president, Professional Rodeo Cowboys Association, Inc., at Colorado Springs, Colo., March 1, 1983.
31. Crawford, p. 50.
32. Edmund Christopher, "World's Roughest Sport," *Holiday* 19 (June, 1956): 90.
33. Gerald C. Lubenow, "Rodeo—The Soul of the Frontier," *Newsweek*, October 2, 1972, p. 72.
34. Edwin Shrake, "Horsing Around with Bull," *Sports Illustrated*, December 3, 1973, p. 43.
35. "Baby Doll the Rodeo Cowboys All Love," *Life*, November 8, 1957, p. 94.
36. Shrake, p. 43.
37. Kinkead, p. 46.
38. "Go West, Pardner," *Los Angeles Herald-Examiner*, September 28, 1980, sec. E, p. 6.
39. Clifford P. Westermeier, *Man, Beast, Dust—The Story of Rodeo*, p. 46.

CHAPTER 9

1. Fred Schnell, *Rodeo! The Suicide Circuit*, p. 108.
2. Douglas Kent Hall, *Let 'Er Buck!* p. 209.
3. Giles Tippette, *The Brave Men*, p. 25.
4. Ibid.

5. Bruce F. Claussen, M.D., "The Sore-Armed Bareback Bronc Rider," *Prorodeo Sports News*, July 22, 1981, p. 3.
6. Tippette, p. 25.
7. Toots Mansfield, *Calf Roping*, p. 56; "Clyde Burk Rides On," *Hoofs and Horns* 14, no. 9 (March, 1945): 20.
8. Charles Wellington Furlong, *Let 'Er Buck: A Story of the Passing of the Old West*, p. 209.
9. Ibid.
10. Ibid., p. 212.
11. Ibid., p. 215.
12. Ibid., p. 221.
13. Claude Stanush, King of the Cowboys," *Life*, May 13, 1946, p. 62.
14. Eugene F. Kinkead, "Cowboy Business," *New Yorker*, October 26, 1940, p. 48.
15. Ibid.
16. Ibid.
17. "Champ Rider," *Life*, October 22, 1951, p. 124.
18. Ibid., p. 123.
19. "A Sport, Not a Show: World's Championship Rodeo, New York City," *Newsweek*, October 26, 1953, p. 100.
20. "Rodeo Schools," *Prorodeo Sports News*, February 23, 1983, p. 21.
21. Advertisement, *Prorodeo Sports News*, April 19, 1978, p. 18.
22. "National Finals Rodeo—1967," *Rodeo Sports News*, Championship Edition, 1968, p. 12.
23. Professional Rodeo Cowboys Association, Inc., *Articles of Incorporation, By-laws and Rules*, 1983, p. 2.
24. "National Finals Rodeo—1967," p. 12.
25. Interview with Freckles Brown at White River, S. Dak., June 2, 1975.
26. Ibid.
27. "New Bronco Breed: Rodeo Cowboys," *Time*, September 2, 1974, p. 86.
28. "Justin Unveils Fully-Equipped Mobile Medical Center, Staffed by Athletic Trainer Don Andrews at '82 NFR," *PRCA News Release*, November 29, 1982; "Special Awards," *Prorodeo Sports News*, Championship Edition, 1983, p. 111.
29. Fred Morrow, "Trainer Tends Rodeo Pains; Spit Is Passé," *Rocky Mountain News*, January 22, 1981, p. 6.
30. Hall, p. 40.
31. Ibid., p. 75.
32. Tippette, p. 350.
33. Ibid., p. 351.
34. Edwin Shrake, "Horsing Around with Bull," *Sports Illustrated*, December 3, 1973, p. 46.
35. Hall, pp. 121–22.
36. Ibid., p. 51.
37. Interview with Shawn Davis at White River, S. Dak., June 2, 1975.
38. "Sporting Life," *Newsweek*, November 11, 1963, p. 80.
39. Hall, pp. 145–46, 201.

40. "The Suicide Circuit," *Time*, November 18, 1957, p. 83; "Mr. Broken Bones," *Life*, September 15, 1961, pp. 87–90.

41. Douglas C. Looney, "Getting in Step with Dad," *Sports Illustrated*, October 4, 1976, p. 44.

CHAPTER 10

1. Professional Rodeo Cowboys Association, *Facts!* p. 28.

2. J. Frank Dobie, *The Longhorns*, p. xv.

3. Stanley Godlovitch, Roslind Godlovitch, and John Harris, eds., *Animals, Men, and Morals*, p. 122.

4. Douglas Branch, *The Cowboy and His Interpreters*, p. 75.

5. Robert Glass Cleland, *The Cattle on a Thousand Hills*, p. 79.

6. Philip Ashton Rollins, *The Cowboy*, p. 276.

7. Peter Singer, *Animal Liberation*, p. 10.

8. Branch, p. 45.

9. Editors of Time-Life Books, *The Cowboys*, p. 100.

10. Ibid., p. 92.

11. R. L. Duffus, *The Santa Fe Trail*, p. 228 (emphasis added).

12. J. Evetts Haley, *The XIT Ranch of Texas and the Early Days of the Llano Estacado*, p. 242.

13. Cordia Sloan Duke and Joe B. Frantz, *6000 Miles of Fence—Life on the XIT Ranch of Texas*, p. 136.

14. *Mobeetie* (Tex.) *Panhandle*, October 18, 1883; "Field and Farm," *Denver Field and Farm*, May 15, 1886, p. 8.

15. Ernest Staples Osgood, *The Day of the Cattleman*, p. 50.

16. H. Glafcke, editorial, *Cheyenne Daily Leader*, July 6, 1872, p. 4.

17. Henry Blackman Sell and Victor Weybright, *Buffalo Bill and the Wild West*, p. 133.

18. *Rodeo Secretary's Results List*, Cheyenne Frontier Days, Cheyenne Wyo., July 24–August 1, 1982 (in files of the National Media Department, Professional Rodeo Cowboys Association, Colorado Springs, Colo.).

19. Don Russell, *The Wild West: A History of the Wild West Shows*, p. 2.

20. Ibid., p. 12.

21. "Cody's Cyclone," *Omaha Daily Herald*, May 20, 1883, p. 8; William E. Deahl, Jr., "Nebraska's Unique Contribution to the Entertainment World," *Nebraska History* 49, no. 3 (Autumn, 1968): 293.

22. Ibid., p. 295.

23. Russell, p. 13.

24. Ibid., p. 7.

25. Zulma Steele, *Angel in Top Hat*, p. 246.

26. "A Novel Race," *Stock Grower and Farmer* (Las Vegas, N.M.T.), November 26, 1892, p. 4; "The Horse World," *Denver Field and Farm*, May 20, 1893, p. 9; ibid., May 27, 1893, p. 9; ibid., June 17, 1893, p. 9.

27. "The Horse World," *Denver Field and Farm*, June 24, 1893, p. 9; ibid., July 1, 1893, p. 9.

28. "Dodged about the Bull," *Rocky Mountain News*, September 30, 1895, p. 1.
29. Ibid.
30. "Genuine Bull Fight," *Rocky Mountain News*, October 2, 1895, p. 6 [?—poor copy].
31. Clifford P. Westermeier, "Cowboy Sports and the Humane Society," *Colorado Magazine* 26, no. 4 (October, 1949): 243.
32. "Weary Wild Westerners," *Rocky Mountain News*, October 9, 1895, p. 8; Westermeier, "Cowboy Sports," p. 244.
33. Interviews with Bob Eidson, executive vice president, Professional Rodeo Cowboys Association, Inc., at Denver, Colo., September 14, 1978, and at Colorado Springs, Colo., August 26, 1981, and March 1, 1983.
34. "Steer Busting," *Wyoming Tribune*, July 27, 1907, p. 4.
35. Ibid.; Westermeier, "Cowboy Sports," p. 245.
36. Roswell C. McCrea, *The Humane Movement*, pp. 18–19.
37. Robert D. Hanesworth, *Daddy of 'Em All*, p. 50.
38. Ibid., p. 59.
39. Clifford P. Westermeier, *Man, Beast, Dust—The Story of Rodeo*, p. 58.

CHAPTER II

1. Clifford P. Westermeier, "Cowboy Sports and the Humane Society," *Colorado Magazine* 26, no. 4 (October, 1949): 249.
2. Genevieve Lipsett-Skinner, "Does the End Justify the Brutality of Bulldogging These Unoffending Steers?" *Calgary Daily Herald*, September 4, 1912, p. 7.
3. Humane Activities Office, International Rodeo Association, *A Humane Look at Professional Rodeo*, p. 6.
4. Joanne Enevoldsen, public relations and education director, Calgary Humane Society, Calgary, Alberta, Canada, to author, August 11, 1978.
5. Westermeier, "Cowboy Sports," p. 249.
6. D. J. A. Cross, honourary associate, Calgary Exhibition and Stampede, Calgary, Alberta, Canada, to author, May 4, 1979.
7. Westermeier, "Cowboy Sports," p. 249.
8. G. P. Putnam, "Pendleton Round-Up; A Classic of American Sport," *Outlook*, October 25, 1922, p. 331.
9. Westermeier, "Cowboy Sports," p. 246.
10. "Rodeos Again in Spotlight," *Union* (Walla Walla, Wash.), August 27, 1926, p. 1.
11. Ibid.
12. Ibid.
13. "Rodeo Must Go, Humane Group Rules," *Christian Science Monitor*, Pacific ed., October 19, 1926, p. 6.
14. *Program of Events, Prize List and Rules for Prescott Frontier Days Celebration*, Prescott, Ariz., July 1–4, 1928, p. 3.
15. *Souvenir Program*, National Western Horse Show and Rodeo, Denver, Colo., January 16–23, 1932, p. 25.

16. Mary Lucile Deaton, "The History of Rodeo" (Master's thesis, University of Texas at Austin, 1952), p. 54; Clifford P. Westermeier, *Man, Beast, Dust—The Story of Rodeo*, p. 243.

17. Professional Rodeo Cowboys Association, Inc., *Articles of Incorporation, By-laws and Rules*, 1983, pp. 73, 75; International Rodeo Association, Inc., *Rules and By-laws*, 21st ed., 1981, p. 97.

18. *Senate Bill No. 476*, California Legislature, 52nd Session, Sacramento, Calif., January 20, 1937; *Journal of the Senate during the 52nd Session of the Legislature of the State of California*, pp. 267–3487 passim; California Law Library, Sacramento, Calif., to author, November 29, 1982.

19. Westermeier, *Man, Beast, Dust*, p. 243.

20. "Secretary's Message," *RAA Bulletin*, n.s. 1, no. 5 (May, 1937), reprinted in *Hoofs and Horns* 6, no. 12 (June, 1937): 15.

21. Ibid.; Roswell C. McCrea, *The Humane Movement*, p. 148.

22. Wanden M. LaFarge, "No Turtles Need Apply," *Saturday Evening Post*, July 9, 1938, p. 46.

23. Robert M. Miller, D.V.M., "Is Rodeo a Cruel Sport?" *Western Horseman* 31, no. 2 (February, 1966): 99.

24. Professional Rodeo Cowboys Association, *Facts!* p. 25.

25. "Bill to Ban Hotshots in California," *Rodeo Sports News*, April 1, 1967, p. 5; "Public Hearing on California Anti-Rodeo Bill May 16," *Rodeo Sports News*, May 1, 1967, p. 1; "State Humane Association Opposes California Anti-Rodeo Bill," *Rodeo Sports News*, May 15, 1967, p. 1; "California Prod Bill Killed in Committee," *Rodeo Sports News*, June 1, 1967; p. 1.

26. James Robey, "All Outdoors," *Dayton (Ohio) Journal-Herald*, February 2, 1966, reprinted (under the title "Despite Negative Legislation Ohio Rodeos Continue") in *Rodeo Sports News*, March 15, 1966, p. 3.

27. *An Act* (Amended House Bill No. 541), 106th General Assembly, Regular Session, Ohio General Assembly, Columbus, Ohio, 1965–66, p. 3.

28. Humane Activities Office, International Rodeo Association, *A Humane Look at Professional Rodeo*, pp. 5, 7; Ellen Boyle, president, International Rodeo Fans, Yonkers, N.Y., to author, September 6, 1978.

29. "Repealer Bill Introduced in Ohio," *Rodeo Sports News*, February 1, 1967, p. 1.

30. "House Committee Votes 'Do Pass' Ohio Amendment," *Rodeo Sports News*, April 15, 1967, p. 1.

31. "Ohio Law Found Unconstitutional," *Rodeo Sports News*, June 1, 1967, pp. 1, 7.

32. Jean Tucker, "Horse Show Curbs? Senate Says 'Nay'!" *Hartford Courant*, March 8, 1967, p. 1; "In Connecticut House It's a Different Story," *Rodeo Sports News*, April 1, 1967, p. 4.

CHAPTER 12

1. Gerald Carson, *Men, Beasts, and Gods*, pp. 156–69. (quote p. 169).

2. William Alan Swallow, *Quality of Mercy*, p. 166; Robert W. Fenwick, "Controversy over Rodeo Flares Anew," *Denver Post*, August 15, 1971, p. 33.

3. Humane Society of the United States, *Policy Statement.*

4. Ibid.

5. Henry S. Salt, *Animals' Rights Considered in Relation to Social Progress.*

6. Ellen Boyle, president, International Rodeo Fans, Yonkers, N.Y., to author, September 6, 1978; Lee Boccagni, "Out of the East," *Rodeo Sports News,* July 15, 1971, p. 2.

7. "Ride 'em Cowboy—Gently," *Newsweek,* June 28, 1971, p. 83; "Despite Humane Hasslers, Garden Pays Off Big," *Rodeo Sports News,* July 15, 1971, p. 1.

8. Charlene Drennon, director—West Coast, Humane Society of the United States, San Francisco, Calif., to author, September 5, 1978.

9. Humane Society of the United States, *Special Report on Rodeos,* p. 5.

10. "Ride 'em Cowboy—Gently," p. 83.

11. Robert M. Miller, D.V.M., "Is Rodeo a Cruel Sport?" *Western Horseman* 31, no. 2 (February, 1966): 99.

12. "Misleading Humane Groups Must Be Exposed," *Rodeo News* 10, no. 6 (June, 1970): 19, reprinted in Humane Activities Office, International Rodeo Association, *A Humane Look at Professional Rodeo,* rev. ed., p. 3; "The Catholic Brochure That Misrepresents," *Rodeo News* 7, no. 5 (May, 1967): 32, reprinted in Humane Activities Office, International Rodeo Association, *A Humane Look at Professional Rodeo,* p. 5.

13. Gerald Carson, *Men, Beasts, and Gods,* p. 125.

14. Humane Activities Office, International Rodeo Association, *A Humane Look at Professional Rodeo,* p. 2.

15. Friends of Animals, Inc., *Rodeo Brochure.*

16. Professional Rodeo Cowboys Association, *Facts!* p. 3.

17. "Special Report on Rodeos," *The Ark* 43, no. 3 (Christmas, 1975): 54–59; "Animal Lovers Spur Drive to Outlaw Rodeo" (Associated Press), *Los Angeles Times,* August 3, 1973, sec. 1, p. 4.

18. Humane Society of the United States, *Special Report on Rodeos,* p. 3; Professional Rodeo Cowboys Association, *Facts!* p. 3; "Organized Fight Waged in Colorado," *Rodeo Sports News,* May 15, 1973, pp. 1, 3.

19. Brian E. Shiffman, "A Report on Effects of Roping Stress Related to Rodeo Calves" (research paper, California Polytechnic State University," 1975), pp. vi–45 passim.

20. Ibid., pp. 58–61.

21. Edwin Shrake, "Horsing Around with Bull," *Sports Illustrated,* December 3, 1973, p. 46.

22. Interview with Warren Cox, director of animal protection, American Humane Association, at Denver, Colo., September 15, 1978.

23. Peter Singer, *Animal Liberation,* p. 243.

24. Interview with Warren Cox, September 15, 1978.

25. Interview with Bob Eidson, executive vice president, Professional Rodeo Cowboys Association, at Denver, Colo., September 14, 1978.

CHAPTER 13

1. *Contest Rules and Local Rules*, Sheridan-Wyo Rodeo, Sheridan, Wyo., July 18–20, 1934, back page.
2. C. M. Black, "Suicide Circuit," *Collier's*, October 26, 1940, p. 41.
3. Ulrich Calvosa, "Cowboys Are Crazy," *Collier's*, October 5, 1946, p. 24.
4. Douglas Kent Hall, *Let 'Er Buck!* p. 103.
5. "Frontier Sketches," *Denver Field and Farm*, July 8, 1899, p. 6.
6. "Stock Notes," *Las Animas* (Colo.) *Leader*, December 15, 1882, p. 3.
7. "A Cow-Boy Contest," reprint from *New York Herald* in *Rocky Mountain News*, January 4, 1886, p. 7.
8. "Frontier Fancies," *Denver Field and Farm*, July 4, 1896, p. 6.
9. Clifford P. Westermeier, "Seventy-five Years of Rodeo in Colorado," *Colorado Magazine*, 28, no. 1 (January, 1951): 15.
10. "The News of the Day," *Denver Republican*, September 27, 1887, p. 4.
11. "Grand Cowboy Tournament" (advertisement), *Denver Republican*, October 14, 1887, p. 8; *Corbett & Ballenger's Fifteenth Annual Denver City Directory for 1887*, p. 146; "Cowboy Tournament To-Day," *Denver Republican*, October 14, 1887, p. 8.
12. "Plainsmen Playing," *Rocky Mountain News*, September 7, 1890, p. 5.
13. "A Novel Race," *Stock Grower and Farmer* (Las Vegas, N.M.T.), November 26, 1892, p. 4; "Cowboys Awarded Prizes," *Denver Republican*, July 2, 1893, p. 2.
14. "The Summer Fair," *Calgary Weekly Herald*, May 17, 1893, p. 4.
15. Ellsworth Collings and Alma Miller England, *The 101 Ranch*, pp. 142–43.
16. Clifford P. Westermeier, "Seventy-five Years of Rodeo in Colorado," *Colorado Magazine* 28, no. 2 (April, 1951): 143.
17. Arthur Chapman, "Rodeo Dollars," *World's Work* 60 (July, 1931): 28.
18. Ibid., p. 30.
19. Clifford P. Westermeier, *Man, Beast, Dust—The Story of Rodeo*, p. 303.
20. Clifford P. Westermeier, "Seventy-five Years of Rodeo in Colorado," *Colorado Magazine* 28, no. 3 (July, 1951): 220.
21. "Rodeo: Riders Bring Wild West Thrills to Jaded Easterners," *News Week*, October 21, 1933, p. 17.
22. Ibid., pp. 17–18.
23. "The Wild West in New York City," *Literary Digest*, October 24, 1936, p. 36.
24. "Career Cowboys," *Time*, October 16, 1939, p. 59.
25. Westermeier, *Man, Beast, Dust*, p. 409.
26. Rodeo Cowboys' Association, *Articles of Association, By-Laws, and Rules*, 1945, p. 4.
27. "Cowboys Ask Higher Pay, Delay Rodeo," *Nevada State Journal*, July 5, 1949, p. 12; "Rodeo Association May Bar Pro Cowboys in the Future, As Result of $4,000 Rhubarb," *Nevada State Journal*, July 6, 1949, p. 2.
28. "Rodeo Association May Bar Pro Cowboys," p. 2; "Keep the Rodeo" (editorial), *Nevada State Journal*, July 6, 1949.
29. J. A. Burkhart, "The Cowpoke Is Always Broke," *Nation*, September 9, 1950, p. 224.

30. Ibid., p. 225.
31. P. Friggens, "Rip-Roarin', R'arin' Rodeo," *Reader's Digest* 51 (October, 1947): 112.
32. Wanden M. LaFarge, "No Turtles Need Apply," *Saturday Evening Post*, July 9, 1938, p. 18; Professional Rodeo Cowboys Association, *President's Year-End Report to Membership*, 1983, p. 1.
33. Approvals Department, Professional Rodeo Cowboys Association, *Year-End Report of Approved Team-Roping Rodeos in 1982*, p. 9.
34. Interview with Jack Hannum, Rodeo Administrator, Professional Rodeo Cowboys Association, at Colorado Springs, Colo. January 29, 1982.
35. Statistical information, National Media Department and Point Awards Department, Professional Rodeo Cowboys Association, Colorado Springs, Colo., January, 1983.

CHAPTER 14

1. John L. Balderston, *New York World* [n.d., 1924], as quoted in "London All Worked Up over an All American Rodeo," *Literary Digest*, July 26, 1924, p. 44.
2. "PRCA and the World All Around Champion Cowboy Tom Ferguson," *Rodeo Sports News*, Championship Edition, 1977, p. 15.
3. "Lybbert Passes $100,000 in Regular Season, Leads All-Around Contenders into the Finals," *PRCA News Release*, November 8, 1982; "Lybbert Cracks $100K in Single-Season Arena Winnings," *Prorodeo Sports News*, November 17, 1982, p. 4; "History-Making, Record-Breaking National Finals Completes Professional Rodeo's 1982 Season," *PRCA News Release*, December 13, 1982.
4. "Trophy Donors for 1939," *RAA Bulletin*, n.s. 3, no. 14 [12] (December, 1939), in *Hoofs and Horns* 9, no. 7 (January, 1940): 18.
5. "Trophy Donors Are Needed," *RAA Bulletin*, n.s. 6, no. 2 (February, 1942), in *Hoofs and Horns* 11, no. 9 (March, 1942): 22.
6. Professional Rodeo Cowboys Association, *President's Year-End Report to Membership*, 1983, p. 1.
7. Professional Rodeo Cowboys Association, *Minutes of Board of Directors Meeting*, Oklahoma City, Okla., December 7–11, 1981, Item No. 3052, p. 4.
8. One award in 1959—an oil painting donated by B. Kalland, Santa Maria, California—was designated for the *fifth-place* winner in the all-around, while in 1975 and 1976 the Triple H, Inc., Los Lunas, New Mexico, contributed a turquoise watchband to award to the cowboy placing fifteenth in the bareback-bronc riding. See "Championship Donors for 1959," *Rodeo Sports News*, Championship Edition, 1960, p. 69; "World Championship Awards," *Rodeo Sports News*, Championship Edition, 1976, p. 90; "PRCA and World Championship Awards," *Rodeo Sports News*, Championship Edition, 1977, p. 108.
9. "1951 Donors for Point Award Winners," *Buckboard* 7, no. 8 (January, 1952): 4; "Championship Donors for 1959," *Rodeo Sports News*, Championship Edition, 1960, p. 69; "Awards Pledged for 1969 Rodeo Cowboys Association Champions," *Rodeo Sports News*, Championship Edition, 1970, p. 115; "1980 PRCA Championship Awards," *Prorodeo Sports News*, Championship Edition, 1981, p. 104.

10. Interview with Stub Hill, manager—sales and promotions, PRCA Properties, Inc., at Colorado Springs, Colo., March 8, 1983; interview with Mel Parkhurst, rodeo and equine team manager, Blue Bell, Inc., Greensboro, N.C., at Colorado Springs, Colo., March 18, 1983.

11. "Special Awards," *Prorodeo Sports News*, Championship Edition, 1983, p. 111.

12. "1977 PRCA Championship Awards," *Rodeo Sports News*, Championship Edition, 1978, p. 110; "PRCA Championship Awards," *Prorodeo Sports News*, Championship Edition, 1979, p. 111; Frontier Airlines, Inc., Denver, Colo., to author, March 30, 1978.

13. "Frontier Steps Up to Support Rodeo," *News Release*, Frontier Airlines, Denver, Colo. [n.d.]; "World Championship Awards," *Rodeo Sports News*, Championship Edition, 1974, p. 57; "World Championship Awards," *Rodeo Sports News*, Championship Edition, 1976, p. 90; "PRCA and World Championship Awards," *Rodeo Sports News*, Championship Edition, 1977, p. 108; "Special Awards," *Prorodeo Sports News*, Championship Edition, 1981, p. 112; "Special Awards," *Prorodeo Sports News*, Championship Edition, 1982, p. 112.

14. Interviews with J. Kelly Riley, rodeo team manager, R. J. Reynolds Tobacco Co., Winston-Salem, N.C., at Denver, Colo., January 14, 1981, and by telephone, February 2, 1982.

15. "Special Awards," *Rodeo Sports News*, Championship Edition, 1972, p. 86; "Winston Rodeo Awards," *Rodeo Sports News*, Championship Edition, 1973, p. 86; ibid., Championship Edition, 1974, p. 40; ibid., Championship Edition, 1975, p. 12; ibid., Championship Edition, 1976, p. 11; ibid., Championship Edition, 1978, p. 113; ibid., *Prorodeo Sports News*, Championship Edition, 1979, p. 110; ibid., Championship Edition, 1980, p. 110.

16. Interview with J. Kelly Riley at Denver, Colo., January 14, 1981, and at Colorado Springs, Colo., March 17, 1983; "Winston Revises Awards Program," *Prorodeo Sports News*, January 23, 1980, pp. 1, 3; interview with Stub Hill, March 8, 1983; "Winston Rodeo Series," *Official Program*, National Finals Rodeo, Oklahoma City, Okla., December 4–12, 1982, p. 141.

17. Sandy Teague, "Winston Scoreboards on the Move," *Prorodeo Inside*, May, 1978, pp. 5–9 passim.

18. "The Circuit System," *Rodeo Sports News*, Championship Edition, 1976, p. 136.

19. Richard B. Barron, supervisor, brand projects, Schlitz & Schlitz Malt Liquor, Milwaukee, Wis., to author, March 9, 1978.

20. "1977 PRCA Championship Awards," p. 110.

21. Richard B. Barron to author, March 9, 1978.

22. "1,000,000 Prize Money Agreement with Coors Brewery," *Prorodeo Sports News*, April 2, 1980, p. 11; Professional Rodeo Cowboys Association, *1981 Official Pro Rodeo Media Guide*, p. 213.

23. Interview with Stub Hill, March 8, 1983.

24. Address by Peter Coors, senior vice president—marketing, Adolph Coors Company, Golden, Colo., at 1980 World Champions' Awards Banquet, Denver, Colo., January 14, 1981.

25. Professional Rodeo Cowboys Association Properties, Inc./Adolph Coors Company, *Addendum I* to Contract, 1980.

26. "$1,000,000 Prize Money Agreement," p. 11; interview with Stub Hill, March 8, 1983.

27. Professional Rodeo Cowboys Association, *Official Pro Rodeo Media Guide 1978*, p. 143.

28. "Black Velvet Sets Award for Stock Contractors," *Rodeo Sports News*, February 22, 1978, p. 1.

29. "Bucking Stock of the Year," *Prorodeo Sports News*, Championship Edition, 1980, p. 66; ibid., Championship Edition, 1981, p. 64.

30. "Special Awards," *Prorodeo Sports News*, Championship Edition, 1980, p. 114; ibid., Championship Edition, 1981, p. 112.

31. Interview with Stub Hill, March 8, 1983.

32. "Special Awards," *Prorodeo Sports News*, Championship Edition, 1981, p. 112; ibid., Championship Edition, 1982, p. 112.

33. "PRCA Announces New Television Format," *PRCA News Release*, April 26, 1982; "PRCA Establishes Television Production Company," *Prorodeo Sports News*, May 5, 1982, pp. 1, 4; "Special Awards," *Prorodeo Sports News*, Championship Edition, 1983, p. 111.

34. "National Finals Rodeo," *Rodeo Sports News*, Championship Edition, 1975, p. 9; "PRCA Championship Awards," *Prorodeo Sports News*, Championship Edition, 1983, p. 58; "Hesston National Finals Radio Station List," *PRCA News Release*, November 29, 1982; interview with Martin Carmichael, PRCA television legal consultant, New York, N.Y., at Colorado Springs, Colo., April 1, 1983; interview with Bob Eidson, executive vice president, Professional Rodeo Cowboys Association, at Colorado Springs, Colo., April 1, 1983.

35. Interview with Bruce Ford, conducted by Larry Mahan during the telecast of the last (tenth) go-round of the National Finals Rodeo, Oklahoma City, Okla., December 12, 1982.

Bibliography

BOOKS, PAMPHLETS, ESSAYS

Adams, Ramon F. *The Old-Time Cowhand*, New York: Macmillan Co., 1961.

Atherton, Lewis. *The Cattle Kings*, Lincoln, Neb.: University of Nebraska Press, 1972.

Branch, Douglas. *The Cowboy and His Interpreters*. New York: D. Appleton & Co., 1926.

Carson, Gerald. *Men, Beasts, and Gods*. New York: Charles Scribner's Sons, 1972.

Clancy, Foghorn (Fred M.). *My Fifty Years in Rodeo*. San Antonio: Naylor Co. 1952.

Cleland, Robert Glass. *The Cattle on a Thousand Hills*. San Marino, Calif.: Huntington Library, 1941.

Collings, Ellsworth, and Alma Miller England. *The 101 Ranch*. Norman: University of Oklahoma Press, 1971.

Corbett & Ballenger's Fifteenth Annual Denver City Directory for 1887. Denver: Corbett & Ballenger, 1887.

Cox, James, et al. *Historical and Biographical Record of the Cattle Industry and the Cattlemen of Texas and Adjacent Territory*. Saint Louis: Woodward & Tiernan Printing Co., 1894. Reprint. New York: Antiquarian Press, 1959.

Crawford, William. *The Bronc Rider*. New York: G. P. Putnam's Sons, 1965.

Dale, Edward Everett. *Cow Country*. Norman: University of Oklahoma Press, 1942.

Deaton, Mary Lucile. "The History of Rodeo." Master's thesis, University of Texas at Austin, 1952.

Dobie, J. Frank. *The Longhorns*. New York: Grosset & Dunlap, 1941.

Duffus, R. L. *The Santa Fe Trail*. London, Toronto, and New York: Longmans Green & Co., 1931.

Duke, Cordia Sloan, and Joe B. Frantz. *6000 Miles of Fence—Life on the XIT Ranch of Texas*. Austin: University of Texas Press, 1961.

Editors of Time-Life Books. *The Cowboys*. New York: Time-Life Books, 1973.
———. *This Fabulous Century*. Vol. 4, *1930–1940*. New York: Time-Life Books, 1969.

Friends of Animals, Inc. *Rodeo Brochure*. N.p., n.d.

Furlong, Charles Wellington. *Let 'Er Buck: A Story of the Passing of the Old West*. New York: G. P. Putnam's Sons, 1921.

Gipson, Fred. *Fabulous Empire: Colonel Zack Miller's Story*. Boston: Houghton Mifflin Co., 1946.

Godlovitch, Stanley, Roslind Godlovitch, and John Harris, eds. *Animals, Men and Morals*. New York: Taplinger Publishing Co., 1972.

Haley, J. Evetts. *Charles Goodnight—Cowman and Plainsman*. Norman: University of Oklahoma Press, 1949.
———. *The XIT Ranch of Texas and the Early Days of the Llano Estacado*. Norman: University of Oklahoma Press, 1953.

Hall, Douglas Kent. *Let 'Er Buck!* New York: Saturday Review Press/E. P. Dutton & Co., 1973.

Hanesworth, Robert D. *Daddy of 'Em All*. Cheyenne, Wyo.: Flintlock Publishing Co., 1967.

Howard, Robert West, and Oren Arnold. *Rodeo: Last Frontier of the Old West*. New York: New American Library, 1961.

Humane Society of the United States. *Special Report on Rodeos*. N.p., August, 1975.

International Rodeo Association. Humane Activities Office. *A Humane Look at Professional Rodeo*. Rev. ed. Nashville: International Rodeo Association, May, 1973.

Journal of the Senate during the 52nd Session of the Legislature of the State of California. Sacramento: State Printing Office, 1938.

Kegley, Max. *Rodeo—The Sport of the Cow Country*. New York: Hastings House, 1942.

Lamb, Gene. *Rodeo Back of the Chutes*. Denver: Bell Press, 1956.

McCrea, Roswell C. *The Humane Movement*. College Park, Md.: McGrath Publishing Co., 1969.

Mansfield, Toots. *Calf Roping*. Colorado Springs: Western Horseman, 1961.

Morris, John W. *Ghost Towns of Oklahoma*. Norman: University of Oklahoma Press, 1977.

Osgood, Ernest Staples. *The Day of the Cattleman*. Chicago: University of Chicago Press, 1970.

Porter, Willard H. *Roping and Riding: Fast Horses and Short Ropes*. New York: A. S. Barnes & Co., 1975.

Professional Rodeo Cowboys Association. *Facts!* Colorado Springs: Professional Rodeo Cowboys Association, 1982.

Reader's Guide to Periodical Literature. New York: H. W. Wilson Co., 1900–. Vol. 11, *July, 1937–June, 1939,* edited by Alice M. Dougan, Bertha Joel, and Jeanette Moore-Smith, 1939. Vol. 21, *March, 1957–February, 1959,* edited by Sarita Robinson, 1959.

Rollins, Philip Ashton. *The Cowboy.* New York: Charles Scribner's Sons, 1927.

Russell, Don. *The Wild West: A History of the Wild West Shows.* Fort Worth: Amon Carter Museum of Western Art, 1970.

Salt, Henry S. *Animals' Rights Considered in Relation to Social Progress.* New York and London: Macmillan & Co., 1894.

Savitt, Sam. *Rodeo—Cowboys, Bulls and Broncos.* Garden City, N.Y.: Doubleday & Co., 1963.

Schnell, Fred. *Rodeo! The Suicide Circuit.* New York: Rand McNally, 1971.

Sell, Henry Blackman, and Victor Weybright. *Buffalo Bill and the Wild West.* New York: Oxford University Press, 1955.

Shiffman, Brian E. "A Report on Effects of Roping Stress Related to Rodeo Calves." Research paper, California Polytechnic State University, 1975.

Singer, Peter. *Animal Liberation.* New York: Random House, 1975.

Steele, Zulma. *Angel in Top Hat.* New York: Harper & Brothers, 1942.

Swallow, William Alan. *Quality of Mercy,* Boston: Mary Mitchell Humane Fund, 1963.

Tippette, Giles. *The Brave Men.* New York: Macmillan Co., 1972.

Westermeier, Clifford P. *Man, Beast, Dust—The Story of Rodeo.* Denver: World Press, 1947.

———. *Trailing the Cowboy.* Caldwell, Idaho: Caxton Printers, 1955.

The World Almanac and Book of Facts 1983. New York: Newspaper Enterprise Association, 1981.

ARTICLES

Advertisement (Grand Cowboy Tournament). *Denver Republican,* October 14, 1887, p. 8.

Advertisement (Rodeo School). *Prorodeo Sports News,* April 19, 1978, p. 18.

Advertisement (World's Championship Rodeo, Madison Square Garden, New York, N.Y.). *Hoofs and Horns* 7, no. 2 (August, 1937): 21.

"All Soldier Rodeo." *Hoofs and Horns* 12, no. 5 (November, 1942).

"Animal Lovers Spur Drive to Outlaw Rodeo." (Associated Press). *Los Angeles Times,* August 3, 1973, sec. 1, p. 4.

Armstrong, Jerry. "The Collegiate Cowboy's Column." *Western Horseman* 7, no. 4, (July–August, 1942); 7, no. 5 (September–October, 1942); 9, no. 3 (May–June, 1944); 9, no. 4 (July–August, 1944); 10, no. 1 (January–February, 1945); 10, no. 4 (July–August, 1945); 11, no. 2 (March–April, 1946); 12, no. 1 (January–February, 1947); 12, no. 3 (May–June, 1947).

————. "Picked Up in the Rodeo Arena." *Western Horseman* 13, no. 3 (May–June, 1948); 14, no. 3 (March, 1949); 14, no. 5 (May, 1949); 16, no. 7. (July, 1951); 17, no. 1 (January, 1952); 20, no. 7 (July, 1955).

"Army Rodeos." *Hoofs and Horns* 15, no. 4 (October, 1945).

"Awards Pledged for 1969 Rodeo Cowboys Association Champions." *Rodeo Sports News*, Championship Edition, 1970, p. 115.

"Baby Doll the Rodeo Cowboys All Love." *Life*, November 8, 1957, p. 94.

Baumann, John. "Experiences of a Cow-Boy." *Lippincott's Magazine* 38 (August, 1886).

————. "On a Western Ranche." *Fortnightly Review*, April 1, 1887.

Beckner, B. "Rodeo." *Popular Mechanics* 46 (August, 1926): 190–200.

"Bill to Ban Hotshots in California." *Rodeo Sports News*, April 1, 1967, p. 5.

Black, C. M. "Suicide Circuit." *Collier's*, October 26, 1940, p. 41.

"Black Velvet Sets Award for Stock Contractors." *Rodeo Sports News*, February 22, 1978, p. 1.

Boatright, Mody C. "The American Rodeo." *American Quarterly* 16, no. 2 (Summer, 1964).

Boccagni, Lee. "Out of the East." *Rodeo Sports News*, July 15, 1971, p. 2.

Bouvee, Sgt. "Red." "Rodeo in Italy." *Western Horseman* 9, no. 5 (September–October, 1944).

Britt, A. "Ride 'im, Cowboy!" *Outlook*, September 26, 1923, pp. 136–39.

"Broadway Cowboys." *Time*, October 21, 1935, p. 52.

"Broadway Rodeo." *Time*, October 18, 1937, p. 57.

Brody, Tom C. "The Roughest Rides to Richest." *Sports Illustrated*, December 18, 1967, p. 22.

"Bronc-Busting in Gandhi-land." *Western Horseman* 10, no. 2 (March–April, 1945).

"The Broncho Busters' Union." *Denver Republican*, September 10, 1910.

"Buckaroos 'Down Under.'" *Western Horseman* 9, no. 1 (January–February, 1944).

"Bucking Stock of the Year." *Prorodeo Sports News*, Championship Edition, 1980, p. 66; Championship Edition, 1981, p. 64.

Burkhart, J. A. "The Cowpoke Is Always Broke." *Nation*, September 9, 1950, pp. 224–25.

"Buster Champion Injured at Big Rodeo in Springs." *Rocky Mountain News*, August 17, 1922, p. 3.

"California Prod Bill Killed in Committee." *Rodeo Sports News*, June 1, 1967, p. 1.

Calvosa, Ulrich. "Cowboys Are Crazy." *Collier's*, October 5, 1946, pp. 22–24.

"Career Cowboys." *Time*, October 16, 1939, p. 59.

Carson, Gerald. "The Late, Late Frontier." *American Heritage* 23 (April, 1972).

"The Catholic Brochure That Misrepresents." *Rodeo News* 7, no. 5 (May, 1967): 32. Reprinted in Humane Activities Office, International Rodeo Association, *A Humane Look at Professional Rodeo*, rev. ed. (Nashville, Tenn.: International Rodeo Association, May, 1973), p. 5.

"Champion Cowboy." *Time*, March 8, 1954, p. 55.

"Champions 'Crowned' as Rodeo Ends with Thrill Packed Show." *Denver Post*, January 18, 1942, p. 10.

"Championship Donors for 1959." *Rodeo Sports News*, Championship Edition, 1960, p. 69.

"Champ Rider." *Life*, October 22, 1951.

Chance, Tabitha. "There's Mindy's Dad on the Trombone." *TV Guide*, November 29, 1980, pp. 14–16.

Chapman, Arthur. "The Cowboy of Today." *World's Work* 8 (September, 1904).

———. "Rodeo Dollars." *World's Work* 60 (July, 1931).

Christopher, Edmund. "World's Roughest Sport." *Holiday* 19 (June, 1956).

"The Circuit System." *Rodeo Sports News*, Championship Edition, 1976, p. 136.

Clancy, Foghorn (Fred M.). "Cowboy Sports and Frontier Contests." *Billboard*, March 17, 1923.

———. "Rodeo Fans of America Proposed." *Hoofs and Horns* 10, no. 10 (April, 1941).

Claussen, Bruce F., M.D. "The Sore-Armed Bareback Bronc Rider." *Prorodeo Sports News*, July 22, 1981, p. 3.

Clinton, Bruce. "Are Cowboys Athletes?" *Hoofs and Horns* 8, no. 9 (March, 1939).

———. "Modern Cowboy Contestants." *Western Horseman* 5, no. 4 (July–August, 1940).

———. "Rodeo Conscious." *Hoofs and Horns* 10, no. 8 (February, 1941).

———. "Rodeos—The New Big-Time Business and Sport." *Hoofs and Horns* 6, no. 2 (July, 1936).

"Clyde Burk Rides On." *Hoofs and Horns* 14, no. 9 (March, 1945).

Coburn, Walt. "Rodeos Don't Die." *Hoofs and Horns* 13, no. 9 (March, 1944).

"Cody's Cyclone." *Omaha Daily Herald*, May 20, 1883, p. 8.

Cole, Eddie G. "From the I.R.A. Office." *Hoofs and Horns* 26, no. 8 (March, 1957).

"College Rodeo." *Time*, May 21, 1951, p. 75.

Connelly, Lex. "Founding and First Years of National Finals Rodeo." *Persim-mon Hill* 4, no. 1 (Summer, 1973).

"Cooperation with Cowboys." *Hoofs and Horns* 6, no. 11 (May, 1937).

"The Cowboy, Like the Indian, Has Passed His Hey-Day of Life Here." *Calgary Daily Herald*, September 4, 1912, p. 7.

"A Cow-boy Contest." Reprint from *New York Herald* in *Rocky Mountain News*, January 4, 1886, p. 7.

"Cowboys and Wild Horses." *Denver Republican*, October 15, 1887, p. 1.

"Cowboys Ask Higher Pay, Delay Rodeo." *Nevada State Journal*, July 5, 1949, p. 12.

"Cowboys Awarded Prizes." *Denver Republican*, July 2, 1893, p. 2.

"The Cowboys of the Western Plains and Their Horses." Reprint from *Providence Journal* in *Cheyenne Daily Leader*, October 3, 1882, p. 4.

"Cowboys Turtle Association," *Hoofs and Horns* 6, no. 7 (December, 1936); 7, no. 10 (April, 1938); 9, no. 8 (February, 1940); 9, no. 11 (May, 1940); 10, no. 2 (August, 1940); 12, no. 1 (July, 1942).

"Cowboy Tournament To-day." *Denver Republican*, October 14, 1887, p. 8.

"Cowboy Union Fines Fifty in Ogden Show." *Salt Lake Tribune*, July 22, 1939, p. 17.

"Cowpokes Form Union to Improve Standards." *Denver Post*, January 20, 1932, p. 8.

Cremer, Leo, et al. "Rodeos of Today." *Hoofs and Horns* 9, no. 1 (July, 1939).

"C.T.A. Headquarters Moved." *Hoofs and Horns* 11, no. 9 (March, 1942).

Cuddy, Roy. "Rodeo Fans of America." *Hoofs and Horns* 10, no. 12 (June, 1941).

Deahl, William E., Jr. "Nebraska's Unique Contribution to the Entertainment World." *Nebraska History* 49, no. 3 (Autumn, 1968).

"Denver Stock Show to Stress Role of Ranchers in National Defense." *Denver Post*, January 5, 1942, p. 8.

"Despite Humane Hasslers, Garden Pays Off Big." *Rodeo Sports News*, July 15, 1971, p. 1.

"Discussion of Some Rodeo Questions." *RAA Bulletin*, n.s. 7, no. 3 (March, 1943), in *Hoofs and Horns* 12, no. 10 (April, 1943).

"Dodged about the Bull." *Rocky Mountain News*, September 30, 1895, p. 1.

Earle, G. W. "Ride 'im, Cowboy." *Popular Mechanics* 53 (June, 1930): 906–11.

"Editor's Page." *Western Horseman* 3, no. 5 (September–October, 1938).

"Empty Saddles." *Wild Bunch* 2, no. 2 (May, 1980): 8.

"Event Winners at Larger Rodeos." *Rodeo Sports News*, Championship Edition, 1969, p. 99.

Fain, Johnie, and Learah Cooper Morgan. "The Cowboy and the Rodeo." *Arizona Highways* 36, no. 2 (February, 1960).

"Fannye Lovelady Resigns." *Hoofs and Horns* 14, no. 11 (May, 1945).

"Fast Action Features Rodeo Opener." *Denver Post*, January 11, 1942, p. 2.

Fenwick, Robert W. "Controversy over Rodeo Flares Anew." *Denver Post*, August 15, 1971, p. 33.

"Field and Farm." *Denver Field and Farm*, May 15, 1886, p. 8.

"First 'Cowboy Union' Ever Organized Will Form in Denver." *Denver Post*, January 18, 1932, p. 5.

"First Finals Rodeo in '59." *Rodeo Sports News*, Championship Edition, 1959, p. 38.

Fort Collins Courier, April 12, 1883, p. 2.

Friggens, P. "Rip-Roarin', R'arin' Rodeo." *Reader's Digest* 51 (October, 1947): 111–14.

Froman, R. "Ornery Critters Are His Fortune." *Nation's Business* 40 (May, 1952): 56 ff.

"From the Secretary" (CTA). *Hoofs and Horns* 9, no. 2 (August, 1939); 10, no. 12 (June, 1941).

"From the Secretary" (RAA). *RAA Bulletin*, n.s. 5, no. 8 (September, 1941), in *Hoofs and Horns* 11, no. 4 (October, 1941); n.s. 9, no. 4 (April, 1945), in *Hoofs and Horns* 14, no. 11, (May, 1945).

"Frontier Fancies." *Denver Field and Farm*, July 4, 1896, p. 6.

"Frontier Sketches." *Denver Field and Farm*, July 8, 1899, p. 6.

"Frontier Steps Up to Support Rodeo." *News Release*, Frontier Airlines, Inc., Denver, 1978.

Gage, E. W. "Ride 'im Cowboy!" *Travel* 65 (June, 1935): 33–35 ff.

Garis, R. "Ride 'im Cowboy!" *New York Times Magazine*, October 8, 1950, pp. 20 ff.

Garland, Tex. "Chuck Wagon Chatter." *Rodeo Fans*, 3, no. 3 (March, 1944).

"A Generous Gift." *Hoofs and Horns* 13, no. 8 (February, 1944).

"Genuine Bull Fight." *Rocky Mountain News*, October 2, 1895, p. 6 (?—poor copy).

Glafcke, H. Editorial. *Cheyenne Daily Leader*, July 6, 1872, p. 4.

Goldstone, Patricia. "Rodeo Cowgirls on the Horns of a Dilemma." *Los Angeles Times*, November 7, 1980, pt. 5, pp. 12–14.

"Go West, Pardner." *Los Angeles Herald-Examiner*, September 28, 1980, sec. E, p. 6.

Grant, Don. "Curtailment of Horse Events." *Western Horseman* 7, no. 3 (May–June, 1942).

"Greatest Show in Neary 20 Years Attracts 25,000." *East Oregonian*, September 18, 1937, p. 1.

"Haircuts for Army Horses Pay Big Dividends." *Western Horseman* 12, no. 4 (July–August, 1942).

Hartwig, John E. "Is Rodeo History Repeating Itself?" *Billboard*, March 28, 1931, p. 17.

"Hesston National Finals Rodeo Station List." PRCA News Release, November 29, 1982.

"He Wants to Be a Cowboy." Stock Grower and Farmer (Las Vegas, N.M.T.), 8, no. 17, July 4, 1891, p. 10.

"History-Making, Record-Breaking National Finals Completes Professional Rodeo's 1982 Season." PRCA News Release, December 13, 1982.

Holme, Thomas. "A Cowboy's Life." Chatauquan 19 (November, 1894).

Hopkins, Ethel A. "Editorial Comments." Hoofs and Horns 5, no. 10 (March, 1936).

"The Horse World." Denver Field and Farm, May 20, 1893, p. 9; May 27, 1893, p. 9; June 17, 1893, p. 9; June 24, 1893, p. 9; July 1, 1893, p. 9.

"House Committee Votes 'Do Pass' Ohio Amendment." Rodeo Sports News, April 15, 1967, p. 1.

"The Humane Society." Denver Republican, October 15, 1887, p. 1.

"In Connecticut House It's a Different Story." Rodeo Sports News, April 1, 1967, p. 4.

"The Japs Take Over." Western Horseman 7, no. 3 (May–June, 1942).

"Justin Unveils Fully-Equipped Medical Center, Staffed by Athletic Trainer Don Andrews at '82 NFR." PRCA News Release, November 29, 1982.

"Keep the Rodeo." (Editorial). Nevada State Journal, July 6, 1949, p. 4.

Kinkead, Eugene F. "Cowboy Business." New Yorker, October 26, 1940.

LaFarge, Wanden M. "No Turtles Need Apply." Saturday Evening Post, July 9, 1938.

Letter from Directors, Rodeo Cowboys Association, Fort Worth, Tex., to Hugh Bennett (CTA secretary-treasurer 1936–40) and King Merritt (CTA steer-roping/team-tying director 1941–45), March 15, 1945. Reprinted in "RCA—Cowboy Organization Makes Changes," Hoofs and Horns 14, no. 11 (May, 1945).

Letter from J. D. McCormick, Council Grove, Kans., to Hugh Bennett (CTA secretary-treasurer 1936–40), December 14, 1939. Reprinted in Hoofs and Horns 9, no. 8 (February, 1940).

Letter from John "Buck" Taylor, Corsicana, Tex., to Hoofs and Horns magazine, Tucson, Ariz. Reprinted in "This and That," Hoofs and Horns 12, no. 6 (December, 1942).

Lipsett-Skinner, Genevieve. "Does the End Justify the Brutality of Bull-dogging These Unoffending Steers?" Calgary Daily Herald, September 4, 1912, p. 7.

Lofting, Colin. "How to Get Rich on a Horse." Saturday Evening Post, August 25, 1956.

"London All Worked Up over an All American Rodeo." Literary Digest, July 26, 1924.

Looney, Douglas C. "Getting in Step with Dad." *Sports Illustrated*, October 4, 1976, pp. 40–42.

"Lorena Trickey Bids World in General 'Good Morning.'" *Colorado Springs Gazette*, August 13, 1922, sec. 2, p. 1.

Lubenow, Gerald C. "Rodeo—The Soul of the Frontier." *Newsweek*, October 2, 1972, p. 72.

"Lybbert Cracks $100K in Single-Season Arena Winnings." *Prorodeo Sports News*, November 17, 1982, p. 4.

"Lybbert Passes $100,000 in Regular Season, Leads All-Around Contenders into the Finals." *PRCA News Release*, November 8, 1982.

McCann, L. P. "Ride 'em Cowboy!" *Sunset* 59 (September, 1927): 18–20.

Maddy, Herbert S. "Eastern Rodeos." *Hoofs and Horns* 4, no. 10 (March, 1935); 4, no. 12 (May, 1935).

Martin, Chuck. "The Place of Rodeos in National Defense." *Hoofs and Horns* 11, no. 9 (March, 1942).

Miller, Robert M., D.V.M. "Is Rodeo a Cruel Sport?" *Western Horseman* 31, no. 2 (February, 1966).

"Misleading Humane Groups Must be Exposed." *Rodeo News* 10, no. 6 (June, 1970): 19. Reprinted in Humane Activities Office, International Rodeo Association, *A Humane Look at Professional Rodeo*, rev. ed. (Nashville, Tenn.: International Rodeo Association, May, 1973), p. 3.

Morrow, Fred. "Trainer Tends Rodeo Pains; Spit Is Passé." *Rocky Mountain News*, January 22, 1981, p. 6.

Moser, Charlotte. "At $100,000 a Year, He's America's Top Cowboy." *Us*, April 18, 1978, pp. 65–67.

"Mr. Broken Bones." *Life*, September 15, 1961, pp. 87–90.

Muir, Jean. "Cowboys on the Campus." *Saturday Evening Post*, February 10, 1951.

"Myriad New Site . . . Sudden Death Out." *Prorodeo Sports News*, February 7, 1979, p. 1.

"National Finals: A Growth Industry." *Rodeo Sports News*, January 25, 1978, p. 4.

"National Finals Rodeo." *Rodeo Sports News*, Championship Edition, 1975, p. 9.

"National Finals Rodeo—1967." *Rodeo Sports News*, Championship Edition, 1968, p. 12.

"New Bronco Breed: Rodeo Cowboys." *Time*, September 2, 1974, p. 85.

"New Service Offered." *Hoofs and Horns* 6, no. 10 (April, 1937). (Misprinted on issue as vol. 11, no. 10.)

"The News of the Day." *Denver Republican*, September 27, 1887, p. 4.

"NFR and World Championships." *Rodeo Sports News*, May 1, 1976, p. 20.

Nimmo, Joseph, Jr. "The American Cow-Boy." *Harper's New Monthly Magazine* 73 (November, 1886).

"1980 PRCA Championship Awards." *Prorodeo Sports News*, Championship Edition, 1981, p. 104.

"1951 Donors for Point Award Winners." *Buckboard* 7, no. 8 (January, 1952).

"1977 PRCA Championship Awards." *Rodeo Sports News*, Championship Edition, 1978, p. 110.

"Non-Pro Rodeo Has No Future, Gardner Says." *Hoofs and Horns* 9, no. 2 (August, 1939).

"Notice." *Hoofs and Horns* 4, no. 7, (December, 1934).

"A Novel Race." *Stock Grower and Farmer* (Las Vegas, N.M.T.), November 26, 1892, p. 4.

"Ohio Law Found Unconstitutional." *Rodeo Sports News*, June 1, 1967, p. 1.

"$1,000,000 Prize Money Agreement with Coors Brewery." *Prorodeo Sports News*, April 2, 1980, p. 11.

"Organized Fight Waged in Colorado." *Rodeo Sports News*, May 15, 1973, p. 1.

"Out of the Wild West They Came." *Literary Digest*, October 19, 1935, p. 34.

"Parade in Ogden Will Open Pioneer Celebration Today." *Salt Lake Tribune*, July 21, 1939, clipping in scrapbook, Everett Bowman Collection, Prorodeo Hall of Champions.

"Paul Mayo and Judge Tolbirt Re-instated." *Rodeo Sports News*, June 15, 1964, p. 16.

"Plainsmen Playing." *Rocky Mountain News*, September 7, 1890, p. 5.

Porter, Willard H. "American Rodeo: Sport and Spectacle." *American West* 8, no. 4 (July, 1971).

———. "Readin', Writin' and Ropin'." *Western Horseman* 21, no. 7 (July, 1956).

Potter, Gib. "Trailering 40 Years Ago—Texas to Calgary." *Western Horseman* 33, no. 7 (July, 1968).

Prattle, Jane. "A Thinking Man's Game." *Prorodeo Sports News*, May 31, 1978, p. 4.

"PRCA and World All Around Champion Cowboy Tom Ferguson." *Rodeo Sports News*, Championship Edition, 1977, p. 15.

"PRCA and World Championship Awards." *Rodeo Sports News*, Championship Edition, 1977, p. 108.

"PRCA Announces New Television Format." *PRCA News Release*, April 26, 1982.

"PRCA Approves Pro Judging System." *Rodeo Sports News*, October 19, 1977, p. 1.

"PRCA Championship Awards." *Prorodeo Sports News*, Championship Edition, 1979, p. 111; Championship Edition, 1983, p. 58.

"PRCA Establishes Television Production Company." *Prorodeo Sports News*, May 5, 1982, p. 1.

"PRCA Pro Rodeo 1977." *Prorodeo Sports News*, Championship Edition, 1978, p. 4.

"Program 'Most Comprehensive' for Wrangler." *Prorodeo Sports News*, February 10, 1982, p. 6.

"Pro Official Staff to Increase in 1983." *Prorodeo Sports News*, November 17, 1982, p. 1.

Pruett, Gene. "Cowboys Turtle Association to Big Time Corporation." *Persimmon Hill* 4, no. 1 (Summer, 1973).

"Public Hearing on California Anti-Rodeo Bill May 16." *Rodeo Sports News*, May 1, 1967, p. 1.

Putnam, G. P. "Pendleton Round-Up; A Classic of American Sport." *Outlook*, October 24, 1922, pp. 330–31.

Ralph, Julian. "A Talk with a Cowboy." *Harper's Weekly*, April 16, 1892, p. 379.

"RCA—Cowboy Organization Makes Changes." *Hoofs and Horns* 14, no. 11 (May, 1945).

"RCA—Negotiations Still Pending Regarding Consolidation of IRA, NRA and RCA Point Awarding Systems." *Hoofs and Horns* 14, no. 12 (June, 1945).

"RCA Point Awarding System." *Hoofs and Horns* 14, no. 11 (May, 1945).

"Real Job Lies Ahead for Rodeo Profession." *RAA Bulletin*, n.s. 6, no. 3 (March, 1942), in *Hoofs and Horns* 11, no. 10 (April, 1942).

"Repealer Bill Introduced in Ohio." *Rodeo Sports News*, February 1, 1967, p. 1.

"Report of Activities under New Business Manager to Be Made Soon." *Hoofs and Horns* 15, no. 1 (July, 1945).

"Report of First Three Months['] Activities under New Manager." *Buckboard* 1, no. 1 (July, 1945).

"Ride 'em Cowboy!" *Popular Mechanics* 72 (October, 1939): 497–504 ff.

"Ride 'em Cowboy—Gently." *Newsweek*, June 28, 1971, p. 83.

Rigdon, Skipper. "Rodeo Foundation." *Rodeo Sports News*, Championship Edition, 1960, p. 109.

Roberts, Barbara. "Sale at Baker [Oregon] Is a Huge Success." *Western Horseman* 9, no. 5 (September–October, 1944).

Robey, James. "All Outdoors." *Dayton* (Ohio) *Journal-Herald*, February 2, 1966. Reprinted as "Despite Negative Legislation Ohio Rodeos Continue," *Rodeo Sports News*, March 15, 1966, p. 3.

"Rodeo: Riders Bring Wild West Thrills to Jaded Easterners." *News Week*, October 21, 1933, p. 17.

"Rodeo Association May Bar Pro Cowboys in the Future, As Result of $4,000 Rhubarb." *Nevada State Journal*, July 6, 1949, p. 2.

"Rodeo Foundation." *Rodeo Sports News*, Championship Edition, 1962, p. 61.

"Rodeo Information Commission." *Rodeo Sports News*, Championship Edition, 1968, p. 81.

"Rodeo in France." *Hoofs and Horns* 15, no. 4 (October, 1945).

"Rodeo Must Go, Humane Group Rules." *Christian Science Monitor*, Pacific ed., October 19, 1926, p. 6.

"Rodeo News Bureau." *Rodeo Sports News*, Championship Edition, 1974, p. 16.

"Rodeo Performers Agree to Settle Labor Disputes." *Denver Post*, January 8, 1938, p. 8.

"Rodeo Picture Shaping Up Better." *RAA Bulletin*, n.s. 6, no. 6 (June, 1942), in *Hoofs and Horns* 12, no. 1, (July, 1942).

"Rodeo Riders' Association Head Resigns." *Salt Lake Tribune*, July 23, 1939, p. 1.

"Rodeos Again in Spotlight." *Union* (Walla Walla, Wash.), August 27, 1926, p. 1.

"Rodeo Schools." *Prorodeo Sports News*, February 23, 1983, p. 21.

"Rodeos Curtailed along Coast." *Western Horseman* 7, no. 2 (March–April, 1942).

"Rodeo's Point-Award System—How to Become Champion." *Rodeo Sports News*, July 1, 1955, p. 1.

"Secretary's Message." *RAA Bulletin*, n.s. 1, no. 5 (May, 1937), in *Hoofs and Horns* 6, no. 12 (June, 1937); n.s. 1, no. 9 (September, 1937), in *Hoofs and Horns* 7, no. 4 (October, 1937).

"Shades of the Old West . . . ." *Literary Digest*, November 25, 1933, p. 25

Sherman, Tex. "Rodeo News." *Hoofs and Horns* 3, no.9 (February, 1934).

Shrake, Edwin. "Horsing Around with Bull." *Sports Illustrated*, December 3, 1973, pp. 40–41+.

Smith, H. H. "New Wild West." *Outlook*, October 28, 1936, pp. 272–73 ff.

Smith, Red. "Home, Home on the Range, New Jersey." *New York Times*, July 23, 1977.

———. "Rodeo School Has Finishing Touch." *Philadelphia Inquirer*, February 10, 1963.

———. "Scandal." *New York Herald Tribune*, November 7, 1963, p. 23.

"Soldier Gene Autry." *Hoofs and Horns* 12, no. 2 (August, 1942).

"Special Awards." *Rodeo Sports News*, Championship Edition, 1972, p. 86; *Prorodeo Sports News*, Championship Edition, 1980, p. 114; Championship Edition, 1981, p. 112; Championship Edition, 1982, p. 112; Championship Edition, 1983, p. 111.

"Special Report on Rodeos." *The Ark* 43, no. 3 (Christmas, 1975).

"A Sport, Not a Show: World's Championship Rodeo, New York City." *Newsweek*, October 26, 1953, p. 100.

"Sporting Life." *Newsweek*, November 11, 1953, p. 80.

Stanush, Claude. "King of the Cowboys." *Life*, May 13, 1946, pp. 59–62+.

"State Humane Association Opposes California Anti-Rodeo Bill." *Rodeo Sports News*, May 15, 1967, p. 1.

"Statement from Everett Bowman." *Hoofs and Horns* 14, no. 12, (June, 1945).

"Steer Busting." *Wyoming Tribune*, July 27, 1907, p. 4.

Stegner, Harry P. "Photographing the Cowboy as He Disappears." *World's Work* 17 (January, 1909).

"Stemler Joins PRCA in New Position." *Rodeo Sports News*, February 1, 1977, p. 2.

Stewart, Horace V. "Happy-Go-Lucky Band of Cowboys Are Real Men, Says Show Chief." *Denver Post*, January 24, 1931, p. 3.

Stewart-Gordon, J. "Winningest Cowboy in the World." *Saturday Evening Post* 243 (Fall, 1971).

"Stock Notes." *Las Animas* (Colo.) *Leader*, December 15, 1882, p. 3.

"Stock Show Will Have Many Added Attractions This Year." *Denver Post*, January 11, 1931, p. 13.

Stout, David. "PRCA's Growing Years." *Prorodeo Sports News*, August 25, 1982, p. 16-A.

"Strike at Rodeo in Boston Ends, Men Re-employed." *Boston Evening Transcript*, November 3, 1936, p. 4.

"The Suicide Circuit." *Time*, November 18, 1957, p. 83.

"The Summer Fair." *Calgary Weekly Herald*, May 17, 1893, p. 4.

Swift, Mike. "The Rodeo Information Commission." *Rodeo Sports News*, Championship Edition, 1958, p. 120; Championship Edition, 1959, p. 43.

Teague, Sandy. "Winston Scoreboards on the Move." *Prorodeo Inside*, May, 1978.

"There's a Difference in Rodeos." *Denver Daily Record Stockman*, Stock Show ed. January 30, 1943, p. 112.

"This and That." *Hoofs and Horns*, 12, no. 2 (August, 1942); 12, no. 6 (December, 1942).

Thistlethwaite, E. W. "Cowboys—Old and Modern." *Hoofs and Horns* 6, no. 10 (April, 1937).

"Trial of Herbert Frizzell, Rodeo Cowboy, Switched from Big Spring to Midland, Texas, *Buckboard* 5, no. 7 (January, 1950).

"Trophy Donors Are Needed." *RAA Bulletin*, n.s. 6, no. 2 (February, 1942), in *Hoofs and Horns* 11, no. 9, (March, 1942).

"Trophy Donors for 1939." *RAA Bulletin*, n.s. 3, no. 14 [12] (December, 1939), in *Hoofs and Horns* 9, no. 7, (January, 1940).

Tucker, Jean. "Horse Show Curbs? Senate Says 'Nay'!" *Hartford Courant*, March 8, 1967, pp. 1, 7.

"Turtle Notes." *Hoofs and Horns* 11, no. 10 (April, 1942).

"TV, War Threat Making It Tough for Rodeo Hands." *Rocky Mountain News*, January 8, 1951, p. 6.

"Two a Year." *Rodeo Sports News*, Championship Edition, 1959, p. 17.

"Two National Telecasts." *Rodeo Sports News*, Championship Edition, 1959, p. 37.

"Upcoming Rodeos." *Prorodeo Sports News*, June 30, 1982, p. 12.

Van Cronkhite, John. "What the National Finals Will Mean to the Sport." *Rodeo Sports News*, Championship Edition, 1959, p. 39.

"Walked Out of Rodeo because of Money." *Boston Daily Record*, final ed., November 3, 1936, p. 7.

Ward, Fay. "Organization." *Wild Bunch*, May, 1916.

"Wartime Status of Rodeos." *RAA Bulletin*, n.s. 6, no. 4 (April, 1942), in *Hoofs and Horns* 11, no. 11 (May, 1942).

Weadick, Guy. "What Are Rodeos Doing?" *Hoofs and Horns* 7, no. 7 (January, 1938).

"Weary Wild Westerners." *Rocky Mountain News*, October 9, 1895, p. 8.

Westermeier, Clifford P. "Cowboy Sports and the Humane Society." *Colorado Magazine* 26, no. 4 (October, 1949).

————. "Seventy-five Years of Rodeo in Colorado." *Colorado Magazine* 28, no. 1 (January, 1951); 28, no. 2 (April, 1951); 28, no. 3 (July, 1951).

Western Horseman 13, no. 4 (July–August, 1948): 2; 39, no. 7 (July, 1974): front cover.

"West Watches First Stock Show since Wartime in Denver." *Denver Post*, January 7, 1942, p. 13.

"The Wild West in New York City." *Literary Digest*, October 24, 1936, pp. 44–46.

Williams, George. "Ike Rude—Rodeo's Iron Man." *Persimmon Hill* 5, no. 4 (Spring, 1976).

"Winston Revises Awards Program." *Prorodeo Sports News*, January 23, 1980, p. 1.

"Winston Rodeo Awards." *Rodeo Sports News*, Championship Edition, 1973, p. 86; Championship Edition, 1974, p. 40; Championship Edition, 1975, p. 12; Championship Edition, 1976, p. 11; Championship Edition, 1978, p. 113. *Prorodeo Sports News*, Championship Edition, 1979, p. 110; Championship Edition, 1980, p. 110.

"Winston Rodeo Series." *Official Program*, National Finals Rodeo, Oklahoma City, Okla., December 4–12, 1982, p. 141.

"World Championship Awards." *Rodeo Sports News*, Championship Edition, 1974, p. 57; Championship Edition, 1976, p. 90.

Wright, Cecil. "California News Items." *Hoofs and Horns* 11, no. 8 (February, 1942); 11, no. 10 (April, 1942).

CORRESPONDENCE

Barron, Richard B., Supervisor, Brand Projects, Schlitz & Schlitz Malt Liquor, Milwaukee, Wis., March 9, 1978.
Boyle, Ellen, President, International Rodeo Fans, Yonkers, N.Y., September 6, 1978.
California Law Library, Sacramento, Calif., November 29, 1982.
Cross, D. J. A., Honourary Associate, Calgary Exhibition and Stampede, Calgary, Alberta, May 4, 1979.
Drennon, Charlene, Director-West Coast, Humane Society of the United States, San Francisco, Calif., September 5, 1978.
Enevoldsen, Joanne, Public Relations and Education Director, Calgary Humane Society, Calgary, Alberta, Canada, August 11, 1978.
Frontier Airlines, Inc., Denver, Colo., March 30, 1978.
Linder, Herman, Cardston, Alberta, Canada, March 19, 1981.
New York Public Library, New York, N.Y., February 18, 1981.

DOCUMENTS

[Boston contestants]. *Petition.* Boston, Mass., October 30, 1936.
California Legislature, 52nd Session. *Senate Bill No. 476,* January 20, 1937.
―――. Regular Session. *Assembly Bill No. 888 (A Bill to Amend Section 597K of the Penal Code),* 1967.
Humane Society of the United States. *Policy Statement.* N.p., n.d.
International Rodeo Association. *Rules and By-laws,* 21st ed. Pauls Valley, Okla.: International Rodeo Association, December 1, 1981.
Ohio General Assembly. *An Act* (Amended House Bill No. 541), Ohio General Assembly, Columbus, Ohio, 1965–66.
Professional Rodeo Cowboys Association. *Articles of Incorporation, By-laws and Rules.* Colorado Springs: Professional Rodeo Cowboys Association, January 1, 1983.
―――. *Minutes of Board of Directors Meeting,* Oklahoma City, December 7–11, 1981.
―――. *1981 Official Pro Rodeo Media Guide.* Colorado Springs: Professional Rodeo Cowboys Association, 1981.
―――. *Official Pro Rodeo Media Guide 1978.* Colorado Springs: Professional Rodeo Cowboys Association, 1978.

————. *President's Year-End Report to Membership*. Colorado Springs: Professional Rodeo Cowboys Association, February 1, 1983.

————. Approvals Department. *Year-End Report of Approved Team-Roping Rodeos in 1982*. Colorado Springs: Professional Rodeo Cowboys Association, 1982.

Professional Rodeo Cowboys Association Properties, Inc./Adolph Coors Company. *Addendum I* to Contract, 1980.

Rodeo Association of America. *Constitution and By-laws and Rules of the Rodeo Association of America*. Salinas, Calif.: Rodeo Association of America, 1941.

Rodeo Cowboys' Association. *Articles of Association, By-laws and Rules*. Fort Worth, Tex.: Rodeo Cowboys' Association, 1945.

Rodeo Secretary's Result List, Cheyenne Frontier Days, Cheyenne, Wyo., July 24–August 1, 1982.

United Cowboys Turtle Association. *Four Rules*, November 6, 1936.

INTERVIEWS

Brown, Warren G. "Freckles," June 2, 1975.
Carmichael, Martin, April 1, 1983.
Chambliss, Hugh, March 8, 1983.
Connelly, Lex, March 20, 1978.
Cox, Warren, September 15, 1978.
Davis, Shawn, June 2, 1975.
Eidson, Bob, September 14, 1978; August 26, 1981; March 1, 1983; April 1, 1983.
Ford, Bruce, December 12, 1982.
Hannum, Jack, January 29, 1982.
Hill, Stub, March 8, 1983.
Irwin, Charles "Sharkey," May 4, 1982.
Kane, Wanden (M. LaFarge), February 9, 1983.
Lindsey, Oscar E. (Earl), August 7, 1982.
McBeth, John, June 4, 1975.
Parkhurst, Mel, March 18, 1983.
Riley, J. Kelly, January 14, 1981; February 2, 1982; March 17, 1983.
Stout, David, August 31, 1981.
Tibbs, Casey, various dates, 1967–69.

RODEO PROGRAMS, PRIZE LISTS, ENTRY BLANKS

Boston, Massachusetts. *Contestants Entry Blank*, Col. W. T. Johnson's World's Championship Rodeo, Boston Garden, November 2–11, 1936.

Boston, Massachusetts. *Official Program*, Colonel William T. Johnson's Sixth Annual World's Championship Rodeo, Boston Garden, November 2–11, 1936.

Cheyenne, Wyoming. *Official Program*, Cheyenne Frontier Days, July 27–31, 1926.

Cheyenne, Wyoming. *Official Program*, 40th Annual Frontier Days Rodeo, July 22–25, 1936.

Denver, Colorado. *Souvenir Program*, National Western Stock Show and Rodeo, January 16–23, 1932.

Denver, Colorado. *Souvenir Program*, National Western Stock Show and Rodeo, January 13–21, 1978.

New York, New York. *Prize List*, World's Championship Rodeo, Madison Square Garden, October 7–25, 1936.

Oklahoma City, Oklahoma. *Official Program*, National Finals Rodeo, December 4–12, 1982.

Pendleton, Oregon. *Contestants' Disclaimer*, Pendleton Round-Up, September 16–18, 1937.

Prescott, Arizona. *Program of Events, Prize List and Rules for Prescott Frontier Days Celebration*, July 1–4, 1928.

San Francisco, California. *International Rodeo Association's 1947 Championship Rodeo in Conjunction with the Grand National Livestock Exposition and Horse Show*, November 1–9, 1947.

Sheridan, Wyoming. *Contest Rules and Local Rules*, Sheridan-Wyo Rodeo, July 18–20, 1934.

Tucson, Arizona. *Tucson*. Official Rodeo Program, La Fiesta de los Vaqueros, February 21–23, 1936.

MISCELLANEOUS

Address, Peter Coors, Senior Vice President-Marketing, Adolph Coors Company, Golden, Colo., at 1980 World Champions' Awards Banquet, Denver, Colo., January 14, 1981.

Lecture, Rodeo School, Sutton Ranches, Onida, S. Dak., June 4, 1975.

Membership records, Membership Department, Professional Rodeo Cowboys Association, Inc., Colorado Springs, Colo.

Statistical information, National Media Department and Point Awards Department, Professional Rodeo Cowboys Association, Inc., Colorado Springs, Colo., January, 1983.

Index